Priorities in Religious Education

ONE WEEK
LOAN

Priorities in Religious Education:

A Model for the 1990s and Beyond

Edited by

Brenda Watson

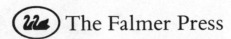 The Falmer Press

(A member of the Taylor & Francis Group)
London • Washington, D.C.

UK   The Falmer Press, 4 John St., London, WC1N 2ET
USA   The Falmer Press, Taylor & Francis Inc., 1900 Frost Road, 101, Bristol, PA 19007

First published 1992

Library of Congress Cataloging-in-Publication data are available on request

A catalogue record for this book is available from the British Library

ISBN 0 75070 016 5 cased
ISBN 0 75070 017 3 paperback

Set in 10/11.5pt Bembo
by Graphicraft Typesetters Ltd., Hong Kong

Printed in Great Britain by Burgess Science Press, Basingstoke on paper which has a specified pH value on final paper manufacture of not less than 7.5 and is therefore 'acid free'.

Contents

Contents

Preface

The potential role of religious education in the 1990s for all schools is as significant as ever. The Education Reform Act has ensured the survival of the subject in state schools and given fresh impetus for its development. Schools outside direct state control often have a specific concern for religious education, at least in theory; some wish to make it the central point of the curriculum. Moreover, for those schools where religion is marginalized there is increasing pressure today — through concern to eradicate racism and sexism, for example — to take more seriously matters concerned with values and beliefs which entail some attention to religion. For whether viewed from the perspective of a consciously pluralist society or approached from that of a concern for Christian heritage, the question of religion cannot be easily dismissed. It continues to exercise a fascination and power. This is even more apparent if seen on a global stage. Religious education therefore matters.

The educational aim of helping children and students to understand religion is easy to state, but exceedingly hard to achieve, because religion is an area of knowledge which bristles with difficulties: its complexity, controversial nature and emotive power can make it a minefield from which many consider it safest to keep well away.

The minimal time, resources, staffing and status which RE normally receives make the question of what shall be done with and in it crucially important. The plea of the classroom teacher for practical help in deciding on priorities must be taken seriously. In most schools only a little can realistically be attempted. It is vital therefore that that little is chosen with care.

In this book leading experts share their thinking on what they see as the most significant way in which religious education should develop. The twelve priorities are summarized in an appendix to the book together with discussion questions and a diagram — materials which could be used for staff meetings or for a study day or conference; it could also prove useful for a governors' meeting, or for consideration by the local SACRE.

One approach to this book for those particularly interested in practical help might be to turn first to the last chapter, followed by the rest of Part 3. The relevance of Parts 1 and 2 to the everyday realities of the teacher's role in RE, whether in primary or secondary school, will then be clearly appreciated.

Acknowledgments

I am grateful to the Hon. Robert Wills, Chairman of the Farmington Trust, for making possible my work in editing this book and in particular to Colonel Robert Hornby for his constant support and encouragement. I also wish to record my thanks to Betty Colquhoun and Helen Gibson for their willing and efficient secretarial assistance.

Introduction: The Need for Priorities

Brenda Watson

Priorities are a fact of life. However much energy, talent, skill or experience we may have, we still cannot do everything and the greater our vision and imagination, the more heavily will our limitations press upon us.

Deciding on priorities is an uncomfortable task. The weight of distraction and countless possibilities can create a sense of hopelessness and resignation in hard-pressed teachers who may settle for 'just coping' rather than resisting pressures and taking initiative. It is well to remember Francis Bacon's aphorism: 'A wise man will make more opportunities than he finds'.

Such advice is in keeping with one of the major priorities behind the 1988 Education Reform Act: the encouragement of a spirit of 'enterprise'. It has important applications beyond any utilitarian concerns of promoting industry, business and wealth-creation.

If we do not choose priorities, they choose us, and their effects are inescapable. An unanswered letter is in fact an answer — one which can, for example, break a friendship, fail to give much-needed help or slam the door on an exciting new venture. Lack of response generally has negative repercussions.

The importance of actively making choices needs to be constantly borne in mind when considering religious education. This subject-area provides a fertile field for the practice of priorities. 'Fertile field' is perhaps mistaken imagery: rather, religion presents to the already overburdened teacher an enormous acreage of vegetation with devastating thorns and prickles to be negotiated. How to bring this under cultivation for the benefit of children and students, or at least how to hack a way through the jungle, requires a clear perception of the purpose and scope of religious education.

This is not easy to come by for several reasons which include the following.

The Nature of Religion

Religion deals with what is fundamental in an attitude to life; it is concerned with what is of ultimate significance. It is, however, extremely easy to ignore

1

such basic issues. Wittgenstein made much of 'the distinction between all the trivia we can talk about, and all the essentials we can't'. This poses a particular problem for religious education worthy of the name, for it must discuss such 'essentials'.

Moreover, it must do so in what is so often an alien environment. This not infrequently has the effect of encouraging teachers to adopt a 'safe' approach avoiding controversy by concentrating on factual material which is capable of appropriate simplification and which is likely to be of immediate interest or relevance.

The emphasis on 'immediate' is significant. Adapting a splendid phrase of Chesterton's, we might summarize the contemporary dilemma as 'the idolatry of the immediate to the exclusion of the ultimate'.

The Enormity of the Subject

So vast and complex is religion that deciding on priorities is bound to be daunting. There has to be a willingness to let go the good in the interests of the best. Without an acute sense of overall strategy, it is easy to be misled by the attention of the moment on something which is in itself commendable and valuable, yet which is not the most needful, central and important task to be attempted. We need constantly to reflect that time and energy spent on one thing cannot be spent on another.

This is a truism which it is mostly convenient to forget. If, for example, we pay the detailed and careful attention to the teaching of Islam which it deserves and requires in order to foster real understanding, we cannot do justice also to Sikhism, to Hinduism, to Buddhism, to ... If we help students towards a vivid awareness of the forms in which Christianity appears today, we cannot at the same time concentrate on difficult skills of biblical interpretation.

Indoctrination by Omission

It is often uncomfortable to consider that perhaps what we omit teaching is more important than what we do teach. The total package we present to children and students contains messages in, as it were, a binary code of 1 and 0. Indoctrination can more readily happen with regard to what their attention is never drawn to than with regard to what is explicitly expressed. If people are directly in touch with something, there is a real possibility of their thinking about it for themselves, thus overcoming any conditioning; but if they are in a state of ignorance, there is nothing on which to reflect and so they remain trapped.

A diet of festivals and rites of passage, can, for example, lead children and students to suppose that religion is a matter of external and often bizarre cultural practices. This fits in well with the secularist view of religion as a cultural phenomenon which appeals to some people and not to others. Such a view assumes that the truth or otherwise of religion cannot be known and therefore need not be taken seriously.

In this way religious education in schools can reinforce the conditioning which society as a whole has pressed upon the child, causing religion to be marginalized, trivialized and misrepresented.

For the child from a religious home these three factors tend to work in a different way which can also cause misunderstandings. The beneficial or harmful effects relate, of course, to the quality of religious upbringing which the children receive.

Pressure of Other Priorities

Many of our priorities are decided for us. Force of circumstances, chance encounters and a thousand other factors influence what in fact takes place and this is always at the expense of something else. The National Curriculum, for example, lays down priorities both explicitly and by implication which will influence profoundly what happens at the chalk-face in most state schools.

Religious education receives honourable mention, but in fact does not appear within the magic circle of the 'core' curriculum, nor even among the 'foundation' subjects. Its special category of 'basic' may sound impressive, yet without being regaled with all the paraphernalia of assessment at Key Stages, and served by national guidelines under the protection of the National Curriculum Council, it is likely to remain the outsider to which scant acknowledgment is given.

The provisions of the 1988 legislation are sufficiently definite for schools to have to account more rigorously with regard to their provision of religious education: SACREs, governors and parents can now more readily act as watchdogs to see that schools play fair. Yet the constraints of a plethora of other priorities upon curriculum organization in schools will continue to have a detrimental effect on the allotment of time, resources and staffing available for this subject. How to make the most of a meagre allocation is therefore a prime requirement.

Pressures of different kinds affect schools which are not within the state system or obliged to follow the National Curriculum guidelines. Often resources and status for religious education is slight in these schools also, and where generous often has to conform to a standard laid down in syllabuses and directives from governors.

The scenario with which religious education has to deal is all too familiar. Elsewhere I have described this as the Doleful Ds: Distraction of other concerns, other priorities, confusion, uncertainty, no room of one's own, too many calls on time, no quietness, etc. The Difficulty of the subject — the concepts seem almost incomprehensible to most people today, they go against the tide, they are extremely controversial, they are also like dynamite and might become extremely dangerous and most teachers are facing these difficulties almost on their own in schools. Delusion — people are led astray by the conditioning of society which affects teachers as well as pupils, by obsession with assessment and examination, by prevalent mistaken views of education as a package of information and attitudes to be presented to pupils by teachers, and of religion as a sociological human phenomenon. Despair — a sense of how can we do anything? of rootlessness, of lack of understanding, lack of confidence, lack of ability, fear of failure.

The question becomes how can we move to what I like to refer to as the Animating As of Attentiveness in place of Distraction, Awareness rather than Difficulties, Appreciation instead of Delusion and Aspiration not Despair. All affect (and, in the case of the Doleful Ds, afflict) each other.

Purpose of This Book

These are some of the factors which all those responsible for religious education need to take into account. So much of current textbook theory makes the mistake of the old-style Agreed Syllabuses — working on the assumption that a great deal of time, resources and energy is available for dealing with a subject which is complex, dynamic and controversial. For a long time I have argued that, in order to be done properly, RE requires four hours a week, and I have always been laughed at as though asking for the moon!

It is more realistic therefore to pose a question such as this: Suppose you had only forty hours in which to pursue the total amount of specifically religious education which these children or students will ever receive in school, what would you choose to do and why?

This book, written by people of considerable experience in teaching, is designed to help teachers and others involved in the curriculum management of schools to think out their own reasoned answers to such a question. I sent all the contributors what basically appears in the first section of this chapter and asked them to write up what they saw as the top priority for religious education.

Their responses have been arranged in three parts. First there are three chapters written from a broad educational perspective. The five writers in the second part approach the subject from various religious faith-perspectives which include Evangelical, Roman Catholic and Muslim and involve an analysis of the Christian School Movement as well as a major overview of the whole subject of cultural diversity. The third part focuses on the classroom in a much more precise way. Practising teachers have written two of these chapters, and the other chapter gives detailed suggestions for a scheme of work in eight units. It is hoped therefore that ideas will become translated into manageable actualities; theories into practice.

In the concluding chapter I have indicated how I see these priorities relating together, mostly in convergence but sometimes divergently. I have indicated problem areas where issues are far from being resolved and where attempted agreement would be premature. Readers may disagree with my synopsis, but I hope it may serve as a stimulus for their own evaluation. There can be no blueprint for such matters.

A Metaphor for the Book as a Whole

This may help readers to see at a glance why I have arranged the chapters in this way. The idea is to take a journey in search of authentic religious education.

The three parts of the book explore different kinds of terrain. The first is open countryside, perhaps downland with long vistas all round, beckoning the walker towards a distant vantage point. John Wilson starts us on our way by advising us to study a map so that we have a route clearly in mind. We may not want to take the path he himself maps out, but that it is important to be clear where we are going needs to be heeded. Otherwise we may be like the old Methodist local preacher who was reported by one of his congregation as saying he 'aimed at nothing and hit it'.

Jack Priestley takes over as our guide by advising us to travel light, moving on with a sense of freedom and breadth which can encourage maximum flexibility. Priestley invites us to reconsider many of the ingrained habits and assumptions about education and about religious education which the system promotes. He advocates courage to live in the present moment and be centred in what actually is happening and can happen where we are. He brings with him someone who has been a guide, philosopher and friend for whom respect for religion came 'as a consequence of an intellectual pilgrimage'. He therefore encourages us to move on and forward.

Nicola Slee then follows with her call for the use of imagination which will fit us for the explorations ahead. She develops the need for vision, relating it to what is central to religion and inviting us to survey the scene from a high vantage-point — that of the arts — to gain inspiration and perspective.

The next section of the journey is a patchwork of cultivated fields and woodland, some of it dense where it is hard to see the wood for the trees. In this area we come across buildings, varied in style but perhaps similar in function. Our guides here are Richard Wilkins, Syed Ali Ashraf, Bernadette O'Keeffe and Kevin Nichols, as they discuss questions of faith-commitment and loyalty to tradition. Edward Hulmes then takes us to another highpoint to survey the ground covered and provide an overview much needed in the world of cultural diversity.

Finally, as we make our way across rough wild country with many obstacles and points where it is easy to miss the way, we are reminded of the classroom situation. Here Michael Poole helps us to negotiate a seemingly impenetrable barrier, with his concern for the relationship between science and religion. Elizabeth Ashton then helps us discover a pathway through the undergrowth of simplistic notions which retard progress in the primary school. Michael Donley then takes us to our final ascent, enabling us to survey the whole area we have walked before bringing us back to our starting-point.

Have we learned anything on the way? Has it been worth it? Hopefully we have taken a few steps further forward in understanding the true role of religious education in schools.

Varying the analogy, some words of T.S. Eliot are perhaps appropriate.

You are not the same people who left that station.
Or who will arrive at any terminus,
While the narrowing rails slide together behind you.
(from *The Four Quartets 'Dry Salvages'*)

Part 1

Educational Perspectives on Religion

Editorial Introduction

Concern for *RELIGIOUS EDUCATION* needs to take seriously both its constituent terms, as do all the contributors to this book. Whilst those grouped together in Part 2 relate their discussion more clearly to specific religious traditions, the authors in Part 1 operate from a broader concept of religion as part of human experience in general. They explore its relationship to educational goals.

The first priority identified is the need to clarify what religion is and therefore what might constitute good religious education. 'Terms do not mean just what we want them to mean: *we* have to do justice to *them*'. John Wilson sees religion as 'peculiarly concerned with what one worships'. The crucial questions here include: 'What should one worship?', or 'Should one worship at all?' He goes on to note that in order to educate, the teacher should encourage children to think for themselves about these matters 'as reasonably as possible'. He sees the skills needed as basically those which he drew up in connection with his well-known moral education programme.

He discusses three possible objections concerning commitment and the place of Christianity in religious education. He then moves on to advocate considerable freedom and experimentation by teachers with regard to actual practice — on the basis of a firm grasp of aims. He urges committed groups to give priority to an educational concern for children alongside their religious or ideological aims.

The chapter provides a valuable introduction to what follows, anticipating a number of issues, such as the question of commitment which is discussed with some vigour later in the book, especially by Kevin Nichols and Edward Hulmes. The chapter will, like the rest, inevitably raise questions in the minds of readers but the purpose of the book is to encourage awareness of the issues not to present dogmatic conclusions.

The next chapter takes a deeper look at what is involved in the word *education* and how religion should relate to it. Jack Priestley, basing his ideas on those of the neglected but seminal thinker, A.N. Whitehead, points out that religious education does not fit current educational theory. Instead of abandoning RE or of trying to accommodate it to what is acceptable today, we should rather question the assumptions governing our notions of RE as out-of-step. Priestley argues that 'the essence of education is that it be religious' (p. 33). This is difficult for people to accept, or even consider, today because of the pervasiveness of positivism with its insistence on knowledge being scientifically provable. He believes, however, that the moment for Whitehead 'has surely come as the bankruptcy of positivism becomes clearer' today.

Whitehead came to see how mistaken the mechanistic view of knowledge was, seeing the world as 'composed of bits of stuff with attributes'. In fact reality is one of fluidity and organic change and knowledge more like a flowing river. Priestley argues for a cross-curricular approach to education, noting that 'true integration' emerges 'from depth not breadth of study, from a teacher who can prise open the smallest crack and reveal what lies below the surface of what initially may appear to be very solid ground'.

A pertinent section on the relationship between academic and vocational education follows and leads on to a discussion on the nature of religion. This is seen as concerned with wholeness — 'the most comprehensive over-view' —, a wholeness which includes both the individual and the communal aspects of life, both solitary experience and the public expression of it within religious traditions. Religious education must therefore maintain a balance between 'knowing and understanding the experience of others and using that knowledge to know and understand ourselves'. In this way the distinction between the academic and the personal becomes irrelevant for 'the subject *which* is being taught becomes fused into the subject *who* is being taught. Education should carry a health warning: it changes people.'

He concludes with a fascinating perspective on time — that precious commodity of which there is never enough. 'Good teaching is the use of the moment, the Now, the Instant', for, quoting Whitehead, 'knowledge does not keep any better than fish'.

The last writer in this part, Nicola Slee, sees knowledge and education in much the same way as Priestley. She is particularly aware of the constraints placed on teachers but considers it would be 'a failure of vision and respon-sibility of incalculable magnitude' to neglect the education of spirituality. She notes that the last ten years have seen renewed concern among religious educators for a more pupil-centred approach in which the spiritual dimension is 'at the centre, rather than the periphery, of religious education'. She offers a substantial critique of the phenomenological approach to religious education which tends to promote a detached study of external behaviour instead of 'an exploration of inwardness ... an encounter with mystery, transcendence'.

Her discussion of the meaning we should give to the word 'spiritual' concludes with her own helpful summary. She goes on to discuss imagination and identifies a crucial role for reason in guarding against the misuse of imagination with its possibly sinister and destructive effects.

She makes some valuable comments on the relationship between religion and the arts. It is important that the arts be seen not simply in the role of illustrating religious understanding. It is only as they are able to be them-selves that they have most to offer to religious understanding. This may be because the arts can often get through to people in a secular age when what is specifically or explicitly religious fails.

A final section explores some practical implications and offers four timely pointers towards a deeper quality of education.

Chapter 1

First Steps in Religious Education

John Wilson

The *first* thing we have to do is to determine what can sensibly be *meant by* 'religious education': how the phrase can appropriately be construed. What is *it to be* educated in religion? Asking this question is obviously our first task, because unless we can give a satisfactory answer to it we cannot determine the scope or aims of religious education: or still less, its practice. We shall, literally, not know what we are talking about.[1]

The question leads us at once to consider (i) what we are to understand by 'religion' as a form of thought or a department of life; and (ii) by what criteria we are to judge a successful performance in that area. Education in science, or history, or other forms of thought, make up respectable and properly-institutionalized subjects only because we are (fairly) clear what is to count as 'science' or 'history', and how to do them well. This is not the case with religious education.

It is equally obvious that the question is a philosophical one: that is, it involves becoming clear about the concepts, values and other factors that are peculiar to what is marked by 'education' and 'religion'. That is of course also a controversial matter, but only philosophically controversial: it cannot be settled by sociology or ideology. Nor is it a matter just of personal taste: not just any translation of 'religious education' will be adequate. The man quoted as saying 'When I say "religion" of course I mean "the Christian religion" and when I say "the Christian religion" of course I mean "the Church of England"' is not just *prejudiced*: he has made a wrong translation, a wrong use of words. (If he had put the terms in inverted commas, as I have, he might have seen that.) Terms do not mean just what we want them to mean: *we* have to do justice to *them*.

'Philosophy' is too grand a term for what I am pleading for. I want those interested in RE simply to *face* the question 'What does "religious education" *mean*?', and to use 'mean' in the proper sense: not 'What does it mean to me?' or 'What would I like to see going on under that heading?', but rather 'What do these words direct us towards?'. I have, in what follows, given my own answer to this question; but whether that answer is adequate is much less important than that the question be faced.

What 'Religious Education' Means

'Education' does not refer to just any way of dealing with human beings. We distinguish it from training, conditioning, indoctrinating, brain-washing and other processes.[2] 'Education' involves initiating people into various forms of thought and activity in such a way that they are helped to become more well-informed, understanding and reasonable. Education in religion, then, cannot (logically) be a matter of inculcating or persuading people into a particular religious faith, or into the religious attitude generally. It must rather be a matter of helping them become more reasonable in the sphere of religion.

This requirement is not satisfied merely by teaching people *about* religion.[3] We could teach people *about* mathematics or science by teaching the history of mathematics or some sociological facts showing the importance of science: but this would not be education *in* mathematics or science. Similarly we could teach children about various moral codes: but moral education also involves giving them the ability required to choose between them, to think morally and reasonably for themselves, to use a set of standards or rules of procedure from within the moral area.

Any programmes designed primarily (i) to sell a particular faith (for example, Christianity) or a particular outlook on life; or (ii) simply to talk in a general way about the history, sociology, etc., of religion, miss the mark. What is required is that we should be clearer about what counts as reason and unreason, success and failure, 'being educated' or 'not being educated' in the sphere of religion.

This remains true however we conceive of religion: whether as some kind of 'faith' or 'commitment', obedience to authority, set of factual beliefs, attitude to life, or pattern of behaviour. We want to know how to judge whether any of these are right, true, appropriate, sensible, reasonable, sane, worth having, or whatever terms fit the case.[4] Presumably most people believe that one or more of these terms apply at least to some cases of religious belief, or some cases of non-religious ideals and outlooks. Most of us think it wrong (unreasonable, misguided, etc.) to worship Hitler or Baal; and some think it right (sensible, defensible, etc.) to worship Jesus. So long as we use any of these terms, religion is in this sense within the scope of reason.

Religious and Other Outlooks

Any activity that could be specifically and plausibly called 'religious' must be distinguished from various other activities that are not specifically religious.[5] Religion is not (i) a matter of scientific explanation or magic: (ii) making particular moral choices: (iii) having some sort of attitude to life as a whole, to 'ultimate reality'. All these may in practice be connected with particular religions, but they are not peculiarly religious; and there have been, and are religions which are not concerned with any of them.

Religion is peculiarly concerned with *what one worships*[6], which is in turn connected with what one thinks one ought to be in awe of, feel humble towards, reverence, and so forth. It is concerned with certain *emotions* being directed towards certain *objects of emotions*: awe and love for God, guilt for sin, reverence for the Buddha, etc. The crucial questions here are of the form 'What should one worship?', 'Should one worship at all?', or 'Is there anything in the universe of which we should be in awe?' The educator's job is not to answer these questions *for* children, but to give them those qualities and abilities that they need in order to work out possible answers for themselves as reasonably as possible.

Religious outlooks and beliefs are only a sub-class of emotion-based outlooks in general. There are many near-religions, such as Marxism, Maoism, Fascism and others: and other outlooks, such as a passionate belief in 'honour', 'not losing face', and 'not backing down', or ideals such as Stoicism or Epircureanism. Everyone, children as well as adults, has some outlook or ideal of some kind, whether or not it takes the form of a religious or metaphysical set of beliefs. This is only to say that everyone directs his emotions in certain ways to certain objects: that he has a specific emotional investment, so to speak, in the world. Religion is one type of investment; and it usually deals not only with emotions peculiar to itself (awe, reverence), but also with other emotions (guilt, fear, love, remorse, pride, etc.).

Thus education in religion is, centrally and crucially, education in the emotions. We all know that emotions can be in various ways reasonable or unreasonable; they can be excessive or insufficient, directed to proper or improper objects, based on true or false beliefs. To worship Hitler, for instance, is in some ways like wanting to marry the wrong girl, or wanting to be like a gangster hero. Education in religion is education in *one* (very important) sphere in which the emotions enter. (See further in Wilson, 1971)

Aims and Components

For this, therefore, as for moral education, we require a list of particular skills, abilities and other qualities which we need to develop in children. To talk generally and globally of 'maturity', 'understanding', etc., is not much help: we need to be as specific as possible. These qualities or 'components' turn out to be essentially the same as those I have listed for moral education as follows (Wilson, 1972): —

PHIL	concern for other people as equals, respecting other people's wants and outlooks.
EMP (1)	awareness of one's own feelings (conscious and unconscious). (AUTEMP)
EMP (2)	awareness of other people's feelings (conscious and unconscious). (ALLEMP)
GIG (1)	knowledge of 'hard' facts relevant to the emotions.
GIG (2)	mastery of techniques relevant to the emotions.
KRAT (1)	bringing the above to bear on real-life situations, which includes

(1a)   being alert to or noticing the situation;
(1b)   thinking seriously and fully about it;
(1c)   thinking responsibly about it (i.e. so as to reach a decision).

KRAT (2)   actually having the right feelings/emotions as a result of the above.

These components are fully discussed and illustrated elsewhere.[7] See also the Practical Postscript on p. 23 which gives an example of how they may be developed by the teacher. They represent all the qualities which are logically required for having the right emotion directed towards the right object: and, negatively, represent all the possible types of failure from which a person may suffer in the sphere of the emotions. Certain of the components are particularly relevant to the religious emotions: we should guess this to be true of EMP (1) (AUTEMP) and KRAT. In other words, without the ability to be aware of one's own feelings — perhaps particularly the unconscious feelings — and to change those feelings by reflection, discussion and other methods, it seems unlikely that any person can be successfully educated in religion; or, indeed, in any sphere where powerful and often unconscious emotions are involved.

We have not yet said anything about the *methods* of education in religion and the emotions; and it is not, of course, implied that children can be given these components simply by telling them what they are. Nor is it implied that much religious and other education, as it stands, may not be effective at developing the components in children. All we have tried to do so far is to produce a clear list of aims, objectives, or criteria of success for what is central to religious education: that is, the education of the religious emotions. A great many facts about religion, experiences of religious worship, etc., may no doubt be so used as to contribute to these aims. What is important is that the aims should be clearly understood.

Particular Difficulties

To some the above will seem rather remote from what they are accustomed to regard as 'RE'. This may be because we have so far said nothing about how these aims may be cashed out into practical teaching methods: but they may also feel that something is being left out of the aims, or that there are difficulties of principle which have been glossed over. So it will be profitable to take a quick look at three possible objections or difficulties.

'How Can One Understand a Religion Without Being Committed to It?'

Some have maintained that a person cannot 'understand religion' in the full sense — perhaps not even in the most important sense — without being personally *committed* to a religion. This objection seems to present us with an impasse: for (a) unless we are in some sense 'committed', we cannot understand it fully; yet (b) unless we are in some sense *not* 'committed', we cannot assess it objectively and rationally. To try and settle this by saying that religion 'is not a rational matter anyway' is, as we have seen, as false as it is fugitive. We need rather to distinguish the senses in which somebody who is to 'understand religion', or to be 'educated in religion', needs to be committed or otherwise.

(i)   Different people have different beliefs and attach their emotions to different objects. They have different gods, different moral codes, like different kinds of music and literature, believe different things about the physical world, fall in love with different people and so forth. We do indeed sometimes say 'I can't understand how he could believe that', or 'I can't understand what he sees in her', or 'I can't understand why she should worship such-and-such or approve morally of so-and-so'. But in fact we also think that, given patience, insight, imagination and practice, we can come to understand such things. Some cases demand much more imaginative effort, and are much more a matter of 'getting the feel', than others: but as long as people speak intelligibly and have human emotions, it is always possible to understand them, even if some cases seem to us extremely odd.

(ii) It is true that, if I am not a totally committed worshipper of (say) Hitler and am trying to understand someone who is, I shall not have 'personal experience' of what it is like to be totally committed in this way. But this is only to say that I cannot *be* the other person and *have* his commitment, any more than I can have his headache. This is a logical truth, not a regrettable empirical limitation; and it may tempt us to say things like 'I can never *really* know what it's like to worship Hitler' or 'One can never fully understand another person' (since one can't *be* that person). But this temptation must be resisted. If one could not understand people without being them, one could never understand them at all. I can know what it is *like* to have a total commitment to Hitler, if I learn enough about the Nazi movement and use my imagination: I can, in any normal sense of the word, *understand* it, just as (though in a more complicated way) I can understand a person's beliefs without actually sharing them.

(iii) Indeed it is sometimes (perhaps often) the case that totally committed people, so far from being in the privileged position of having unique knowledge about that situation, may in many ways understand themselves and their situation *less* well than an outsider might. They may be too involved, biased, prejudiced, unable to see themselves objectively and compare themselves with others and so forth. This is surely a commonplace with human emotions generally: it is doubtful whether Hitler or Hitler's followers understood themselves better than a competent and uncommitted psychologist understands them.

(iv)   Nevertheless there is a sense in which one may say that someone who wants to understand religion (or many other emotion-based activities) must be 'committed'. He/she must be committed fully to the business of 'getting the feel' of such activities, and this (as we have said) involves far more than just learning some bleak psychological or sociological or other empirical facts about them. In the same way, someone who wanted to understand music or drama would have to do more than learn the dates of Beethoven or Shakespeare: he/she would have to launch him/herself into the world of the Eroica or *Fidelio* and *Hamlet*, to 'commit' him/herself to it imaginatively. This is sometimes said in the case of drama to involve 'suspending one's disbelief': but it is better to say that one believes when one is *in* the world, and suspends all questions of belief or disbelief about the world as a whole until later, when perhaps one may want to criticize or assess it. Learning what it is like to be a Christian would certainly involve engaging in characteristically Christian activities and forms of thought — going to church, praying, being moved by the words of the Bible, etc.: just as, for a full understanding of Fascism, one would go to the rallies, march with the goose-step, try and think oneself into the mental postures demanded by 'racial purity' and 'German destiny' and so forth.

(v)   But this is perfectly consistent with, indeed necessary for, the ability to *assess* these things objectively at *other* times: just as, to use a humble example, one may 'get the feel' of cricket by actually playing quite a lot of it, yet at other times make judgments about whether it is a good or bad game. If we must use the word, we can say that one is 'committed' to it *at the time of playing*. Conversely, the ability to make these objective and (in one sense) 'uncommitted' assessments is itself necessary to the concept of *understanding* the phenomenon fully. For understanding involves being able to stand outside, as well as inside, the game: being able to make comparisons, determine where the game is silly or neurotic and where it has point and reason, and in general evaluate it. A person could not be said fully to understand Christianity and Fascism unless he/she could do *both* of these: just as, for instance, a mother who fully understood her daughter's being in love with a man must both be able to see it from her point of view *and* be able to look at it objectively.

'Shouldn't the Form of Religious Education be Christian in this Country?'

This is rather a difficult objection to phrase, because it can easily be muddled up with others. I shall not take the objector to be saying 'Children should be turned into good Christians' or 'Children should be indoctrinated with

Christianity': that represents a point of view which we have dealt with else-where. I shall rather take the objector to be saying something like 'Children should be taught Christianity because it is part of our common culture': or, more fully, 'Look, we teach English children English and not Chinese: we even think it right to concentrate to some extent on English history, rather than the history of the ancient Aztecs or the contemporary Pygmies. Since this is a Christian country — in some sense, anyway — shouldn't our RE be chiefly concerned with Christianity? So surely you are wrong in suggesting that children should be taught to "get the feel" of lots of other religions'.

(i)   The point here depends on a clear understanding of the concept of education and educational aims. As we said before, this might justify teaching about Christianity because it is helpful to historical, or sociological, or some other form of understanding: but these reasons have nothing to do with *religious education as such*. To put it briefly, the notion of 'cultural transmission' is only relevant to *educational* aims insofar as it is the transmission (or simply teaching) of various forms of thought and factual information. And these are not themselves culture-bound: they may or may not flourish in particular cultures, but that is not why we transmit them — they are valuable in their own right.

(ii) Of course it may be granted that there are other sorts of aims. Not everything we actually do and should do in schools is to be justified specifically on educational grounds. Part of the point of teaching the British system of measuring distance in miles, for instance, is simply that it will be useful for a child in Britain to know these. But it is not on those grounds that we would justify it as *education in mathematics*. The aims of education in mathematics, as in all other subjects, derive from the nature of the subject itself. Certainly teaching about British 'miles' may be a useful *method* of achieving those aims; but that is not the point. Similarly the notions of 'education in history', 'education in literature', etc., are not culture-bound; 'education in history' does not *mean* 'education in British history', but something more like 'education in the principles and skills which history as a subject involves'. Again, it may be the case that one of the best ways of teaching a British child history and literature is to start, at least, by using British history and literature: but this implies no difference in aim.

(iii) Exactly the same goes for 'religious education'. Our aims are to get the child to be better able to understand, access and develop his/her rationality in respect of religion: and I have argued that our central concern here is with the education of the religious emotions. It may be that this aim can best be achieved, in Christian or quasi-Christian countries, by making a good deal more use of Christianity, as subject-matter, than of other religions: and the same might go for Buddhism in Buddhist countries, Baal-worship in ancient Palestine and so forth. But equally this may not be so: it may be that presenting children with less familiar examples has an equally valid claim on the teacher's time — on the grounds, perhaps, that the child needs a good many different examples in order to get a grip on religion in general at all. In the same way, some historians would argue that, to give the child a good grasp of what history is and how to do it, we should proceed better by taking fairly remote examples (ancient Greek history, for instance) than by taking familiar ones. I am not arguing any specific empirical thesis here: I am arguing only that it is a question about methods, which cannot be settled *a priori*.

'Surely Teachers who are Committed For or Against a Religion can't be Non-partisan?'

Although this question also presents no difficulties once we are clear about the concept of religious education, it is very commonly asked: so perhaps something needs to be said even at the risk of being repetitious (see further Wilson, 1972),

(i) When teachers are trying to educate pupils in various subjects they are very likely to have particular views of their own on particular points. Thus I may favour one scientific theory of the origins of the universe, or one historical interpretation of the fall of the Roman empire: I may like or dislike Shelley or Dickens: I may be thrilled or bored by pop music or Bach. The same is true in the spheres of morality and religion. As an individual I am committed to, or favour, these particular beliefs or values. But this has no logical connection with my role as an *educator*. Nobody would suppose that I should teach science, or history, or English literature in accordance with my own individual beliefs or values, however strongly I may feel about them. Indeed the more strongly I feel about them — as is likely to be the case with morality and religion — the more careful I should be to avoid stepping out of my role as educator.

(ii) This is perfectly consistent with a number of quite different points:

   (a) It is often *difficult* for people who feel strongly about beliefs or values not to be partisan, and no doubt this applies to teachers as well as anyone else.

   (b) When in the course of teaching teachers are asked what their own beliefs or values are, nothing is to be gained (and something to be lost) by their refusing to tell. Indeed it may be quite helpful for them to use their own beliefs, like anyone else's, as subject-matter for discussion and investigation.

   (c) No doubt in practice teachers' own beliefs and values will influence their pupils to some extent; and this influence may go far enough to merit the term 'indoctrination'.

17

(iii) But no one should conclude from this that teachers cannot or should not act as educators, at least for some (I would hope, most) of the time. It is all right to say 'You can't help your own beliefs affecting the pupils' or even 'You can't help indoctrinating', if all you mean is 'It is utopian to suppose that anyone can be completely neutral all the time'. But it is very far from all right if you imply that teachers do not have a role — and that the most important role — as educators and since they do have that role, it is not sense to say that they 'indoctrinate' when they play it. For 'indoctrinate' only has meaning by contrast with other methods of dealing with people, one of which we refer to by the term 'educate'.

(iv) The point about the role of the educator as such, which I have been trying to sharpen throughout, has important practical implications. Teachers will not, I should guess, succeed in preserving neutrality in RE and other subjects if they adopt a merely negative attitude: that is, if they simply try to *avoid* indoctrinating or expressing their own viewpoints. They will succeed only if they have a clear conception of the *positive* role of the educator. The warmth and enthusiasm which each of us as an individual feels for his/her own particular beliefs and values must, for those of us who are teachers, be transmuted into warmth and enthusiasm for the *subject*, for education. It is this which we need to generate in our pupils: and if we have a real interest in generating it, we shall not need to worry too much about whether our own beliefs and values are creeping in. Teachers are required to have a stronger commitment to education than their own particular views: if not, they are not earning their money.

Methods and Contexts

If the aims stated in (c) on page 17 can be taken as common ground, we next need to know what sort of teachers, teaching-methods and social arrangements in the school are likely to fulfil these aims: that is, are likely to develop the 'components' mentioned on page 12. Much research is needed before we can say anything certain about this: we offer here some fragmentary suggestions, as much to show the sort of lines on which teachers should be thinking as from any great confidence that the particular methods mentioned are effective.

(i) Many features of current RE teaching would not merit a supposed subject called 'religious education', but may nevertheless be highly relevant to that subject if they are attached to its central concern with the emotions. For example, teaching comparative religion as a kind of sociology or anthropology, or teaching children about church history, or explaining to them Christian doctrine as represented in the creeds, could hardly be justified on specifically

religious grounds. But if these things are relevant to a better understanding of religious and other emotions — to an understanding of
what it is, or what it feels like, to have a religion — and if they are
taught in that light and with that aim, then it is plain that we shall
hesitate before throwing them out of the window. Thus (to choose
an instance at random) we might reasonably think it important for
children to be able to entertain the kind of feelings represented in,
and evoked by, the Psalms or the first chapter of Genesis, if they
are to have an emotional grasp of what one type of religion, at
least, is actually like.

The teacher will thus probably want to use some of the
traditional material as subject-matter or as affording examples of
particular religions (in much the same way as the teacher of
morality may wish to use particular moral codes or *mores* as illus-
tration-material). But this material will not be inculcated: and the
selection of it will depend on whether it fulfils this particular
purpose. Probably the most important kinds of material here will
not consist of 'hard' historical facts (the journeys of St. Paul, the
history of the rise of Islam, etc.) but of psychological illustrations
(what it felt like to believe in Jehovah, Aphrodite, etc. — do we
feel anything of the same kind nowadays? — and so forth). We are
concerned here with making real to the child such considerations
as what sorts of objects (gods) various people today, and in past
history, are or have been in awe of and worshipped; why they have
done so; how the children themselves feel about various objects of
emotion (their parents, nature, artistic productions that evoke
emotion, etc.); what beliefs, conscious or unconscious, underlie
these feelings; whether these beliefs are reasonable; and so forth.
Psychological study of primitive and polytheistic religions may be
particularly important here, at least as important as the study of the
'higher' religions.

(ii) Nor is this a matter merely of *instruction*: the child also requires
experience. In trying to educate children in those areas commonly
called 'musical appreciation' or 'drama', we are not content merely
to instruct them about music and drama: we also make them take
part in concerts and plays. So too with religion. Provided we keep
our aims clearly in mind, there is an obvious case to be made out
for giving children that experience of religion which may be gained
by particular forms of worship. 'Communal acts of worship' in the
school may in principle be thus justified: and the experiences which
a child might gain by taking part in many different types of worship — not only Roman Catholic, Church of England, Methodist,
etc., but also Jewish, Muslim, Buddhist and so forth — are obviously valuable (see Wilson, 1971; also Cox and Cairns, 1989). Like
other aspects of religious education, this falls into place once we
realize that we are out to educate children in religion, not to
inculcate a particular religion; and again, much imaginative thinking,

and much trial and error is needed before we know just what experiences are educative for what sorts of children. What is important is that we should stop acting as if religion were just something we hoped would *rub off* on children, and start thinking seriously about what methods and social contexts are in fact likely to fulfil our aims — to increase EMP, develop PHIL, and so forth.

(iii) Although the educator will be concerned with various objects of emotion as found in religion, he/she also needs some methods of getting the children to admit to, and hence to be better able to understand and control, their own emotions (awe, fear, loneliness, admiration, guilt and so forth), in relation to the objects to which they are *already* attached: for these will be the stuff out of which their outlook — whether eventually religious or not — will be made. The relevant type of education here is perhaps more analogous to psychotherapy than to subject-teaching. Naturally one must be careful in dealing with the child's feelings here, and caution is appropriate. But enthusiasm is just as important: and to give up this task altogether would be, in effect, to give up the notion of any serious religious education. For, amongst other tasks, the teacher has to create a situation in which pupils are able and willing to express and consider their own emotions; and this includes considering their own outlooks, ideals or pictures of life. Unless the pupils can be, at least temporarily, detached from those outlooks, there is no chance whatsoever of their being able to consider them and alter them if need be. It is no good merely *talking to* or *instructing* a person who, say, is totally immersed in a fascist or an 'honour ethic': who has a compulsive need to prove him/herself to be tough and daring, tries never to lose face, worships an immoral bully, and has an ingrained code of behaviour based on the emotions which lie behind this code. A relationship of trust must be built up, without which the real job of getting down to an analysis of emotions cannot even be started. Teachers have much here to learn from the psychoanalysts: and it is a pity that such terms as 'psychotherapy' and 'psychoanalysis' have clinical and medical connotations; when in fact they are *educational* techniques which are highly relevant to this subject (see further in Wilson, 1990).

(iv) Once we get rid of the idea of uncritically accepting particular contexts (which may make neither for security nor for therapy) simply because they are there, or are part of some tradition for which we still have some hankering, it will be seen that teachers have a far wider choice in practical matters than might have been supposed. Thus the question 'What shall we do about the school assembly for worship required by the 1988 Education Reform Act?' has to be tackled in an appropriately wide framework. The right questions to ask are: 'Do we want to have the whole school together in one place? Where? When? For what sort of purpose —

reinforcement (social solidarity, etc.) or education? What sort of activities will achieve this purpose?' These questions go far beyond such issues as whether they should be Christian or multi-faith in content.

(v) Again, once we are thoroughly weaned from the notion of RE as a means of inculcating the religious attitude or a particular religion, we shall easily see that we shall want to put before the child not only what we take to be 'good' religions or outlooks, but also ones which we take to be thoroughly wrong-headed, or even lunatic. Just as we think it possible for the child to learn from the conduct of villains as well as heroes in literature, so it would be useful to show him/her (for example) the irrationalities of the Nazi movement, the Inquisition, Baal-worship, and so forth. For we want the child to internalize, to appropriate for him/her self, the *reasons why* some religions and outlooks are sane and sensible: and this cannot in principle be done without the child also being able to see why others are insane and stupid.

(vi) As we have said, 'religion' is a topic-area within which we may try to educate our pupils' emotions. Some may hold that the best plan is to retain this topic area, add others ('sex', 'money', etc.), and divide up 'the education of the emotions' in this way. Others — and a case for this can also be made — may feel that the divisions should correspond, not to topics, but to some at least of the *logical* components relevant to the education of the emotions, which, of course, cut across all the topics. Thus one could envisage different separate types of teaching — perhaps even separate curricular periods — devoted to (a) the development of insight (AUTEMP); (b) the development of skills and aptitudes in expressing and controlling emotion (GIG); (c) psycho-therapeutic sessions designed to free pupils from unconscious counter-motivation and hence developing KRAT; and so forth.

It is too early to say how far any of these approaches may be successful. What is important, however, is that we do not lose sight of the aims, and of the need for a clear assessment of whether the aims are being achieved. There is at present a good deal of work going on which is topic-based: children are encouraged to discuss war, sex, the family, the problem of old people, and so forth. This approach may be very useful: but we need (i) to have a clear idea of what particular components this sort of discussion is intended to develop; and (ii) some attempt to assess whether it actually does develop them, or merely arouses interest in the classroom and gives the impression of a more 'modern', 'progressive' or 'non-authoritarian' approach.

(vii) Finally, readers will, of course, be aware that a great deal of work has been done which is highly relevant to teaching-methods for religious education, though it has not in general been done under this title. I am thinking of such things as mime, impromptu acting, drama, music and movement, therapy groups, role-playing, the use of film, tape-recorders and video-tape. Once we realize that understanding religion is basically a matter of understanding emotions, and not a matter of understanding a complicated set of intellectual propositions, it is easy to see the value of such methods as these: and easy to see, too, that RE is not something only suitable for intelligent sixth forms. Our components — PHIL, EMP, GIG and KRAT — are not confined to those of high IQs. This does not mean that a good deal of hard 'academic' work need not be done by those children for whom it will be profitable: but it does mean that the sort of difficulties we are likely to meet are not so much lack of intelligence or reasoning power, but lack of emotional security, autonomy, and insight.

Future Tasks

Teachers

The teacher's first task is to gain a clear grasp of the aims outlined above. Armed with this, teachers can then take a look at their school's social arrangements, the methods they use and that other people use, and decide for themselves whether these are likely to achieve the aims. The teachers can, and should, try out new methods and social contexts in an endeavour to develop the components more effectively. Ultimately, however much research may be done, the teacher is the best person to decide what methods and arrangements suit his/her particular children: no research will ever be detailed enough to by-pass the need for the imaginative teacher's own judgment. All we have tried to do here is to direct that judgment along the proper conceptual lines.

Committed Groups

I use this title to refer to particular bodies such as the Church of England, the Humanist Society, Communist groups and so forth. What is required of them is in essence simple. The aims of anything that can respectably be called religious *education*, as we have seen, are common ground to any rational person. These aims, then, can and must be shared by Catholics, atheists, humanists and all other such groups. To talk about Jewish or Protestant education in religion must be seen to be as silly as talking about Jewish or Protestant education in science or literature.

This does not mean that it is wrong for groups or individuals to be committed. It simply demands a distinction, both in theory and in practice, between education and other aims. So long as they do not interfere with, or trespass on, the interests of other groups, the educator has no quarrel with those of any faith or of none: it is only when they attempt to pass on their particular and partisan commitments to children that danger ensues. For children are not the property of their parents, or of any group (even a sovereign state) which has a partisan commitment: they are potentially rational and autonomous adults.

Conclusion

I should like to reiterate the point with which I began. Religion is a form of thought and experience, a department of life, in its own right: and 'religious education' means something like 'initiation into the religious form of thought'. Because it exists in its own right, we must do justice to it as such. We must not be distracted by particular pressures, fears or desires arising from our own particular circumstances (that we live in a 'pluralistic' or 'multi-faith' society, that we want to pass on a particular 'cultural heritage', or whatever). The form of thought, and the education appropriate to it, are both time-free and culture-free: they are, as it were, transcendent and not defined sociologically — any more than are the forms marked by 'mathematics', 'science', 'history' or any other.

Any serious practical attempt at religious education must start from this point: it must have (i) an adequate definition of 'religion'; and (ii) an adequate list of qualities, attributes or 'bits of equipment' that any person (of any time, creed, culture or background) needs and must (for logical reasons) have in order to make progress and perform well in that department of life. On any account, religion is a matter of central importance: and we shall not even begin to do it justice until we take it with the timeless and trans-cultural significance that it requires.

Practical Postscript

It may be useful to list some of the questions and activities that would be relevant to developing the components mentioned earlier in relation to a particular topic. Out of many I choose the contrasting notions of purity and beauty in religious worship and practice.

(i) Take the children to contrasting practices: for example, (a) a low-church Christian or Islamic context, where there are no pictures, ornaments, etc.: (b) a full-blown Roman Catholic service with music, candles, images and so on. Inform them in relation to this of Cromwell's destruction of images, the Byzantine iconoclastic and anti-iconoclastic movements, etc.

(ii) Discuss with them their feelings about these variations. What did the people doing these things feel? Contrast the ideas of 'nothing standing between oneself and God/Allah' and 'celebrating the richness of God's creation by art and beauty'.

(iii) Discuss also the justice/injustice of forcing certain kinds of worship on other people.

(iv) Give the children experience of different kinds of 'religious music' (Gregorian chants, Bach, Verdi's Requiem, Haydn's Creation, modern 'pop' liturgies). Which of these seem really 'religious'? What does that imply for their picture of 'religion'?

(v) Discuss the contrasting merits of (a) a polytheism (for example, Greek polytheism) which does justice to all the forces/emotions in ourselves and the world; (b) a severe monotheism (Jehovah/Allah) which focusses attention on unity but perhaps at the cost of disowning some forces/emotions (for example, sexuality). What ought 'religion' to do about this?

In these and other such activities, we can develop PHIL by considering the equal rights of people to worship in their own way (see (iii)); GIG by teaching them historical facts, and giving them contemporary experience of religious practice; most importantly, EMP by encouraging them to become aware of their own and others' feelings; and eventually KRAT by enabling them to become freer from their own compulsive attachments to one or the other of these two ideas.

To these might be added an attempt to get the pupils to consider their feelings about hypocrisy or insincerity in adults; about the Dionysian/ orgiastic nature of some quasi-religious practices (pop concerts, etc.): about the attractions of simplicity (fundamentalism): and in general about the problem of incorporating many conscious emotions in one's own mind without sacrificing unity and integrity.

This represents just one example out of many: practising teachers will be able to think of many others.

Notes

1 There is general confusion about education in controversial areas (religious education, moral education, political education, education in personal relationships, etc.). The best discussion is in Loukes *et al.* (1983) chapter 6.
2 For useful discussions of the concept of education see Loukes *et al.* (1983) chapter 2 and Wilson (1979) chapter 1.
3 I hope this distinction, here made briefly, will be reasonably clear. There is obviously some sort of difference between (i) looking at various enterprises or disciplines as social or psychological phenomena, without regard for their truth or merits; and (ii) looking at them as having some claims to truth. Thus we could (i) consider, say, astrology as a social or psychological phenomenon; but this would be very different from (ii) considering astrology as a candidate for truth.
4 See previous note. It is remarkable that, in many areas (religious education is one), many writers fight shy of references to truth or objective criteria of reason: perhaps out of an undue fear of giving offence to various cultures, creeds, or social groups.
5 If we are to consider the truth-claims of religion — that is, if we are to contemplate educating people *in* this form of thought and life — then clearly we have to define what the form is. Many writers are extremely reluctant even to attempt this.

6   Of course there are borderline cases, such as Theravada Buddhism. But if we want to do justice to religion as a form of thought, and to the way in which the term 'religion' is normally used, the criterion of awe and worship seems best. We normally distinguish religion from just *any* kind of outlook or set of principles by this criterion.

7   The nature and relevance of these components are discussed more fully in Wilson (1990).

References

Cox, E. and Cairns, R. (1989) *Reforming Religious Education*, London, University of London Press.

Loukes, H. *et al.* (1983) *Education: An Introduction*, Oxford, Martin Robertson.

Wilson, J. (1971) *Education in Religion and the Emotions*, London, Heinemann.

Wilson, J. (1972) *The Assessment of Morality*, Windsor, NFER.

Wilson, J. (1979) *Preface to the Philosophy of Education*, London, Routledge.

Wilson, J. (1990) *A New Introduction to Moral Education*, London, Cassell.

Chapter 2

Whitehead Revisited — Religion and Education: An Organic Whole

Jack Priestley

The Thing Which Will Not Fit

Near the beginning of her book, *Teaching and the Religious Imagination*, the American writer Maria Harris comments that, 'the beginning of all genuine wisdom is the acknowledgement of the thing which does not fit but which, if acknowledged, leads to reform and re-creation' (p. xvi).

Religious education in Britain is increasingly just such a thing. Within the curriculum its uniqueness was established in 1944 when it became the only compulsory subject. In the run-up to the 1988 legislation there were many who hoped that the distinction would cease when it was learned that there were to be many more compulsory subjects. Their hopes were dashed. No place was found for RE within the core subjects. Perhaps that was to be expected, but it was soon established that it would not feature among the foundation subjects either. Whatever the comfortable words 'Basic Curriculum' might have been intended to suggest, RE felt to be even more separated than before, omitted from a debate which centred around assessment for the ten subjects (eleven in Wales) and initially overlooked by the new National Curriculum Council, which clearly regarded it as something of an embarrassment.

Religious education does not fit. There are three possible reactions to such a state of affairs, two of which are obvious and claim support from rival factions which dominate the debate as they have done for the past half century and more.

The first is simply to argue for the abolition of this anachronism and to do away with the subject altogether. Its exponents range from the crude to the subtle. There are those who simply attempt to get round the legislation, by underresourcing, refusing to employ relevant or appropriate staff and generally making life as difficult as possible whenever an inspector is not in sight. On the other hand there are the much smoother band of skilled political operators in the Civil Service and elsewhere whose divide-and-rule instincts are deeply inbred. Nothing is more easily divided than religious factionalism and it has clearly been noted that the enthusiastic encouragement to denominational schools and colleges to take the subject back within their monastic walls is more likely to have the desired effect of reversing an educational tide which has flowed for two centuries, than any amount of confrontational opposition.

The second reaction to the observation that RE will not fit is that of many professionals and specialists within the realm of the subject itself. This reaction takes the form of seeking to adapt and modify the subject so that it will become educationally respectable. In its more extreme forms this has led to a constant attack on anything which even remotely resembled what is termed 'confessionalism' and has led to attempts to make the subject value-free. In broader terms the debate over the past thirty or so years has centred around the felt need to satisfy educational criteria and to justify the subject on educational grounds.

This is a tempting argument and it has led to some significant and, at times, highly valuable developments. Whatever else its opponents may accuse it of, the world of professional religious education has rarely been dull and has never lacked genuine and lively debate. In itself that debate has been religiously educative although, by and large, it has failed to break through into the wider debate and has largely remained a private language-game for those initiated into the mysteries of its dialogue. Therein lies the problem — such an approach itself does not fit. More than that, however, I suspect that ultimately it is doomed to failure simply because it is based on a false assumption and a totally false premise. The false assumption is that somewhere there exists a set of discrete criteria for an activity called education. The totally false premise is that at root that activity can somehow be value-free.

The third possible reaction is the one to which Maria Harris' statement points us. It is to ask why the minor entity does not fit and to face the possibility that the answer might lead to some creative response which affects the greater whole. It is all too easy to assume that if a tiny fringe curriculum area causes discomfort then there is something wrong with it and it must either disappear or adapt. The alternative requires a strong head, a large slice of arrogance and a bold artistic temperament. It is to argue, like the words of the old monologue, that 'they're all out of step but our Albert'. It is, in other words to suggest that RE does not fit because there is something amiss, not with the adjective 'religious' but rather with the noun 'education'. In fact such an assertion is not quite as arrogant as it might at first appear when it is recalled that our whole modern concept of education came out of religious institutions and religious thinking, even though there is a widespread reluctance to acknowledge that fact.

However, no such acknowledgment is necessary with regard to one of the twentieth century's greatest but most disregarded British thinkers. It was Alfred North Whitehead (1970) who, towards the end of his book on *The Aims of Education* concluded that, 'the essence of education is that it be religious'. It is Whitehead's thought upon which I shall draw for the rest of this chapter in attempting to state why it is that this misrepresented subject which we call religious education represents the best hope for restoring a true perspective of the notion of education itself.

The Man Who Would Not Fit

Whitehead himself did not fit. Many who have vaguely heard of him assume that he too was an American. In fact he was 62-years-old and on the point of retirement when he was invited to become a Professor of Philosophy at Harvard and to take over the mantle of William James. James is known for many things but perhaps most of all for his Gifford lectures of 1902 which were published as *The Varieties of Religious Experience* (James, 1982).

The first, and perhaps the most significant, point to make both about Whitehead's comment and James' work is that neither of these authors were noticeably religious in any conventional sense. Not only did they rarely go to church, for example, but, mild-mannered though both were, they each reserved a particular venom for certain aspects of institutional religion. Nevertheless, James, essentially a psychologist, had concluded that the efficacy of religion was that it worked. It was 'pragmatic' in the sense that Peirce, who had coined the word, originally intended. Religion could be shown to be a major cohesive factor in a huge number of individual lives and, because of its variety of forms, cohesive of individuality, rather than of corporateness, except where it was institutionally abused. Similarly Whitehead's respect for religion came, not out of upbringing, but as a consequence of an intellectual pilgrimage.

Whitehead was first and foremost a mathematician. He boasted often that as an undergraduate he had never attended any lecture other than those in mathematics. His greatest contribution to the field is in the seminal *Principia Mathematica* on which he worked for ten years with his former student Bertrand Russell. It was after the completion of that publication that Whitehead's thinking took him on a differing course from the then narrowing orthodoxy of English intellectual life. As linguistic positivism began to dominate he found himself broadening into a thought-world of ever more general ideas, first in the philosophy of science and then into history, the classics and finally religion. Cambridge, England, became too intellectually claustrophobic for him. London offered some respite, particularly as he sought to extend opportunities for higher education for mature, external students through Birkbeck College, but it was unexpectedly in Cambridge, Massachussetts that he discovered that great liberation of the spirit which resulted, not only in another twenty years of creative writing, but also in the establishment of a school of thought of which Maria Harris is just one among many contemporary exponents.

It is time to bring Whitehead home with gratitude to those who have kept his spirit alive. His moment has surely come as the bankruptcy of positivism becomes clearer by the day and as we struggle to find some philosophical foundation for the growing awareness of the organic wholeness and interrelatedness of the world in which we live. Whitehead's philosophy of organism can increasingly be seen as half a century ahead of its time and has still not begun to penetrate the increasingly closed-shop, bureaucratically-controlled education-speak which more and more appears as a substitute for educational thinking on curriculum matters, with all but the faithful debarred from direct influence and some language seemingly outlawed. 'Holism' and 'hidden curriculum', for example, are apparently now (at the time of writing, April 1991) censored from all National Curriculum Council documents. This is not to say that such words and phrases have not themselves often become mere cliches in the past. Rather it is to suggest that superficiality is better disposed of by deeper thinking than by the mere substitution of one set of banalities for another. Whitehead, I want to argue, is a thinker for a new age if not for what is termed *the* New Age. He is of particular relevance for religion and education and, above all, for exploring the relationship between the two.

Like the Cambridge philosophers of his day Whitehead had turned against the old metaphysics which had held up the development of science ever since the Middle Ages. Where he came into real conflict with the new generation of philosophers, however, was in their assumption that they could do without metaphysics altogether. Their confident assumption was that all their deductive thinking was based on pure reason. Whitehead tried in vain to point out that they were as dependent on a particular assumption of the nature of the universe as those who had gone before. If that assumption, or metaphysic, should be wrong then science sooner or later was going to run into the buffers just as surely as traditional theology had done when it failed to detach itself from the medieval idea of a three-decker universe. Moreover, the hidden assumption was wrong. Of that he was convinced. With his gift for reducing great and sophisticated ideas into very common language he put the matter very simply. The fallacy was in believing that, 'the world is composed of bits of stuff with attributes' (Whitehead, 1927, p. 103). The truth, he asserted, is that no boundaries are distinct and permanent; everything is in a constant state of flux. The world is not made up of 'bits of stuff' at all. Rather it is a gigantic living organism in which every component part relates to the whole and to every other part and in which everything is constantly dying and being replenished. Whitehead began to develop his 'organic philosophy'. No-one wanted to know — until he went to Harvard.

Now we do want to know. Organic ideas are springing up everywhere. The 'bits of stuff' of our physical environment are seen to be dying before our very eyes, but always to be replenished, but the old scientific fundamentalism ploughs on, not, let it be said, amongst scientists, so much as in the general thought patterns of a culture indoctrinated into earlier generations and still seemingly intent on outdated notions of inevitable progress.

A New Era From an Old Era

Nowhere is this tendency to think in terms of 'bits of stuff' more evident than in the formulation of the 1988 Education Reform Act and in the ensuing debate about curriculum. It began by listing subjects, continued by attempts, often crude in the extreme, to measure attainment in those subjects and only now is beginning to think about values and to add them as other 'bits of stuff' in the form of cross-curricular dimensions and themes. In short it is an assumption based on 'stuff' or matter. Put another way it rests on a materialistic metaphysic. But this goes totally unrecognized. Chaos and disillusionment are bound to ensue because the values being stuck on the cover bear no relation to the contents of the parcel. The whole package reeks of hypocrisy. What is more, religious education is in some danger of being used in the role of an aerosol sweetener to take away the smell.

It follows that the 'stuff' has to be organized. The inevitable model is one of fields. We are presented with countless diagrams of rectangles representing 'fields of knowledge' now grouped into three core (four in Welsh-speaking schools) and seven foundation (eight in non-Welsh-speaking schools in Wales). Occasionally a small isolated field is added; that is religious education. The game then becomes one of knocking down the walls or grubbing out the hedges between various combinations of these 'fields'. Is religious education a humanity, an art or a science? The answers vary and for good reason. No-one can go very far in the study of religion without coming to recognize pretty quickly that the study involves no boundaries. This is not to say that there are not specific bits of content which should be known but to know them is to acknowledge that they draw on all other subjects. Just as an artist cannot be told that there are certain objects which cannot be painted, so religious people have always used the whole world of objects and events as symbolic of their beliefs. Religions, by definition, claim the most comprehensive overview, the highest vantage point in making sense of human affairs and all human activity and knowledge is included within the picture. This fact alone substantiates Whitehead's claim that the essence of education is that it be religious.

The problem is that the 'field' or 'bolt-on' model does not lend itself to this fact and the reason it does not do so and cannot do so is simply that it is static when the reality of the world is one of constant change and dynamism. As soon as we begin the attempt to think only in dynamic or fluid models our whole perception changes. The image created by 'streams' or 'rivers' of learning is much closer to Whitehead's basic premise. Wherever we start our learning it will, if we pursue it, lead into other subjects and ultimately into areas which can only be described as religious. 'Teach few subjects but teach them well', was one of Whitehead's dictums.

This stream of knowledge model is not a sequential model. It does not necessarily begin with mathematics, for example, and lead eventually into religious issues by means of a contemplation of eternity, infinity and the impossibility of the square root of minus one, although it does not exclude that. Good teaching can, with any subject matter, always take even the less able pupil through new knowledge to the point of unknowing, although few teachers attempt it.

This is not, let it be said, to advocate a return to the sort of integration which has bedevilled the curriculum in recent years — a superficial treatment around a shallow theme which demands no real penetration of any discipline. True integration comes from depth not breadth of study, from a teacher who can prise open the smallest crack and reveal what lies below the surface of what initially may appear to be very solid ground. We train our teachers all too often on the assumption that their job is to make the unfamiliar familiar. The mundane instructor will do just that. The creative teacher will do just the reverse. To make the familiar unfamiliar is what makes learning exciting, stimulates the mind and leads to the ultimate questions.

Relevance and Rhythm

As with integration, so with relevance. The question once more is not whether education should be relevant but what it should be relevant to. Much of our current debate assumes that the only worthwhile relevance is an economic or materialistic one. No-one would deny that the ability to earn a living is a necessary component of education. Where it fails is when that idea is placed in too narrow a context.

A great deal of argument is once again taking place on the relative merits of academic or vocational education. It is not a new argument but nor, sadly, does it seem to have advanced throughout our present century. The dichotomy is, in fact, a false one. Whitehead was himself much caught up in trying to make that point some seventy years ago.

It was precisely because the twentieth century was introducing new types of activity, demanding new curricula that it seemed to him, even in the 1920s that the restatement of general principles had once again assumed such great importance. The grave danger, as he saw it, was that the theorists seemed prone to divorce themselves from any concern for the useful, leaving those intent on developing usefulness to proceed without regard to theory. Does anything change?

For Whitehead the challenge came with the creation of the Harvard Business School, the first of its sort in the world. There were, of course, many who scoffed at the idea that business studies had any place within a real university, not least amongst many of Whitehead's former colleagues in Cambridge. His response was to go on the offensive. Asked in 1970 to give a lecture to commemorate the opening he chose the occasion to speak on the nature of a university. All that he had to say could equally apply to younger pupils, and the following passage loses nothing if the word 'school' is substituted for the word 'university' throughout.

Universities, he argued, were commonly regarded as places of learning and of research but, seen as separate activities, each of these could be performed much more cheaply elsewhere and, 'so far as the mere imparting of information is concerned, no university has had any justification for existence since the popularization of printing in the fifteenth century. Yet the chief impetus to the foundation of universities came after that date'. Within the reasons for this lie the true educational worth of such institutions and the function of those who work in them. What a university, and for that matter a school, does, is to bring young and old together in the adventure of curiosity, but it is not just curiosity for facts, it is curiosity for the use of facts, and it is the very intervention of the notion of usefulness projected onto the future which creates the demand for imagination.

> The university imparts information, but it imparts it imaginatively.... A university which fails in this respect has no reason for existence. The atmosphere of excitement, arising from imaginative consideration, transforms knowledge. A fact is no longer a bare fact: it is invested with all its possibilities. It is no longer a burden on the memory: it is energising. (Whitehead, 1970, p. 139)

The use of language here is again significant. Process, as we have seen, presupposes movement and constant dynamism. Teaching is, therefore, to do with such verbs as 'energizing', 'transforming', 'exciting'. Teaching is, above all else, a creative act. It is not merely the passing on of facts but the illumination of them, the constructing of an 'intellectual vision of a new world', and the preserving of the 'zest for life by the suggestion of satisfying purposes'. Herein lies the *raison d'être* of all institutional education and, especially, universities where teaching and research come together. However, and this is the major point, managers and those working in the world of commerce need these attributes as much as anyone. Imagination is the basic requirement of anyone who needs to anticipate the market or develop new products: sensitivity is essential to those who wish to organize others. Management does not have to be mechanical. Without some sort of vision it not only becomes arid and stale but ultimately it fails. At all levels we need people who will exercise curiosity. In a passage which is redolent with relevance for today's debate he states,

> Do you want your teachers to be imaginative? Then encourage them to research. Do you want your researchers to be imaginative? Then bring them into intellectual sympathy with the young at the most eager, imaginative period of life.... For successful education there must always be a certain freshness in the knowledge dealt with. Knowledge does not keep any better than fish. (*ibid*, p. 147)

By this last comment he does not infer that only new knowledge is desirable. Rather the analogy suggests that ideas only die and become inert when removed and stored for long periods outside of a context which gives them meaning. For as he goes on to add, all knowledge, whether it be new or old, 'must come to the students, as it were, just drawn out of the sea and with the freshness of its immediate importance'. Without that style the latest technological information is as inert as anything from the past but with such a style the giving of facts becomes the communication of real knowledge and the growth of wisdom. Imagination is, therefore, not just a desirable extra in a teacher; it is a *sine qua non*. The process of teaching is nothing less than a way of life.

> Imagination is a contagious disease. It cannot be measured by the yard, or weighed by the pound, and then delivered to students. It can only be communicated by a faculty whose members themselves wear their learning with imagination.... Imagination cannot be acquired

once and for all, and then kept indefinitely in an ice box to be produced periodically in stated quantities. The learned and imaginative life is a way of living, and is not an article of commerce. (*ibid*, p. 145)

What makes knowledge educative is its application to the here and now and what the teacher requires to make that connection is both imagination and rhythm. 'Rhythm' is not a word which appears frequently within our educational text books but it is a key word in Whitehead's vocabulary and nowhere is it more important than in religious education. The rhythm to which he refers is that of constantly relating the particular to the whole. First, children should be given the whole outline of a new area of work, then they can explore it in particular parts before finally they see it again as a whole and, ideally, then see that within a greater whole. This last concern is ultimately that of religion in education. There is no place for the despising of work and the ways of earning a living. Work is a religious concept as much as an economic one. The teacher who cannot link the two is failing in creative imagination.

Religion and the Essence of Education

We come then to the core of the discussion. What is the nature of the relationship between religion on the one hand and education on the other? In what sense is education in its essence, religious?

It was Whitehead who coined the definition of religion as, 'what the individual does with solitariness'. It runs as a refrain through his book, *Religion in the Making* (1927).

Religion *is* solitariness; and if you are never solitary, you are never religious. Collective enthusiasms, revivals, institutions, churches, rituals, bibles, codes of behaviour, are the trappings of religion, its passing forms. They may be useful, or harmful; they may be authoritatively ordained, or merely temporary expedients. But the end of religion is beyond all this. (p. 16)

Inevitably this view of religion has been attacked, often by those who have not gone on to read Whitehead properly and by those who cannot distinguish between solitariness and loneliness. Far from failing to recognize corporateness Whitehead points us to the real nature of community. Those with whom we most genuinely commune, or have communion, are those with whom we can share our moments of deep solitude. By contrast socializing is shallow. Community is only explicable in terms of individuals and the individual is only comprehensible in terms of the community of which he/she is a part. The problem is one of expression and communication. 'Expression ... is the return from solitariness to society' (*ibid*, p. 124). The real danger arises when those expressions become first of all turned into group dogmas and then are given priority over new experience.

Religion is primarily individual; dogmas are clarifying modes of expression. As such they are absolutely essential but not only in religion. They are essential for science too. However, like everything else, they are not static. The man who had begun his intellectual life as interested in nothing but mathematics was to end it by declaring, 'Exactness is a fake' (Whitehead, 1941, p. 700). It is of the essence of dogma that it should change and develop. The impatience with dogma has come about because it has been abused. Its function is to be a means of expression but we are back to the point that it all too often comes to be used as an end itself. When this happens its usefulness is destroyed. No dogma can ever be final: at best it can only be adequate.

> You cannot claim absolute finality for a dogma without claiming a commensurate finality for the sphere of thought within which it arose. (Whitehead, 1927, p. 124)
> Dogmas, however true, are only bits of the truth, expressed in terms which in some ways are overassertive and in other ways lose the essence of truth ... though dogmas have their measure of truth, which is unalterable, in their precise forms they are narrow, limitative, and alterable: in effect untrue, when carried beyond the proper scope of their utility. (*ibid*, p. 139)

The need for the rhythm of teaching is once again to the fore. The solitary experience must be related to the experience of the community; the expression of the individual must be held against the dogma which is the expression of the group. The one feeds the other and each is changed by contact with the other.

There is nothing new in this. Good teachers have always followed such a method but constantly we need to be reminded of it. The child's poetry possesses its own validity but can be improved by bringing it into contact with the publicly-acknowledged great poetry of a society. At the same time only the student who has ever really tried to write poetry, paint a picture or create a piece of music can really begin to enter into a realization of what the acknowledged poet, artist or musician has achieved. The bad teacher, by contrast, is the one who uses the work of the great exponents to diminish and destroy the creativity and the faltering first steps at expression of the young.

Religious teaching is no exception to this. At one extreme the outpouring of individual experiences without the check of tradition leads to an assumption that every expression is of equal validity. On the other an insistence on doctrinal orthodoxy and a refusal to countenance any form of heresy is, perhaps quite literally, soul-destroying. Religious 'knowledge' can be the most rancid form of intellectual decay. The juxtaposed signs at the top of the bookshop stairs which read, 'Mind Your Head' 'Second Hand Theology' would have summarized Whitehead's whole approach to the teaching of religion. For theology as usually understood he would have had little time; for theologizing as a process of bringing the greatest thoughts of the past into contact with the experiences and expressions of the present he would have had the highest regard, seeing in it the greatest educational opportunity. For religion when it is alive is a consciousness of that very dynamism which is the real world, whereas to reduce that of all things to 'bits of stuff with attributes' is to ossify, and thus destroy, the life force itself.

Here then is both the problem and the possibility for religion in education. Those who would limit the scope of its thought engage in a contradictory process, and there are many who do. Religionists, especially theologians, have shown less imagination over the years than perhaps any other group of scholars, and those who have displayed it have usually been persecuted for their efforts. Just as scientific method could not be developed by those whose thinking was contained within scientific limitations, so the history of human spirituality is the history of those who dared to step outside of any credal position and, by refusing to be contained within dogma, became recreated out of it. Yet at every level, and perhaps especially in the primary school, we find otherwise imaginative teachers holding back from the full flow of imaginative expression in religious education lest they be guilty of transgressing some sort of credal barrier.

However, while a creed must not shut off from future enquiry there is a discipline to be recognized about understanding how those in the past came to formulate their experience in the credal statements which have come down to us. At its best, speculative reasoning is not merely a leaping around after something novel; it can only come out of a deep understanding of what has been experienced before.

There is, therefore, a balance to be struck between knowing and understanding the experience of others and using that knowledge to know and understand ourselves. The great purpose of education should be to give people a greater reliance on the validity of their own inward and private experience rather than a distrust of it as so often appears to be the case. In a democracy it is the function of education, before all else, to produce thinking people. Only a tiny minority may become philosophers. But mere knowledge without the capacity for thought makes for slavery rather than for the emancipation of the individual spirit which is the true end of education.

For creativity is not given from outside in lumps of information. It exists within, and only within, human beings, where it is developed by the proper exercise of imagination or destroyed by the lack of it. It is the ability to interject imagination at the moment of transmitting facts which separates the teacher from the instructor. It is by this means that the growth of the human spirit keeps pace with the growth of knowledge and feeds upon it, whilst, without it, the accumulation of knowledge can diminish or destroy the fire of that same spirit. Knowledge itself does not constitute education. It is the fuel of the process and like all fuels it can smother and extinguish if not properly mixed. For Whitehead imagination is not an optional extra but a fundamental aspect of the process — the projection of the subjective into even the most apparently objective elements of knowledge because, at the end of the day, the two meanings of the word 'subject' coincide. The subject *which* is being taught becomes fused into the subject *who* is being taught. Education should carry a health warning: it changes people. What we learn affects what we

35

become, not just in the narrow, mechanical sense of finding a job but as total persons.

Can We Find the Time or Can the Time Find Us?

Finally, there is the essential ingredient of time. For teachers this is the most precious commodity of all and there is never enough of it, especially for teachers of religious education. In a strange way Whitehead brings us reassurance on this point by telling us, in effect, that there is really none at all. At least, there is a past and a future but the only time we can possess is the present and that is a mystical point which we can never contain. It joins together the past and the future but it is never there. The moment we think about it it is gone. Or, as another American writer has put it, 'The opposite of present is not past or future: the opposite of present is absent' (Moran, 1974, p. 97). It is an existentialist point and one in which Kierkegaard himself revelled. Its educational significance has rarely been unpacked, but as soon as we go back over our own education it is amazing how often we pin-point the chance moment as being decisive in the path our lives have taken — a moment seized by a teacher out of nothing, rather than the carefully-constructed scheme of work. A reading of the gospels illustrates this point over and over again.

Good teaching is the use of the moment, the Now, the Instant. The past is all we have to draw on; the future is what all education is about. Ultimately the teacher's power is restricted to infusing the point at which they meet. We cannot stop the flow of time; we can only affect its direction.

Central to this difficult idea is the notion of vision. Life can be different from what it has been; the future is not pre-ordained. Religion has always provided men and women with alternatives to the world as it is. We can only understand their utopias when we understand something of the context in which they created them. We can only create our own when we grasp the fullness of the world we inhabit.

The world of school is such a world. For all its deficiencies the new National Curriculum provides us with an opportunity we have never before possessed. The Basic Curriculum encompasses all the core and foundation subjects. Together they make up the learning world of the child's experience and we know, at least in broad detail, just what it consists of. Religious education is perfectly poised to construct itself in such a way that it helps children and young people to make a meaningful whole out of the various parts. There is no need to duplicate. If Celtic Christianity is within the history syllabus what need is there for the content to be done again in RE? If both mathematics and music concentrate on the nature of symbolism why start again from scratch?

But even more importantly we can begin to show the relationship between the parts. This has always been the essential task of the theologian and the religious thinker. The important thing, however, is the process — to theologize about all that is going on in other parts of the curriculum and to relate it to life as it is lived and as it might be lived, to realize its potential in terms of each individual's future growth.

It sounds an enormous task. In one sense it is, but in another it is realizable. The hub of a wheel may be of very small dimensions. It may appear to consist of little else than the spokes joined together but it is the fact that they are held together at all which makes it possible for the whole to function as a wheel and to move forward. The teacher's job in general and that of the RE teacher in particular is to take what has been and is and to show what might be.

Dwayne Heubner, Professor of Religious Education at Yale and another modern American follower of Whitehead, summarizes all of this perfectly when he says,

Education is the lure of the transcendent — that which we seem is not what we are for we could always be other. Education is the openness to a future that is beyond all futures. Education is the pro-test against present forms that they may be re-formed and trans-formed. Education is the consciousness that we live in time pulled by the inexorable otherness.... To interpret the changingness of human life as 'learning' and to rein in destiny by 'objectives' is a paltry response to humankind's participation in the divine or the eternal. (Heubner, 1985, p. 460)

References

HARRIS, M. (1987) *Teaching and the Religious Imagination*, San Francisco, CA, Harper and Row.

HEUBNER, D. (1985) 'Religious metaphors in the language of education', *Religious Education*, **80**, 3, summer.

JAMES, W. (1982) *The Varieties of Religious Experience*, Glasgow, Collins Fontana.

MORAN, G. (1974) *Religious Body*, New York, Seabury Press.

WHITEHEAD, A.N. (1927) *Religion in the Making*, Cambridge, Cambridge University Press.

WHITEHEAD, A.N. (1941) 'Immortality' in SCHLIPP, P. (Ed.) *The Philosophy of A.N. Whitehead*, Evanston, IL, Northwestern University Press.

WHITEHEAD, A.N. (1970) *The Aims of Education and Other Essays*, New York, Macmillan Free Press.

Chapter 3

'Heaven in Ordinarie': The Imagination, Spirituality and the Arts in Religious Education*

Nicola Slee   *How a good education involves artefacts.*

Introduction

'The art of being wise is the art of knowing what to overlook', according to William James,[1] whilst Alan Gregg expresses the same idea a little more suggestively in his aphorism, 'a good education should leave much to be desired'.[2] No educational programme, school curriculum or subject syllabus, however comprehensive or compact, can hope to transmit all that is desirable to be known about what is considered valuable in a society. In a world of rapidly expanding knowledge and ever-shrinking boundaries between races, cultures and nations, education can only aspire to introduce students to a fraction of what is to be known and discovered within any single field of study. This is as true of religion as it is of any other subject, and perhaps more so. Religions, representing as they do complex patterns of belief, ritual, story and behaviour developed over centuries, are not readily reducible to manageable curriculum packages and the attempt to do so may lead to unhelpful over-simplification and misleading caricature. The aim of education must be to set the flame of learning alight in students' minds so that it will carry on burning long after schooling is over (rather than to fill the pail of knowledge, to draw on Yeats' well-know comparison)[3] or, to change the metaphor, to set them out on the road of discovery equipped with the essential tools and skills for the journey rather than try to map out the whole territory which might be traversed. If 'a good education leaves much to be desired', a bad one kills off the innate and infectious curiosity which is the hallmark of the intelligent human being.

* This chapter is a revised and lengthened version of an article originally written for *A Catholic Spirit: Festschrift for Jim Bates*, edited by Robert Butterworth and published by the Department of Theology and Religious Studies at Roehampton Institute in 1989, and is reproduced here by the permission of the editor.

In this process of 'lighting the flame of learning', stark choices have to be made and priorities formulated. There are no easy guidelines for those who must stake out the priorities in current educational policy, but at least three considerations should inform the choices. First, there must be a realistic recognition that much that is worthy of study will have to be omitted: the good must frequently give way to the better. Second, there must be an equally acute consciousness that what is *not* taught or considered worthy of note (what Elliot Eisner designates the 'null curriculum') (Eisner, 1979, pp. 74–92) is as powerful in shaping the curriculum and the values of students as what is explicitly presented for study. Third, as all teachers know, it is the *method* and *context* of teaching as much as the content which determines the extent to which pupils are stimulated and encouraged to take responsibility for their own education.

With regard to religious education in the state maintained sector, recent legislation provides a set of parameters within which priorities must be framed, albeit some rather confusing ones. On the one hand, religious education is charged, along with all other subjects in the basic and National Curriculum, with the noblest and weightiest responsibility imaginable, namely, to foster and promote 'the spiritual, moral, cultural, mental and physical development', not only of individual pupils, but of society as a whole (HM Government, 1988, p. 5). On the other hand, the content and focus of religious education and worship have been much more precisely and narrowly prescribed than has ever been the case in English law, requiring the school curriculum to reflect faithfully 'the fact that the religious traditions in Great Britain are in the main Christian whilst taking account of the teaching and practices of the other religions represented in Great Britain' (*ibid*, p. 6); and worship is required to be even more specifically focused, at least in so far as the majority of acts in a term are required to be 'wholly or mainly of a broadly Christian character' (*ibid*, p. 5). However these clauses are interpreted — and the rapidly growing literature testifies both to the wide breadth of interpretation possible and to the complexity of the hermeneutical process itself[4] — it is clear that religious educators in the state-maintained sector are required to pay much closer attention to the content of their syllabuses than ever before, and to be able to justify it within the terms of the Act.

Whilst the interpretation and implementation of these later clauses will doubtless continue to command the lion's share of attention from those 'at the chalk face' of teaching and management, it would represent a failure of vision and responsibility of incalculable magnitude, if religious educators were to neglect to respond to the broader charge bequeathed by the Education Reform Act in its opening paragraphs to contribute to society's spiritual development and well-being. This chapter argues for the prioritization of this daunting, but not impossible, task, in the discussion, research, policy-making and curriculum development of religious educators in the 1990s. If religious educators do not make the spiritual well-being of pupils and society a priority, it is hardly to be expected that mathematicians, geographers and historians will. If religious educators have nothing positive and distinctive to offer the curriculum at this point, we shall have failed the needs of our children and our society, however ingenious our implementation of the new legislation in its detailed particulars.

I am not alone in my conviction that religious education must be centrally concerned with the education of spirituality. Indeed, it is heartening to note a renewed concern amongst religious educators in Britain during the past decade for the realms of the imagination, spirituality and the arts, and their various interconnections. Partly in reaction to the excessive objectification of religious education proposed by the advocates of the phenomenological approach, in which questions of personal values, commitments and beliefs are safely bracketed out, a number of writers have sought to develop a more pupil-centred, personalistic approach in which the imagination, the arts and the quest for spirituality are at the centre, rather than the periphery, of religious education. The movement towards a more personalistic and existential model of religious education can be detected in many quarters, for example, in the collection of essays on religious education and the imagination edited by Derek Webster and Molly Tickner in 1982; in recent issues of the *British Journal of Religious Education* on spirituality across the curriculum, and fantasy in religious education;[5] in the work of the Religious Experience Research Unit in Oxford[6] as well as in the independent research of David Hay (1982) and others; in the innovative Exploration into Experience series of curriculum materials edited by Brenda Lealman and Edward Robinson; and in some of the newer Agreed Syllabuses which exhibit a concern with the development of pupil's spirituality (for example, Bradford City Council, 1983). And now, these hints and intimations towards the spiritual have received official sanction in the major piece of educational legislation in the last quarter of the twentieth century. The choice of legislators in placing the spiritual development of pupils at the forefront of the Education Reform Act not only confirms the insights of those who have been working with this notion for several years; at the same time, it is a very eloquent testimony to the inadequacy of any merely utilitarian model of education and provides a clear mandate to all who seek to challenge policies which appear to contradict the Act's explicit commitment to the spiritual dimension of society's life.

In what follows, I shall draw on the recent literature to explore something of the significance of the imagination and the arts in religious education, and to elucidate their role in opening up the realm of the spiritual. I shall begin by considering a model of religious education which goes beyond the phenomenological study of religions to a concern with pupils' spirituality. This will lead into an examination of the notion of spirituality and the spiritual realm, and then to a consideration of the intimate relationship between the imagination and spirituality. Having suggested the fundamental role which the imagination can, and should, play in religious education, the role of the arts within religious education will be briefly considered and, finally, a number of practical implications for the approach of the teacher will be suggested.

Beyond the Phenomenological Approach

A number of contemporary British religious educationalists share a deep sense of unease with the prevailing orthodoxy of educational philosophy, in which the purpose of religious education is limited to the development of an understanding of religion and its role in society, achieved through an object- ive and sympathetic study of the phenomenon of religion, as far as this lies within the capabilities of students at their various stages of development. For these thinkers, whilst the phenomenological study of religions is an import- ant component of religious education, it is by no means enough; by itself it is inadequate and sterile. Thus, Edward Robinson (1977) concedes that 'the phenomenological approach enables us all to look at religion, and religions, from a new angle' and he acknowledges that 'this can be refreshing'. 'But', he goes on, 'this new objectivity, encouraging curiosity at the expense of involvement, does enable people to know a great deal about religion without really knowing what religion is about: without relating it, that is, to any personal experience' (p. 80).

Brenda Lealman (1982a) writes:

> Examine the main focus of religious education and it is often on the production of miniature scholars, tolerant citizens, or ... 'church people'. At least, the emphasis is on the acquiring of knowledge about religious institutions. The main focus is rarely on the develop- ment of the person through the stimulation of religious insight and religious understanding within an awareness of mystery.... Religion in religious education has become phenomenon, a matter of learning the skills and techniques with which to understand religions, to learn about and from them. It is hoped that the material will have personal significance to the students, that their experience will be engaged but, so often, this is in order to provide a phenomena hanger. This is not enough. (pp. 59–60)

Jack Priestley (1982) goes further and suggests that the very methodology advocated by the phenomenologists leads (inevitably?) to the trivialization and de-sacralization of religion:

> The methods we do employ, essentially those of the empiricist rather than those of the poet and artist, come into direct conflict with the subject matter under review. We then deal superficially with depth (content to draw Moslem prayer positions rather than reflect on the inner mental state which the bodily movements indicate), analyti- cally with wholes (drawing maps and collecting statistics of Calcutta as a way of 'understanding' Mother Theresa) and resolve ultimate questions with finite answers along the lines of 'Hindus believe...'. (pp. 17–18)

Even if it is granted that the phenomenological approach itself allows, even encourages, the exploration of the 'inwardness' of religious belief and behaviour as a necessary ingredient of religious education (as, for example, the Schools Council Working Paper 36 argues[7]), there is still a danger that this aspect of 'inwardness' is, itself, trivialized and relativized by a method which does not acknowledge the centrality of pupils' own inwardness in the learning process.

If religious education is inadequately conceived as phenomenological religious studies, how, then, is it to be understood? The writers and thinkers we are here considering suggest that religious education must move beyond an objective study of religions to an exploration of inwardness, a grappling with existential questions, a search for spiritual identity, an encounter with mystery and transcendence. Thus, according to Raymond Holley (1978), religious education is essentially 'the provocation of spiritual insight', the development of 'spiritual awareness' and 'religious understanding'. Brenda Lealman (1982b) suggests that religious education is best conceived as a 'method which encourages awareness of mystery and seeing within the perspective of transcendence': 'it must make possible experience within religion and not simply stimulate interest in religion, important though this is' (p. 76). According to Judy Ollington (1982), religious education must 'assist pupils in their search for meaning, in their synthesis of experience', through reflection upon 'the pervading symbol structures within which significance is to be found' (p. 63). David Hay (1985) argues that religious education 'must honestly present religion for what it claims to be — the response of human beings to what they experience as the sacred' and 'must help pupils to open their personal awareness to those aspects of their experience which are recognized by religious people as the root of religion' (p. 142).

Without denying a rich diversity amongst these writers, one can detect a certain common mind among them. For each of them, religious education is far more to do with method than content, it is essentially process rather than programme. It is a process which is characteristically inquisitive and explorative, rather than instructive and explanatory; experiential and inductive rather than didactic and deductive; open-ended and therefore risky rather than predetermined and safe; personal and relational rather than academic and detached; holistic and integrative rather than abstract and analytical. It is a process which fosters spiritual growth and identity rather than the religious beliefs of any particular tradition (though, clearly, for many pupils, spiritual growth and identity will be found within the particular religious tradition into which they have been initiated); and, whilst the acquisition of knowledge and the development of understanding are not decried in this process, they are perceived to be secondary to religious education's more fundamental concern with pupil spirituality. It is this dimension of spirituality, which resides at the core of all religion, that constitutes the unique contribution of religious education, qua religious education, to the curriculum, these writers suggest, although, paradoxically, they also emphasize that religious education does not have a monopoly on the spiritual. Thus, Ursula King (1985) argues that an education towards spirituality 'is not the exclusive concern of the religious education teacher but should be fostered right across the curriculum, especially in the teaching of the arts subjects but also from certain perspectives of the sciences'. She continues:

> However, the religious education teacher ought to have a special interest in spirituality, for this is the very heart of religion. If there is not a message about the disclosure, invitation and challenge of the spirit, both human and divine, at the very heart of every religion ..., what else matters in religion? (p. 138)

Just as ethical considerations arise in many, perhaps all, areas of the curriculum, but remain the primary concern and responsibility of moral education, or, again, as literacy is fostered by the total curriculum but remains a particular objective of the teacher of literature, so, whilst spirituality may be fostered throughout the curriculum, religious education has a special responsibility for, and commitment to, its development. Edward Robinson (1985) argues this point well:

> If we are going to justify religious education ... we have got to see it as fulfilling a unique and irreplaceable function: we have got to show that it can help us to understand life spiritually, that it can awaken the mind, indeed the whole person, to a dimension of experience that no other subject can touch. Well, others may touch upon it; they may well indicate the existence of this spiritual dimension and the need that our species has always felt for it, but religious education alone can explore it. Religious education alone can answer the question, 'What would it be like, what would it mean, to experience life spiritually?' (pp. 246–7)

Spirituality and the Spiritual Dimension

What, then, is meant by this talk of 'spirituality' and 'the spiritual dimension'? For all the elusiveness of the concept, the framers of educational legislation, politicians, peers and educationalists alike join with the writers under consideration in affirming that we cannot do without it. From the 1944 Education Act onwards, all major English educational legislation has made it the duty of local education authorities to promote the spiritual development of the pupils and the communities they serve, without making any attempt to define what this might mean or how it might be done (HM Government, 1988). Successive reports from the DES have reaffirmed the spiritual dimension as one among a number into which pupils should be initiated through the curriculum, although, again, the Department has not done a great deal to clarify the notion.[8] Perhaps such wariness is hardly surprising. Even those recent writers who assert the centrality of the spiritual dimension in education acknowledge a fundamental difficulty when it comes to the attempt to specify what is meant by the term. Thus, Derek Webster (1985) writes:

> The notion of the spiritual is ultimately impenetrable. This is because it draws attention to what is invisible but not illusory, to what is powerful but not explicable, and to what is non-rational but not meaningless. There will be no final logical clarity here, no rational demonstration or accurate conceptualization. Talk about the spiritual is opaque. It is 'the ineffable incomprehensibility' of God at 'the very heart of our existence', or 'that which succeeds in bringing (human beings) to inner transformation.' Such talk veils as much as it reveals. It can point but does not fix, it may evoke but will not beget, it will illuminate but not explain. (pp. 12–13)

The elusiveness of the notion is further compounded by the fact that talk of spirituality and the spiritual has been largely devalued and discredited in the secularized and 'despiritualized' Western world, and has acquired negative and unhelpful connotations for many people, such that the spiritual is perceived in sharp contrast to the physical, the social or the political realm, for example, rather than being intimately related to each of them. Frederick Tristan, a contemporary French writer, talks about this problem of the soiled and radically unsatisfactory nature of our speech about the spiritual:

> The word 'God', for instance, is totally devalued and I think this is a major cause of the despiritualization of the West. Neither does the word 'spirituality' mean anything any longer, or by the same token the word 'spirit'. All such concepts are in need of complete revision. And I'm well aware that the way in which I talk about these things may appear ambiguous or contradictory, while in fact I believe I am simply being honest. I am attempting by means of using devalued words to put across something living. And that's not easy! One has to keep on correcting everything one says. I say 'God', but its not God. I say 'spirit', but I'm speaking of the body. And when I speak of the body, I'm also speaking of spirit. Each time there is paradox, because we have to use a language that is founded on black and white, in other words on dualism. Now dualism is precisely what I refuse to accept. (quoted in Gascoyne, 1988, p. 34)

Yet the limitations of our conceptual tools do not 'excuse us from the attempt to say something intelligible about spirituality', as Webster (1985) insists; they 'just mean that such attempts will offer starting points from which to quest, rather than a map of the territory' (p. 13). Bearing these warnings in mind, it is helpful to consider a number of statements about spirituality, not in the hope of arriving at some exhaustive and definitive demarcation of the concept, but rather to highlight the range of qualities and characteristics that may be associated with the concept of the spiritual.

The DES document, *Supplement to Curriculum 11–16*, provides two contrasting and somewhat contradictory statements on spirituality. The first speaks of the spiritual area of experience as being

concerned with the awareness a person has of those elements in existence and experience which may be defined in terms of inner feelings
and beliefs; they affect the way people see themselves and throw light
for them on the purpose and meaning of life itself. Often these
feelings and beliefs lead people to claim to know God and to glimpse
the transcendent; sometimes they represent that striving and longing
for perfection which characterizes human beings but always they are
concerned with matters at the heart and root of existence. (DES,
1977)

The second statement gives a much narrower view of the spiritual area
as 'concerned with everything in human knowledge and experience that is
connected with or derives from a sense of God or Gods', suggesting that
'spiritual is a meaningless adjective for the atheist and of dubious use to the
agnostic' (*ibid*). Both Webster (1982) and Priestley (1982) dismiss this second
view as 'unhelpful and rather silly' (p. 86), and 'simply mistaken' (p. 114),
respectively, arguing that the category of the spiritual is much wider than
that of the explicitly religious, and is a term which has meaning for a very
wide number of people. Dorothy Dixon, taking account of the wide spectrum of associations, both religious and non-religious, which talk of the spiritual, suggests: 'from the sensing of divine presence to the recognition of a
heightened quality in an event or an encounter, and a response of awe and
wonder' (Dixon, 1984, p. 329). Priestley (1982) lists a number of characteristics of the spiritual, suggesting that the spiritual 'manifests itself first of
all in feelings and emotions from which it has to be translated into thought if
it is to be talked about at all'; that the spiritual is essentially dynamic and can
only be communicated in dynamic images or models; that the spiritual 'is
most directly connected with being rather than doing, knowing or saying',
and finally, that the spiritual dimension is, itself, a-moral, requiring to be
educated morally (pp. 114–5). Ursula King (1985) distinguishes between a
number of ways in which the concept of spirituality is used, but, at its most
fundamental, existential level, she suggests that

> spirituality refers to the lived quality of a person ... It is the way in
> which a person understands and lives within his or her historical
> context that aspect of his or her religion, philosophy or ethic that is
> viewed as the loftiest, the noblest, the most calculated to lead to the
> fullness of the ideal being sought. (p. 137)

Perhaps the most adequate and concise summary is provided by Webster
(1985), who suggests that the spiritual

> is that category of being which is the form of the personal. Its
> coordinates are thought, freedom and creativity; its expression is
> through commitment, valuation and aspiration. It implies openness
> and self-transcendence within (humanity) in community. (p. 13)

Together, these attempts at definition point to the spiritual as a dynamic, all-pervasive dimension of human existence which has to do with 'matters at the heart and root of (that) existence', which is intimately connected with personal identity, with the 'lived quality of a person', but which transcends personal identity and suggests a mystery, an unseen reality, beyond the life of the individual, pervading the entire world order, with which human persons are invited to enter into relationship and communion. This mystery is variously experienced and expressed in personal or impersonal terms, within or without the framework of a religious perspective, as transcendent to or immanent in the present world order, but, however it is construed, there is a common conviction that it is only by attending and responding to this mystery at the heart and root of existence that the earth with all its peoples can live in the fullness of justice, harmony and peace which is its birthright.

Imagination and the Spiritual Dimension

To foster pupils' spirituality and spiritual development, then, religious educators will be concerned with promoting exploration of 'matters at the heart and root of existence' in such a way as to provoke awareness of the interrelatedness of all things and the mystery inherent in all things, and to invite personal response to that mystery — a personal response which incorporates the political and the contemplative within a unity of heart, mind, body and will. As Brenda Lealman (1982a) puts it:

> Mystery is at the heart of religion. Or, rather, religion is our response to, our articulation and interpretation of mystery. The underlying purpose of religious education is to provoke awareness of this mystery as mystery — and to make it possible for young people to be educated in religion, to learn within religious awareness. It is to make it possible for them to see from within a religious perspective, to experience *myself* within the perspective of transcendence; and so, to perceive ordinary life in a new way, to see the strange within the familiar. (p. 59)

Imagination, and especially the creative imagination of the artist, is crucial to this process of fostering the spiritual, according to these writers, because it is the unique and characteristic function of the imagination precisely to open up awareness to what lies beneath and beyond and within the appearance of things, to perceive the mystery in the mundane, the depth beneath the surface, the beyond in the midst, or, as the poets themselves suggest, to discern 'Heaven in ordinarie'[9]:

> To see a World in a Grain of Sand
> And Heaven in a Wild Flower,
> Hold Infinity in the palm of your hand
> And Eternity in an hour.[10]

Imagination, according to Ollington (1984), is 'that human power which enables us to go beyond the immediate situation ... in order that we may grasp what is really possible, gain vision to extend frontiers and recognize that there is more in life than the mundane' (p. 161). It is, as Robinson (1987) describes it, 'that capacity for conceiving that the world, and our life in it, need not always be the way it is now' (p. 8). For Paul Ricouer (1987), 'the imagination is par excellence, the instituting and constituting of what is humanly possible' and thus, 'in imagining possibilities, human beings act as prophets of their own existence' (p. 3). In Robinson's words, it is 'our natural, inborn faculty for transcendence' (Robinson, 1987, p. 12).

This capacity of the imagination to perceive 'heaven in ordinarie' is perhaps most clearly demonstrated in the creative works of the great artists who, as Naum Gabo (1980) puts it, 'remind us that the image of the world can be different' (p. 9) or, in Barbara Hepworth's words, 'rebel against the world as (they) find it because (their) sensibility reveals to (them) a world that could be possible' (Hepworth, 1980, p. 44). The artist is one who, whilst remaining profoundly faithful to the 'ordinarie' mundaneness of the objects, events, persons and forms he/she depicts, describes or creates, at the same time is capable of transmuting the ordinary and mundane into something redolent of mystery, beauty, terror and awe. Or, to put this more satisfactorily, it is precisely the creative genius of the artist to be able to both perceive and express, at one and the same time, without any sense of incongruity or untruth, the mystery within the mundane, the awesomeness of the ordinary. I think at once of Van Gogh's brilliant yellow sunflowers, which seem to pulsate on the canvass with life and colour and joy; or again, of his huge, brute, clumsy, peasant's working boots which yet somehow exude a beauty and a compassionate reverence for the dignity within the squalid poverty of their unseen owner's harsh life.[11] I think of Winifred Nicholson's exquisitely delicate jars and bowls of flowers opening out onto vistas beyond the unseen window frames, which, as her art developed, are increasingly bathed in a kind of luminous light and purity of colour (for example, Collins, 1987). I think of the stark simplicity of Frances Horovitz's verse, in which earth, air, sky, plant and living creature are each stripped down to the bare minimum of line, texture, image and voice, and yet are wholly present to the reader in all their fullness (Garfitt, 1985). Thinking of Horovitz sets me thinking of the pure, clean colour and lines, and the almost surrealist, larger than life, quality of Georgia O'Keefe's shells, bones and flowers (for example, Cowart and Hamilton, 1987). From there it is but a step to the sheer love of form itself which one finds in the sculptured contours and shapes of Moore, Hepworth, Gabo and others, or to the riotous glory in colour of Hoffman's huge, paint-spattered canvasses and Rothko's strangely awesome slabs and walls of colour, which seem to resist stubbornly all attempts at interpretation and which yet possess an uncanny power to move, to comfort and to disturb (cf. for example Tate Gallery, 1987).

Although there is a progressive movement away from representation towards abstraction in the artists I have mentioned, each of them evoke uniquely, for me, the utter 'thusness' and 'isness' of ordinary, mundane objects and forms in such a way that they become somehow luminous and transparent to significance, meaning, perhaps even glory, far beyond what I habitually perceive or notice when I am confronted by an old pair of boots, a vase of flowers, a sheep's skull or animal bones out on the hills, whitened by wind and rain. These are, of course, personal 'favourites' and 'acquaintances'; each reader must supply his/her own examples. What is common to each of the examples I have cited is that, within the frame of the artist's vision, the mundane and superficial become sacred, numinous, holy; they become *sacrament*; and here, the aesthetic imagination moves to a point of convergence with the religious vision, for, underlying both is the 'persistently central assumption that certain objects or actions or words or places belonging to the ordinary spheres of life may convey to us a unique illumination of the whole mystery of our existence, because in these actions and realities ... something numinous is resident, something holy and gracious' (Scott, 1987, p. 14).

If this begins to sound rather grandiose, Mary Warnock helpfully reminds us that human beings habitually employ this same creative facility to perceive things as other in the most ordinary, humdrum ways, as well as in the more elevated realms of science, the arts and religion. 'The imagination', she suggests, 'ranges from the very ordinary, by which we see a tree as a tree, and not a vague mess of shapes and colours, by which we hear a series of sounds as a melody, to the most exalted, by which people can formulate and pass on to others, though perhaps not by the use of literal words, the vision or understanding they have' (Warnock, 1980, p. 405). Indeed, there is, Warnock argues, an essential continuity between our everyday uses of imagination and the sublime achievements of the poets, artists, musicians and other creative geniuses whom we tend to elevate to a higher spiritual plane.

> There is a continuum of imagination. At its most humdrum, it is that by which we interpret sense experience in accordance with the ordinary presuppositions we need and use in everyday life, by which I interpret a red light not just as a coloured light but as a prohibition, or I interpret someone's stance as indicating misery or fatigue. Children who are described as 'imaginative' are those who readily see the tree as a house, or the chest as a ship. In its highest function, the imagination of the creative artist enables him to see, and present to others, the particular significance of a place or an event or a pattern of colour or sound. Somewhere along this continuum comes the aesthetic imagination by which those who are not themselves creative artists are enabled to enjoy and to feel that they understand the creative works of others. And allied to this is the imagination by which in the experience of nature ... people may sometimes feel that what is before them speaks of something urgent, but something which words or other symbols are necessarily inadequate to express. (*ibid*, p. 404)

It is this ability to conceive of things being different from the way they are, as being, in some sense, significant of something other than what is present at the purely objective level of sheer data, which distinguishes human beings from all other species, Robinson (1987) suggests (p. 8), and which lies at the heart of all that is characteristically and uniquely human, such as 'ritual, art, laughter, weeping, speech, superstition, and scientific genius', according to Suzanne Langer (1948, p. 34). And it is this ability to conceive of things being other, as being 'more than', what is immediately apparent, which can open up the spiritual dimension of reality, Robinson (1987) suggests, for:

> it is the peculiar gift of the imagination, and its prime function, not to keep its eyes on the horizon but to speculate continually on what lies beyond it; not simply, as the word might suggest, to create images, or even to pass from one image to another, but to conceive of a reality that may be beyond all conceivable images. (pp. 23–4)

And again:

> If we ask what is the one faculty above all which differentiates us from the rest of the animal creation, it is surely this capacity in us to conceive of things being different from the way they are. More than this, we can conceive the inconceivable, we can believe the unbeliev-able — and all this through that imaginative openness to the infinite possibilities of life, scattered, in Gabriel Marcel's beautiful image, like pollen on the summer air. And it is in this openness that we become aware that reality is not neutral, is not indifferent to our search; that there are powers and forces so sensitively responsive to our initiatives that we can only describe them in personal terms. It is by virtue of our possession of this unique faculty that our species can be described as a spiritual one. Our spirituality is a function of that imagination which is rightly called creative because it is open to the source of all creation. (Robinson, 1985, pp. 250–1)

Thus Robinson goes so far as to define imagination in terms of spiritual capacity, 'that spiritual openness by which men and women ... have become aware of a reality that comes to meet them, of a mysterious initiative that responds to, perhaps even anticipates, their search' (Robinson, 1987, p. 22).

The imagination here comes very close to the biblical notion of faith (as John Taylor points out in his preface to Robinson's book), and is the means whereby the individual perceives, welcomes and receives the gift of transcendent mystery offered in the ordinary and everyday. Robinson here echoes the insight of Wallace Stevens that 'the wonder and mystery of art, as indeed of religion in the last resort, is the revelation of something wholly "other" by which the inexpressible loneliness of thinking is broken and enriched' (Stevens, 1957, p. 238).

Understood in this way, and to use theological language for a moment, imagination is a gracious gift indeed, the bestowal and guarantee of a dynamic openness to life and to future, the first-fruits of the Christian belief in the resurrection, symbol and token of our nature as creatures with a hope and a future. Put more simply, and to use the language of poetry, it is the power of imagination to transform even the most mundane or bleak and apparently meaningless experience which enables us to trust that:

> Every day, something is given —
> Even on black day, blind day
> As though a force,
> Itself immune,
> Indicates sudden balsam,
> Consolation. (Earle, 1987, p. 15)

Nevertheless, to think in such terms is not to suggest a naive and simplistic identification of imagination with spirituality, as if the mere exercise of the imagination, in and of itself, were to guarantee spiritual development. Rather, whilst the two are, indeed, intimately interrelated, it is important to recognise that both imagination and spirituality may be pursued and developed in a number of ways and directions, not all of which are equally desirable or commendable. If imagination is the capacity for openness to mystery which can lead to an encounter with transcendence, it is also a capacity which can be misused and channelled into self-indulgent fantasy and delusion or more sinister and destructive acts of human invention. Such uses of imagination, far from fostering spirituality, are more likely to deaden and corrupt spiritual growth. For all Robinson's 'high doctrine' of imagination, he insists that, although 'imagination is necessary to the development of spirituality, it is not sufficient' (Robinson, 1987, p. 26). It needs the support of reason and of tradition if it is not to assume demonic proportions and wreck havoc. Webster (1982) likewise affirm the need for imagination to work hand in hand with reason as well as with passion, and he suggests that there is no antithesis between the two: 'imagination does not dethrone reason; it enriches it by extending its boundaries' (p. 90).

Spirituality, Imagination and the Arts in Religious Education

If it is part of the task of religious education to foster pupils' spirituality and spiritual development and if the exercise of the imagination is crucial to such a process, then it is clear that the imagination will play a central role in religious education. Can we be more precise than this?

Ollington (1984) has suggested three main contexts in religious education within which the imagination will necessarily play a crucial role. First, the imagination is crucial in life experience themes which form much of the content of religious education in the primary and middle years, and where the concern is to explore experience in depth; it is through imagination that the child is able to link diverse experiences and thus gain a sense of the wholeness and meaning of life. Second, the imagination is crucial in the recognition and exploration of the symbolic, metaphoric and narrative form of religious expressions such as story, gesture, ritual, music, drama, dress and food, through which religions suggest the transformation of the every day and give symbolic meaning to time and place. Third, the imagination is crucial in the exploration and affirmation of different views and ways of life such as mufti-faith religious education requires (p. 161).

Others such as Lealman, Robinson, Priestley, Hay and King, have emphasized the vital role which the creative and expressive arts may play in religious education. According to them, the fostering of pupils' creative imagination through the medium of the arts is at the heart of religious education because, they argue, the arts allow a unique entry to the exploration of experience at depth and the encounter with mystery which are, themselves, the key to pupils' developing spiritual sensitivity and awareness.

The role which these writers envisage for the arts in religious education goes far beyond the merely illustrative, or the explicitly religious, as Webster (1982) argues:

> To associate the expressive arts and religious education should not mean using literature to point a moral, pictures to illustrate points of view, music to serve a religious purpose, dance to derive a liturgy and drama to enact religious tales. Each of these ignores the integrity of the expressive arts, treats them as means to religious education's ends and fosters a destructive distinction between the sacred and the secular.... The unconscious demand by religious education for 'useful propaganda' from the arts stifles their originality. (p. 90)

If 'religious education will not sanctify the arts by employing them as so many puppets to dance for itself', Webster suggests that 'it will, however, gain a more profound understanding of itself by listening to the questions which the expressive arts raise' (*ibid*), and he goes on to suggest that:

> Curiously, it is when the arts do not take explicitly religious myths, pictures, symbols and literature that they most clearly focus on what religious educators find most valuable. Religious education today occurs for most children outside of church and family in schools which are largely secular. Where the arts can discern the religious nature of the questions raised by the secular, they can enhance contemporary spiritual development very significantly. (*ibid*, p. 92)

In an age which is deeply inimical to the spiritual, and whose root metaphors reify a 'hermeneutics of suspicion' which is in direct opposition to the 'hermeneutics of faith' shared by religious believers (Hay, 1985, pp. 140–1), it is suggested that the arts can perhaps penetrate the sceptical consciousness of secular human beings in a way which religious language and myths can no longer do. Thus Robinson (1987) suggests that the arts may be capable of 'seducing' contemporary consciousness into spiritual alertness where religion has failed:

> Given the kind of education that is standard in our secularized system, with perhaps the additional inoculation against religion

provided by compulsory church attendance, it is hardly surprising that large numbers of young and not-so-young people today show all the symptoms of a totally undeveloped or even pathological spirituality. Something almost akin to seduction may then be necessary if that dormant spirituality is to be activated.... We are fortunate to live in a culture still rich in such potential means of seduction — by which of course I mean a still living tradition of the arts in all their creative variety. (pp. 82–3)

For these writers, the arts at their best represent a way of knowing and being in the world which is fundamentally continuous with the ways of knowing and being enshrined in the great world religions, and yet which is also in touch with the scepticism and doubt, the bewilderment and hesitancy, the struggle and the search of an age which many perceive as deeply unsure of itself, bordering on the edge of world crisis, perhaps even catastrophe. The arts express and enshrine, for these writers, an essentially 'religious' attitude towards reality, and yet do so with an indirectness, a tentativeness, an openness, and at the same time, a compelling authority and truthfulness to contemporary experience which, somehow, for many, the religious traditions do not possess. The arts express and enshrine a way of knowing and being in the world which integrates mind, body, emotion and will; which reveres and cherishes the mundane world of matter, form and energy and finds spirit and transcendence there; which is rooted in 'profane' and secular experience and which yet transforms that experience so that the world is recreated anew; which continually challenges, relativizes and subverts the present world order, things as they are, in the light of an envisaged future, things as they might be; a way of knowing and being in the world which balances disciplined attention, patience, labour and struggle with a basic trust in, and openness to, the essential goodness of things and the human capacity for imagination; a way which is rooted in a rich heritage but which is always straining forward, launching out into uncharted territory; a way of knowing and being which embraces paradox and apparent contradiction and lives fruitfully out of the meeting of opposites; a way which seeks to bring order out of chaos, meaning out of the insignificant, pattern where before there was only randomness, and in this sense may be called, without exaggeration, redemptive, salvific, suggesting and revealing healing and wholeness where fragmentation and alienation appear to reign.

If the arts may represent such a way of knowing and being in the world, then, to begin to develop one's own creative artistic skills, on the one hand, and to learn to respond with sensitivity to those works of art created by others, on the other, is to begin to be in touch with those springs of vision, truth and life-giving energy which lie at the heart of religions. The arts are thus seen to have a central, rather than a peripheral, role in religious education because, as F. David Martin (1972) has suggested, they may lure persons into participation in the religious (or spiritual) dimension and they may help to interpret that dimension. In aesthetic experience, 'self-consciousness is lost', one becomes 'absorbed in empirical grounds', and one finds direct access to 'a further reality'. If such an experience of participation is deeply felt, Martin suggests, one senses the 'awe-ful-ness' of that further reality, and one desires even deeper participation and feels a sense of reverence, awe, and concern for the ultimate (p. 91, pp. 27–28). The human being is drawn into Being, and art then achieves its desired goal: 'to break the narrow boundaries of the finite and open a window onto the infinite, for the benefit of the (human) spirit, yearning in that direction' (Pope Pius XII, quoted in Lealman and Robinson, 1981, p. 29).

Some Practical Implications

The exploration and development of the spiritual dimension through creative acts of the imagination for which I have been arguing in this chapter is not, ultimately, something which can be guaranteed by legislation or prescription. Legislation charges educators with the task of promoting spiritual development, and I have suggested that the creative arts have a central role to play in this task by stimulating the imagination, that capacity for transcendence which is perhaps the faculty by which we share most nearly in the 'image of God'. Beyond that, it is difficult to prescribe in detail the content or method of such an education in spirituality, though arguably, one might recognize it where it is taking place according to the extent to which pupils display an awe and reverence for the world in which they live, a thirst for truth and understanding, a recognition of their own unique giftedness and creativity, and a commitment to ongoing self-discovery and relationships with others marked by mutual trust and openness.

Yet it is right that visionary ideals should be pressed for their practical applicability and relevance, especially at a time when educators face increasing pressures on their time, attention and resources. So, at the risk of descending into banality, I offer the following practical priorities as pointers towards a quality of education which might be expected to fan the flames of curiosity, imagination and insight which, themselves, may become the gateway to spiritual discernment and growth.

Attention to the Concrete and Particular

When there is so much to be 'covered' in the curriculum, it is a besetting temptation of teachers to opt for breadth at the expense of depth, to go for the broad sweep rather than the narrow focus, to opt for the 'overview' which can so easily flatten and deaden the unique individuality of each particular thing and hence strip the learning experience of the very colour and vivid detail which might demand attention and provoke insight. Yet, so often it is attention to the precision of the particular which opens access to the profound awareness of the universal. We need to submit to the wisdom of Blake's flower, Van Gogh's peasant's shoes, O'Keefe's shells and bones and learn that it is often better to tell a rabbinic story to catch the flavour and humour of Jewish faith than wade one's way through pages of Torah, better to spend fifteen minutes contemplating and scrutinizing a single Nicholson canvas flooded with light than hear an hour's discourse on the spiritual quest of her art, better to make and eat chapatis and curry together as a way of gaining insight into Sikh hospitality than learn it as a tenet of faith divorced from its concrete expression. In each case, it is not so much the attraction of instant appeal over painstaking effort which should dictate the choice — the long, slow, ruminative attention to a painting may demand just as much in the way of work as reading a book or listening to a speaker — as the discernment by the teacher of the 'one thing necessary' out of a possible hundred which, within the limited time and space available, will do most to capture the spirit of a tradition, a quest, a life-story or an insight, and which will provoke a genuine encounter with the 'thusness' and the particularity of the other.

Looking for Shape and Pattern

Attention to the concrete and particular is not the antithesis of searching for universal truths and wider meanings but precisely its partner. It is by attention to the grain of sand that the world in its wider dimensions is revealed, and the wild flower contains the secret of heaven itself, if Blake is to be trusted. Yet the wider insights born of the contemplation of the artist are perhaps more likely to be expressed in the discernment of shape, image and pattern than in the conceptualization of abstract thought. It is all too easy for the religious education teacher to seek to reduce all tension and conflict between the particularities of divergent religious traditions in a bland and lazy relativism. This is not the way suggested by the artist, whose vision demands that we look at each particular thing in its own utter uniqueness, refusing to reduce it to some common formula; yet whose art equally is witness to the truth that, by the disciplined exercise of contemplation, gradually an unfolding pattern may begin to emerge which is not a denial but rather an enrichment of the diversity of the world. This truth is testified to not only by artists, but also by the mystics of many traditions, whose contemplation of the 'dazzling darkness' some name God has issued in a fundamental conviction of the oneness of all things which holds in relation the apparent conflicts and contradictions described by conceptual thought. It is perhaps by a growing ability to discern the shape, pattern and coherence of things in the work of the creative artist, that pupils may be enabled to discern such shape and pattern in their own lives and in the wider world of confusing and disparate experience.

Letting the Symbol Speak

Having chosen the 'one thing necessary' — the story, the painting, the building, the person, the object, whatever it be — teachers are often tempted to 'explain' and 'interpret' the choice, instead of allowing the symbol to do its own work of creating its own invitation and response. This process of letting the symbol speak for itself is hard for educators to exercise, because it requires a letting-go of power and control, and a simple trust in the potential of subject-matter to reveal its own truth as well as in the potential of the students to recognize it. The teacher is invited to relinquish a certain measure of control over the educational process in order to allow the student to engage with the subject-matter at hand, and to jettison the false and arrogant assumption that she 'owns' the meaning of the object or event. Perhaps most difficult of all, if the symbol is to speak, the teacher is required to trust the potential of each student for insight and growth, and to invite that insight and engagement with new understanding into the open by his/her attitude of welcome and respect towards the student. Such an attitude cannot be aped but can only be exercised by teachers who genuinely recognize that they have much to learn from their students.

Space for Spontaneity and Reflection

Creativity cannot flourish where there is not an openness and space for at least some measure of free exploration, reflection and questioning of the boundaries of what is 'safe', 'accepted' and 'known'. The imagination flourishes precisely at the point where what is known, long gone unchallenged to the point where it is hardly even noticed, becomes suddenly questionable, mysterious, provocative. This plea for space may seem wildly romantic at a time when every inch of curriculum time has to be fought for and won at the expense of some other good, yet without it learning is likely to be both sterile and relentlessly exhausting. Only where there is the space for spontaneity can the spiritual find room to breath and expand.

Such practical priorities, so baldly stated, risk rejection on the one hand for their imprecision and generality, and on the other for their mundane banality. Yet teachers who attempt to practise their art by such simple rules know that their exercise is neither easy nor cheap. They demand a commitment to the vocation of teaching as a creative work of art which is every bit as visionary as the vocation of the artist or the mystic and which has every bit as much to offer the spiritual well-being of a society.

Notes

1 In Fitzhenry (1986), p. 367.
2 *ibid*, p. 111.
3 'Education is not the filling of a pail, but the lighting of a fire', *ibid*, p. 112.
4 Cf, for example, 'Religious education after the 1988 Education Reform Act', *British Journal of Religious Education*, **13**, 3, summer 1991.
5 *British Journal of Religious Education*, **7**, 3, summer 1985 and 10, 1, autumn 1987.
6 Cf, for example, Robinson (1977).
7 Schools Council (1972) *Religious Education in Secondary Schools*, London, Methuen/Evans.

Nicola Slee

8   Cf, for example, Department of Education and Science (1977).
9   The phrase is from George Herbert's poem 'Prayer' in Patrides (1974) p. 71.
10 BLAKE, W. (1958) 'Auguries of innocence' in BRONOWSKI, J. (Ed.) *William Blake*, Harmondsworth, Penguin, p. 67.
11 Cf, for example, van Gogh (1974).

References

BRADFORD CITY COUNCIL (1983) *Religious Education for Living in Today's World*, Bradford, Bradford City Council.
COLLINS, J. (1987) *Winifred Nicholson*, London, Tate Gallery.
COWART, J. and HAMILTON, J. (Eds) (1987) *Georgia O'Keefe: Art and Letters*, Washington, DC, National Gallery of Art.
DEPARTMENT OF EDUCATION AND SCIENCE (1977) *Curriculum 11–16: Supplement to Curriculum 11–16*, London, HMSO.
DEPARTMENT OF EDUCATION AND SCIENCE (1988) *Education Reform Act*, London, HMSO.
DIXON, D. (1984) 'Spiritual area of experience' in SUTCLIFFE, J.M. (Ed.) *A Dictionary of Religious Education*, London, SCM.
EARLE, J. (1987) 'Every day', *Visiting Light*, Bridgend, Poetry Wales Press.
EISNER, E.W. (1979) *The Educational Imagination*, New York, Macmillan.
FITZHENRY, R.I. (Ed.) (1986) *Chambers Books of Quotations*, Edinburgh, Chambers.
GABO, N. quoted in LEALMAN, B. and ROBINSON, E. (1980) *The Image of Life*, London, CEM.
GARFITT, R. (Ed.) (1985) *Frances Horovitz: Collected Poems*, Newcastle, Bloodaxe.
GASCOYNE, D. (1988) 'Flowers in the precinct', *Resurgence*, **129**.
HAY, D. (1982) *Exploring Inner Space*, Harmondsworth, Penguin.
HAY, D. (1985) 'Suspicion of the spiritual: Teaching religion in a world of secular experience', *British Journal of Religious Education*, **7**.
HEPWORTH, B. quoted in LEALMAN, B. and ROBINSON, E. (1980) *The Image of Life*, London, CEM.
HOLLEY, R. (1978) *Religious Education and Religious Understanding*, London, Routledge and Kegan Paul.
KING, U. (1985) 'Spirituality in secular society: Recovering the lost dimension', *British Journal of Religious Education*, **7**.
LANGER, S. (1948) *Philosophy in a New Key*, New York, Mentor.
LEALMAN, B. (1982a) 'The ignorant eye: Perception and religious education', *British Journal of Religious Education*, **4**.
LEALMAN, B. (1982b) 'Blue wind and broken image' in WEBSTER, D.H. and TICKNER, M.F. (Eds) 'Religious education and the imagination', *Aspects of Education*, **28**.
LEALMAN, B. and ROBINSON, E. (1980) *The Image of Life*, London, CEM.
LEALMAN, B. and ROBINSON, E. (1981) *Knowing and Unknowing*, London, CEM.
LEALMAN, B. and ROBINSON, E. (1983) *The Mystery of Creation*, London, CEM.
MARTIN, F.D. (1972) *Art and the Religious Experience: The 'Language' of the Sacred*, Lewisburg, PA, Bucknell University Press.
OLLINGTON, J. (1982) 'Images for life?' in WEBSTER, D.H. and TICKNER, M.F. (Eds) 'Religious education and the imagination', *Aspects of Education*, **28**.
OLLINGTON, J. (1984) 'Imagination' in SUTCLIFFE, J.M. (Ed.) *A Dictionary of Religious Education*, London, SCM.
PATRIDES, C.A. (Ed.) (1974) *The English Poems of George Herbert*, London, Dent.
PRIESTLEY, J. (1982) 'Teaching transcendence' in WEBSTER, D.H. and TICKNER, M.F. (Eds) 'Religious education and the imagination', *Aspects of Education*, **28**.

RICOUER, P. quoted in HARRIS, M. (1987) *Teaching and Religious Imagination*, San Francisco, CA, Harper & Row.

ROBINSON, E. (1977) *The Original Vision*, Oxford, Religious Experience Research Unit.

ROBINSON, E. (1985) 'The experience of transfiguration', *Religious Education*, **80**.

ROBINSON, E. (1987) *The Language of Mystery*, London, SCM.

SCOTT, N. quoted in HARRIS, M. (1987) *Teaching and Religious Imagination*, San Francisco, CA, Harper & Row.

STEVENS, W. (1957) *Opus Posthumous*, New York, Alfred Knopf.

TATE GALLERY (1987) *Mark Rothko: 1903–1970*, London, Tate Gallery.

VAN GOGH, D.W. (Ed.) (1974) *Vincent Series*, Amsterdam, National Museum Vincent Van Gogh.

WARNOCK, M. (1980) 'Imagination — aesthetic and religious', *Theology*, **83**.

WEBSTER, D.H. (1982) 'Spiritual growth in religious education' in 'Religious education and the imagination', *Aspects of Education*, **28**.

WEBSTER, D.H. (1985) 'A spiritual dimension for education?', *Theology*, **88**.

WEBSTER, D.H. and TICKNER, M.F. (Eds) (1982) 'Religious education and the imagination', *Aspects of Education*, **28**. Hull: Institute of Education, University of Hull.

Part 2
Faith-Perspectives on Religious Education

Editorial Introduction

The first three writers have approached the question of priorities for religious education primarily from an educational perspective, bringing together much which is discussed today with regard to the importance of the emotional, the experiential and the spiritual dimensions. In many respects what they write can be readily seen to cohere, but have they moved too far away from the real world of religion?

Part 2 considers this question. It consists of five contributions from people whose understanding of religion is much more closely associated with specific religions and religious traditions.

The priority which Richard Wilkins identifies draws attention to pupils' experience of religion outside school. He considers that this is frequently ignored or disparaged within school, so that the impression of religion which is conveyed does not do justice to what it really is. Even when the religion of the home or religious group is acknowledged, it is often used simply as resource-material. This cannot lead to real understanding of religion. He argues that instead 'education depends on partnership'.

He then considers in some detail the apparently simple question: what does religious education achieve? Using the example of a Johannesburg van-driver, Wilkins raises questions about the aims of religious education. What he has to say is hard-hitting, controversial and with a strong vein of irony. He has important criticisms to make concerning assessment and experiential religious education and believes that controversy should be taken seriously. 'The teacher needs to encourage the question whether or not a faith stands up intellectually, culturally and morally in the modern world' and he notes that this applies not only to religious faiths but also to faiths such as secular humanism.

He writes as a Christian evangelical with full awareness of the pluralism of society, and notes that a fundamentalist background can be an excellent preparation for multi-faith dialogue.

The fluidity and vision argued for by Priestley and Slee receive in this chapter by Wilkins a reminder of the reality of difference, disharmony and difficulty which needs to be brought into the overall vision. The current pluralist view can tend too easily to delight in diversity by subsuming all beneath one overarching aim of human tolerance which, as Wilkins points out, ignores the complexities and realities of religions as they are, and of the commitment which religious faith arouses and sustains in people.

This matter is also very much to the fore in Syed Ali Ashraf's chapter which begins by noting that the attempt to educate people in a broad and balanced way, taking account of the whole of life, normally ignores the question of religious awareness. The prevalence of secularism has caused teachers to be so fearful of any charge of attempted religious indoctrination, that even the obligatory religious education 'becomes not merely partial, but defective'.

Like Priestley, Ashraf considers that 'religious sensibility is an integral part of human consciousness'. He develops his argument by noting that children have an inborn sense of justice, truth, love, mercy and compassion, indicative of our 'higher self' in tune with what is immutable and transcendent. Each individual has constantly to wrestle with the conflict between the selfishness which would ignore this higher self and the selflessness which manifests it. He has a high view of the true function of religion which is to 'uplift the heart beyond the narrow confines of the material worldly self, an expansion of the heart beyond all calculations, a transcendence which for Muslims, Christians, Hindus, Sikhs and Jews cannot occur without the presence of a supreme being, God'.

The rest of the chapter considers appropriate methods 'for enabling pupils to become conscious of the religious sensibility, of rousing it and refining it ... without at the same time making religious education a means of indoctrinating children into a particular faith'. He makes some pertinent points here about commitment, worship and the alignment of 'formal external profession of faith' with a sincere attempt 'to follow in thought and action the moral and religious code of their religion'. Mistakes and failures give rise to genuine contrition. He notes also how all religious traditions witness to the need for divine guidance. Religious sensibility is not a solitary phenomenon, nor is practice in it to be made perfect just by an individual's lone efforts.

Writing as a Muslim, he presents a powerful case for a truly world-religions approach which shows real respect for what is at the heart of particular diverse traditions. There is much in common to be drawn on 'from the great moral and religious literature of the world irrespective of particular religious doctrines'; he terms this 'the Religious Tradition'. Religious education must help pupils to overcome narrow sectarianism and prejudice and realize 'for example, those who follow Jesus Christ or Mohammed should not condemn each other. If religious education cannot succeed in doing this, that education and its methodology must be seriously defective'.

In conclusion Ashraf makes clear that his concern in schools is with religious education not with religious instruction. He argues, as does Wilson, for that 'willing suspense of disbelief' which can promote 'willing adventure' into the experience of religious sensibility.

In an important postscript to the chapter he finds a way of including Buddhism within the scope of his understanding of what is at the heart of religion. A vision is thus unfolded in this chapter of how the real world of diversity can be accommodated whilst being taken seriously on its own terms.

Readers may find this chapter instructive to explore in that he does not water down the importance of a specific religious commitment. Like Priestley's chapter, this is directly challenging to current concepts of education, as also is the one that follows.

Bernadette O'Keeffe's chapter reflects on priorities for religious education in a rather different way. She writes as a sociologist, and most of the chapter is descriptive of the Christian Schools Movement which she is making the subject of a research project. She achieves an impressive level of impartiality and the picture she unfolds is illuminating. The Christians involved see the purpose of education in terms of the nurture of pupils in Christianity which can inform the rest of their lives. Religious education quite naturally supports this overriding priority with specific knowledge and skills concerning the Bible, church history and specifically Christian attitudes to issues, moral and general.

There is little doubt that confessionalism of this type will not be considered acceptable by the majority of educationalists today. It assumes what they do not assume — that there is a guaranteed and absolute certainty available which it is neither possible nor desirable to doubt. For children to be brought up and educated within what is generally seen as a closed system is to infringe their freedom to develop as persons in their own right.

The last part of the chapter seeks to add to the curriculum of these Christian schools a concern for the wider world-perspective. In so doing O'Keeffe offers a priority for state schools also. She argues for the positive contribution of religious education to global and environmental education. If this is not acknowledged we can argue that secular indoctrination is taking place.

Her priority cleverly takes the leading objection of most educationalists to the Christian schools movement and turns it against their accusers. She says in effect, 'Yes, they should not indoctrinate, but neither should you, and you are doing so at the moment'. O'Keeffe is surely right indeed in seeing the Christian schools as a response to the taken-for-granted secularism and relativism which have informed state education for a very long time now and to which all the other contributors in this book are equally opposed.

The emphasis O'Keeffe puts on environmental education is one which also fits in with the kind of concerns expressed in other chapters. Religious education has a major contribution to make to fresh thinking in this area and to awakening a sense of responsibility. The quotations she gives from S. McDonagh are very much to the point, for religious faith per se has not been enough to guarantee wise stewardship of the earth. Discernment and openness to find insight and new forms of cooperation with other inhabitants of this planet are essential.

Kevin Nichols' chapter addresses some of the questions most likely to be in the minds of readers after studying the last three chapters. The place of religious commitment raises quite acute educational anxieties which Nichols' discussion may help to allay. In so doing he puts forward a strong argument *for* the positive role of religious faith in informing education. He is careful to distinguish this from any hint of an imperialist attitude towards other subject-areas whose specific integrity must be preserved and respected. There is therefore no need to fear that we are being offered an 'RE bid for the whole curriculum' as one teacher expressed it in a recent conversation with me on religion and the arts.

The principal reason emerging from his discussion of these issues relates to the need to participate in order to understand, because 'parts' gain their significance from an intuitive grasp of the 'whole' which is more than the sum of the parts. This echoes Priestley's contention about the nature of knowledge just as it reflect's Slee's emphasis on the importance of spirituality. It also reinforces the priority which O'Keeffe identified of a holistic, ecological view of life and of the contribution of religion to that perspective.

Quoting extensively from the writings of Cardinal Newman, whose work is increasingly being seen as relevant for today, Nichols first analyzes the strengths and weaknesses of current religious education theory and practice. He then asks what might be learnt from considering the story of religious education within a particular tradition of faith, taking Christianity as his example. His comment 'No doubt all such traditions have their educational stories' can be seen as an invitation to members of other religions to articulate their stories in the same way as he does for Christianity.

He notes how after an initial period of suspicion towards rational enquiry, Christian tradition formed a fruitful partnership between faith and education in the work of the great third-century theologian and teacher, Origen. The educational atmosphere of his school is described by one of Origen's students, and it indicates the possibility of a vision of education in which religion, reason, openness and diverse views can produce genuine exploration and genuine commitment.

The rest of the chapter argues indeed such commitment is the means of searching for understanding. The distinction between what is only academic and what is of powerful practical and emotional significance for people is crucial; religion can never release its secrets to the purely clinically-minded enquirer. 'True learning begins in wonder, goes on in humility and ends in gratitude'.

He considers that religion is a potentially unifying force which can enable the connections between different curriculum-areas to be grasped. Interdisciplinary enquiry is therefore supremely important for religious education as a means of exploring this interconnectedness.

Readers may feel that the question to which Nichols has not given sufficient attention is the one he identifies towards the end: has 'such a vision of education ... any bearing on a society like ours, in some sense pluralist, in some sense secularized'?

This leads us into the next chapter for Edward Hulmes begins at this point, taking the full weight of the apparent dilemma posed by pluralism. He offers a panoramic view of the world religions scene and combines analysis in depth with wide perspective, bringing together many of the themes discussed earlier in the book. Hulmes foresees a constructive, tension-reducing role for religious education provided there is 'a shift in attitude to the whole question of confessionalism'. For religious education should enable students 'to discover a sense of their religious and cultural identity' (for which Nichols has also argued), as well as helping them 'to appreciate the merits of alternative systems of belief and action'. Students need also 'to acquire the capacity as they mature to review, and if necessary, modify or change their own convictions in later life'. Religious education is indeed a 'risk-venture'.

He goes on to discuss the question of commitment in depth and argues that a pluralist society has to define clearly the limits of tolerance. He argues that this must happen within a concern for inclusiveness. This is not easy, and so, 'in a culturally diverse society *religious* education may best serve the common interest by helping individuals to acquire some degree of fluency in the language of affirmation. Its acquisition marks an important stage in the development of religious literacy'. Such affirmation does not preclude, but rather enables, open and critical enquiry. He considers that teachers should not be afraid of the exploration of differences which 'far from consolidating existing social divisions, may reveal hitherto unsuspected sources of shared experience and common aspirations'.

He then goes on to describe the three essential functions of religious education: the descriptive, the evaluative and the integrative. The first 'challenges every kind of cultural provincialism', the second enables clearer self-knowledge of assumptions, prejudices and beliefs and the third can enable students 'to discern possible links between the separate subject courses which they take in school and the lives they have to live outside'.

In recent years religious education has concentrated on the first and been weak on the second. There is need also for a less selective approach to the task of description. 'The destructive aspects of religious commitment, especially when personal beliefs are expressed in fundamentalist or nationalistic terms, also have to be considered if a fair and balanced evaluation is to be made'.

He notes that there is a question-mark today beside the idea of the multi-cultural society, quoting the example of India where some think it 'cannot *afford* the luxury of cultural diversity'. The problem is much deeper than many are willing to accept. There are alternative views about what is to count as knowledge, as well as about the ways in which such knowledge is to be acquired, which are ignored by the monocultural assumptions of most current Western theories of pluralism. Tolerance in Britain, for example, is only up to a point. 'That point is seldom publicly admitted, and rarely discussed'. It is easy to give the impression that different systems of belief are really only options which are at best relatively true and therefore perhaps it is wiser to ignore them all, and this does not satisfy those in whose name ostensibly tolerance is advocated.

This bogus form of pluralism cannot provide the integrative function of RE which must be based rather on a search for common identity — a unity chiselled out of diversity, not presented by reducing the status of all diversity to that of insignificant difference. He gives an extended section on Islam to illustrate why a common identity is something that must be searched for and not assumed.

At the end of the chapter he has an important quotation from the Jewish thinker and mystic, Martin Buber, who draws attention to the 'elation which education should engender' and the way in which religious concepts have the function of promoting such elation.

Chapter 4

Identify the Educators

Richard Wilkins

Introduction

A neglected truth is that education is much more than schooling. We all profess to know this. But beyond such school-originated activities as home-work, what we often seem to mean is that learning happening out of school is not education in our professional sense. Religious education in particular needs to reverse this attitude.

My point therefore in this chapter is simple and potentially drastic. It is that as religious educators we should recognize that agencies outside the school have for many children a decisive effect on their religious development. We always knew that, but we have tended to think it was rather deplorable. The priority as I see it is to welcome such influences wherever possible. As professionals, careful of our reputation, we have tried to believe that we were in control of young people's religious development according to strictly educational principles. We might be hindered by the unreflective secularism of the culture; we might observe the effects on children of their involvement in 'faith communities', but these were aside from what we were about, which was a strictly educational task for which strictly (and uniquely?) educational attainment targets and assessment procedures were applicable.

We have had time for extra-curricular religion when its national leaders and community institutions (for example, churches, mosques, synagogues, gurdwaras) applied weight to the case for retaining or reforming RE. They could be useful in the drawing up of a new agreed syllabus and they might provide sites for fieldwork, liturgical artefacts or representative spokespeople for curriculum enrichment. Their role has been very largely to demonstrate to pupils something about *other people's* religions.

The effect of a child's religious upbringing or experience on his/her religious development has been treated with considerable reserve. Our expectation that early catechizing would retard later growth has been like the fear that parents would teach their own children to read by phonic methods; they meant well, but ultimately they have made our job more difficult. Worse still, anything like a 'conversion' or 'enlightenment' experience would be profoundly unsettling, almost like a cardiac arrest in the orderly development of true religious education; pupils affected in this way take time to get over it.

Such reactions by RE professionals are entirely understandable. To build on catechizing or to utilize conversion is to run the risk of being implicated in them, and everything about RE from the passing of the Cowper-Temple Clause to the present day warns us against that. Again, the present emphasis on testing encourages the wish to have pupils' development in every subject area under total teacher scrutiny. Educational outcomes are, we believe, a measure of educational input.

Yet every teacher of RE knows that life is not like that. Religious training and out-of-school experience certainly have an initial effect on many pupils' performance in RE. This is not to say that RE in school never initiates and prolongs a pupil's interest in the subject. It is to say that a considerable proportion of the young people who take an initiative in RE, such as entering for GCSE, will have private religious reasons for this interest.

In the examples which follow, this point will be reiterated from various angles. RE, for all its low esteem, has blazed many trails in education. By accepting positively the impact of out-of-school experience on measurable educational performance it may throw a spotlight on a wider educational truth. This is that education depends on partnership. Standards can be raised only if scapegoating is replaced by acceptance of responsibility throughout society for the full education of all our children.

What Does RE Achieve?

If this question were addressed to a professional religious educator at a public meeting s/he would say that s/he was glad someone had asked it. It is a perfectly straightforward and indeed a necessary question; answering it is, however, difficult, complicated, delicate and important.

It is *difficult* because so far as I know there is no research which is sufficiently precise and comprehensive to give us a snapshot, let alone a sequential video, of the middle or long term effects of religious education. That is the negative side.

The positive side is the reason why the question is *complicated*. We actually do have research findings about, for example, young people's religious attitudes in the last years of statutory education. However, two notable examples serve to increase our perplexity. Leslie Francis' surveys of the attitudes towards Christianity record increasing negativity in four successive groups of 16 year-olds tested at four-yearly intervals (Francis, 1989). But the survey asks no questions about the kind of religious education that has been received.

William Kay, on the other hand, researching the religious thinking, attitudes and personality of secondary school pupils, did include questions about the kind of RE which might have contributed to the religious conditions that he found (Kay, 1981). Quite rightly, however, he asked other questions about influences such as church attendance by parents, which were quite independent of schooling. This is most important. Even if we knew where young people were at religiously, it would be extremely difficult to tell how much of these outcomes were solely attributable to religious education received at school.

The question is *delicate* because of the great fear amongst RE specialists that they might be charged with indoctrination. Indoctrination is the unforgiveable sin in modern RE. Various possible 'achievements' by religious educators could bring them under deep suspicion. If RE were shown to have 'achieved' something, in the way of changing young people's religious thinking and attitudes, it is almost certain that RE teachers could be accused of indoctrinating them. There is an enormous variety of beliefs about religion, including the belief that religion is baloney. These convictions are passionately held by important people such as parents, community leaders and, now and again, by educationists in senior and influential positions. If RE actually *caused* young people to adopt a set of attitudes towards religion there would almost certainly be trouble.

Bite the Bullet

Yet however attractive it might seem to suppress the question or say that it is unanswerable, there are various reasons why the answer to it is extremely *important*. For one thing, it is one of those Clapham omnibus, person-in-the-street questions which anyone would think of asking unless s/he had something to hide. More than that, it is important because the people in the street actually pay for RE to be delivered in schools and they want to know if they are getting their money's worth. Jeremy Bentham is supposed to have shaken the foundations of many English institutions in the nineteenth century by asking 'What is the use of it?' It is simple questions like 'What does RE achieve?' which, if answered unconvincingly for too long or not at all, reveal that the Emperor is unclothed.

Of course, RE enjoys a particular immunity to utilitarian questions. All public education depends on two prescriptions: firstly, teachers must be seen to be teaching the right thing; secondly, teachers must be seen to achieve the right results. The reputation of all school subjects alternates between one and the other; RE has depended heavily on the first. If this were not so it could hardly have survived its failure to produce the right-thinking, clean-living generations evidently hoped for in 1944. Public outcry about the ending of school RE would break out chiefly because the disappearance of RE would seem to say something about us as a nation that we did not want to say, namely that religion was irrelevant to life or, alternatively, religion was too hot for the elected authorities and their employees to handle.

This symbolic function of RE is no less potent now that RE is multi-faith than when it was largely Biblical and Judaeo-Christian. The role of multi-faith RE in 'affirming' pupils whose family religion is Buddhism, Hinduism, Islam or Sikhism, is deemed to be very important. Whether they actually feel affirmed as a result is part of the question we are considering. That apart, multi-faith RE is evidence in the curriculum that the effort has been made.

Yet having given due weight to such security as RE enjoys because its presence makes the nation feel better, the question of what RE delivers in the lives of young people cannot be ignored. Even the curriculum symbolism of RE involves a belief that the subject makes a difference, and that the difference is one which is desired by educators and the public that employs them.

Understandably, in view of what I have said, I cannot give a conclusive answer to the question 'What does RE achieve?' I can only address it so far as to examine substantial doubts that RE is solely responsible for young people's progress in religious education.

Religious Literacy

Let us begin with a passage from Trevor Huddleston's highly influential book about apartheid, *Naught for Your Comfort*[3] (Huddleston 1956).

Father Huddleston (as he was then) describes how a party was being held at the secondary school in his Johannesburg parish.

> I happened to be around when the van bearing the meat pies drove in at the gate. The young man driving the van — an Afrikaner of, I suppose, 25 years of age — got out and asked me where he could deliver the meat pies. 'What is this place?' 'An African Secondary School run by the Anglican Mission.' 'What do they learn here, these natives?' 'The same as European children: it was, in fact, the first African school in the Transvaal to reach Matric standard.' 'But what's the use? Isn't Dr. Verwoed right in starting Bantu Education?' I told the young man that, as a result of Bantu Education, St. Peter's School would soon be closing down. It was at this point that we began to talk theology. This young van-driver was a devout member of his Kerk. I can remember his exact words as he clinched his argument with apartheid and the necessity for segregation: 'Our difference' he said, 'is eschatological'. I wondered how many Anglican van-drivers, speaking incidentally in a foreign language, could have used that term so accurately. And he was right. (p. 51)

Among the thoughts which this passage evokes is this: the van-driver was, within limits, religiously literate or, as the more self-consciously educational term has it, 'religiate'.

Religious literacy is one apparently blameless aim of modern RE. Renouncing any idea of affecting young people for or against a particular religious commitment, RE seems to be safe with this. Only the most fanatical parent could possibly object to children knowing what particular concepts of particular religions actually mean.

The Johannesburg van-driver knew what 'eschatology' meant. Not only did he know what it meant in his Afrikaans Dutch Reformed Kerk, he identified the concept in the rather different theological culture of an Anglo-

Catholic priest. Without the Oxford- and Mirfield-trained Englishman mentioning the subject, the van-driver spotted it as the crucial difference between them in a discussion on the education of black Africans. The difference was eschatology; he knew the word, he knew what it meant, and he knew what was implied by different beliefs about it. He used it to demonstrate the 'pluralism' involved in their dialogue. So far as we know, he discussed theological differences in a perfectly civil manner, as befitted 'inter-faith' dialogue in a religiously plural society. His religious education had achieved something.

Could a religious educator ask for more? Well, yes; to be satisfied with the outcomes of this bilingual, religiate van-driver's religious education would seem positively incriminating. But the more we enquire what else a religious educator ought to have achieved to alter the young man's attitudes to apartheid, the nearer we edge to the ditch of indoctrination. His society has taken the political decision; was it not incumbent on the state's teachers, if not its van-drivers, to work within the limits of agreed public policy? If this controversial difference about separation of races depends on such concepts as 'eschatology' it is indeed controversial. What business has an RE teacher to transcend the ideals of his elected employers? This is the kind of language used by RE teachers in Britain to hold themselves aloof when under pressure to achieve particular religious or moral results. If RE teachers import to their work sets of aims and objectives 'higher' and more 'enlightened' than those of the majority of the electorate, by what mandate do they do it? And if they 'achieve' such objectives, have they not gone beyond their brief as public servants?

This digression cannot be pursued further. Our immediate interest should be with the positive achievements of the van-driver's religious educators, whoever and whatever they were. We recap:

(i)   He understood the word 'eschatology' in a foreign language, and he could use it correctly in a discussion with a theologically-trained clergyman who was speaking in his mother-tongue.

(ii) He could deploy the concept, so to speak, inductively, by applying it without verbal prompting, in a debate which was not theological in origin. He could also discuss theological concepts with confidence and courtesy; admittedly he and those who agreed with him held most of the political cards, so he could afford to be courteous.

(iii) He had a positive attitude towards religion. That is to say, he was a devout member of his Kerk, and he adopted a theological outlook on life. Father Huddleston cited this conversation as evidence of the South African Dutch reformed Church's exceptional ability to foster such an outlook in its members.

(iv) All of this was still true of him at the age of 25.

Beyond this we can only speculate, but with some assurance. Liberal-minded educators who find this a repulsive example may interject: 'Ah yes, but this man is deficient in truly phenomenological religious education. There is no evidence that he can empathize with believers of another faith'. On the contrary, we have as much evidence as an example like this can provide. We don't know how he felt, but his clinching statement to Father Huddleston is saying, 'If I believed what you believe about eschatology, I might believe what you believe about the education of blacks. I happen not to believe the first, so I don't believe the second, for reasons that seem to me entirely satisfactory. Good day.'

There is more than that to phenomenologically-based empathy, but it will do until the customers have had their meat pies. We might, in any case, question whether phenomenologically-based empathy is entirely concordant with other objectives that school RE might be asked to achieve to justify its existence. Father Huddleston, for example, maintains that the Afrikaners' racial attitudes arose from their religious beliefs *which the Afrikaners ought not to have believed* (*ibid*, p. 50). Many phenomenologists in Britain would agree with him. Sometimes, empathy is not enough.

For all our moral reservations, the van-driver's religious educators had achieved results which are, in certain respects, enviable. But who were his religious educators? Not necessarily his schoolteachers, although they may have played a part in establishing for him the concept of eschatology and its relevance. Father Huddleston linked the man's theological competence to the fact that 'he was a devout member of his Kerk'. He was probably right. Many RE teachers would be highly satisfied with a van-driving ex-pupil who showed this amount of theological competence nine years after leaving school. The competence, however, may not have been wholly attributable to practitioners of open, non-confessional RE.

What Makes Them Grow?

What follows from this is not hung on one exotic example. Kay (1981) found amongst pupils a very high correlation between positive religious attitudes and church attendance by parents (pp. 186 and 241–2). While a positive attitude to religion is not the same as educational attainment, it seems difficult to deny that a positive attitude to religion at age 16 is a promising mental environment for religious studies.

This kind of correlation has a long history. In 1964, Ronald Goldman published some highly influential research findings which seemed to show that Bible-based RE did not achieve the satisfactory development of children's understanding. Such conclusions required, of course, the stating of criteria against which his survey sample's answers could be measured, and what Goldman would accept as *understanding* of such religious concepts as 'miracle' was not universally accepted. Nevertheless, it is Goldman's assertion that Bible-based RE did not achieve its own objectives of religious understanding that leads us to the relevant point. This was identified by Kenneth Howkins (1966) whose critique of Goldman's work received far less attention than it deserved. Howkins showed that when Goldman identified groups of children by religious background he did not comment adequately on the statistical correlation between that background and the children's religious understanding. For Goldman's research showed that children from a background category politely described as 'gospel-sect' included some who scored exceptionally highly on Goldman's own scale of criteria for religious understanding.

It is highly unlikely that the 'gospel-sect' churches which these children attended had anticipated Goldman by throwing out Bible-based nurture in favour of life-themes. It is much more likely that the children's heavily Biblical diet in highly confessional communities, was achieving results in terms of mature understanding, which is what Goldman said was not being achieved by Bible-based RE. This was clearly in defiance of the Goldmanian principle that children are too young to benefit religiously from the text of the Bible. Some would say that, whatever the rights and wrongs of that, religious maturity was not achieved by Goldman's alternative teaching methods either.

It may be objected that in the cases of the van-driver and of Goldman we have looked for results in attitudes and understanding of *Christian* concepts. There is much more than that to an adequate understanding of religious concepts relevant to life in the modern world. Positive attitudes towards one's own faith and confidence in handling its concepts, are not enough.

I confess that my response to this is largely anecdotal, perhaps because there has been little or no relevant research, or because there has been and I am ignorant of it.

In 1975, as a teacher of RE in a comprehensive school in the South-east of England, I used the last half of the summer term in a way that I now blush to recall. After two years and two terms on Judaeo-Christian topics, my third year (now Year 9) groups were set the task of writing an individual project on a world religion or religious denomination of their choice. Only the paucity of world religions textbooks at that time made sense of such a preposterous exercise. What its long-term educational value was I do not know, but one piece of data emerged that I took to be highly significant.

The children were, without exception, from at least nominally Christian or entirely secular families. Those with the least visible religious allegiance of their own nearly all chose a project on something like 'Christianity'. Those who, largely unknown to me until then, had parental or personal religious observance on the darker side of their private lives, tended to choose a particular Christian denomination. But the children whose personal Christian commitment was most visible at school, in terms of the wearing of a Crusader badge, active involvement in the school's Christian Union and/or forthright expression of orthodox Christian views in discussion, chose to write on Buddhism, Hinduism or Islam, in that order of popularity. These children nearly all chose a religion other than Christianity; and almost without exception they were the only ones who did.

Various explanations could be offered for this soft data. One that will not do is that the children were sick to death of evangelical Christianity and were using this opportunity to kick it out. On the contrary, I know that several of them went on to become senior leaders in the Christian Union, some went into full-term Christian music or theatre groups, one worked for an evangelical voluntary social-work agency and one taught in a Christian school in India.

Another example concerns a 14-year-old pupil of mine who was reported to have had a conversion experience at a Christian camp in the summer holidays. He had never before shown a spark of interest in RE, and if he had deep wells of understanding they had been hidden. Early in the October of his fourth (tenth Bakerian) year, I presented his group with three views of life after death from, respectively, a Buddhist, a Jew and a Humanist. The group was given a series of tasks comparing, contrasting and evaluating. No previous work had been done on the subject at this level. Anthony settled firmly for the Jewish option as being closest to his own. This showed a markedly improved discernment of religious concepts, and I am quite sure that he did not acquire it from me.

The evidence is too slender to bear heavy conclusions, but there is more, equally impressionistic, which confirms its general drift. I have in the last fifteen years met many leading thinkers who reflect the variety as well as the consensus about professional RE. I do not know one who was without a strong confessional background, at least in terms of parentage. Several are, or were, ministers of religion. However much they have 'broadened', 'shifted' or 'apostasized', they provide no evidence at all that a confessional upbringing has inhibited their capacity to understand religious concepts in an educational way. One advocate of multi-faith RE who was prominent in the early seventies invariably began or ended his contributions by saying 'I am a Cornish Methodist, and yet ...'. He was especially candid. In getting to know other multi-faith enthusiasts I came to think that he should have said 'I am a Cornish Methodist, therefore ...'.

What is much more difficult to prove is that the foundation of their present professional religious interests was laid by the RE which they experienced at school. Some at least described as depressingly bad or non-existent the RE they received, while being paradoxically certain that unless RE in schools was improved, very few students would go on as they themselves had to advanced religious studies. In general, however, I do not know whether their school RE achieved its educational objectives. Nor do I know whether RE in primary and secondary schools today, multi-faith and phenomenological as it may be, is producing *on its own* an enthusiasm for religion and religious studies that will deliver us a new generation of religious educators.

It begins to look as though the very qualities of attainment and development for which RE teachers are striving in their pupils might more often be attributable to factors outside the school than within it. Moreover, the activities and environments which produce these educational effects are ones which many RE specialists would deplore as non- or anti-educational, and which some would describe as 'indoctrinatory'. The irony of this last point needs stressing. Among my 14-year-old groups, it was the pupils who attended Bible-classes at weekends who showed *fewest* signs of having been prejudiced against consideration of non-Christian religions.

The Impact of Assessment

The possibility that agreed procedure for assessment might enable us to know more closely what level of understanding RE is enabling pupils to achieve is likely to prove a mirage, even though in the post-1988 era RE may indeed be provided with some such viable means. In the absence of a National Curriculum Council Working Party, various projects have sought to establish attainment targets for the National Curriculum Key Stages ending at 7, 11, 14 and 16.[1] Tribute must be paid to the industry and rigour of these groups. Their efforts, or at least the movement that they represent, have had persuasive effect.[2] There is therefore every indication that RE's effectiveness will be measured by frequent and regular testing over most of the country.

Nevertheless, any optimism should be tempered by the reflection that, if tests show improvement in religious understanding, we can never be quite sure that we are measuring an effect caused by RE in school. Conversely, absence of progress might endorse negatively the view that extra-curricular factors such as the secularism of society are decisive (see Norcross, 1989; also Wilkins, 1989).

Furthermore, we need to be aware that attainment targets which are likely to be defined within an educational framework are not necessarily enough to prove that genuinely religious learning has occurred. There is a special quality about tested religious attainments that makes them comparable to those apocryphal holders of 'A' level French who could not converse with a French person.

This needs expansion. Measurement of religious development did not begin with the 1988 Education Reform Act (ERA). The progress of 'curriculum development' in the 1960s and 1970s produced many specific 'taxonomies' or orderly arrangements of purposeful educational experience. These were often derived from the work of B.S. Bloom (1956) who edited a seminal work on the cognitive domain of learning, and of Krathwohl (1964) who wrote the companion volume on the affective domain. David Naylor, in a helpful paper in the mid-seventies which took account of this work and criticism of it, applied the latter's model for the affective domain to RE in this way:

> The lowest level (*receiving, attending*) is when the pupil is attentive in the RE lesson most of the time but does not respond with any great enthusiasm. The second level (*responding*) is achieved when the pupil shows interest, likes answering questions and occasionally does not hear the bell for the end of the period. At level three (*valuing*) our hypothetical pupil shows signs of commitment, follows up references in his own time, and seeks out additional data. Level four (*organization*) is reached when the learner successfully internalizes values, for example, he becomes as keen on *religious studies* (my emphasis) as some boys are on football. The highest level can be said to have been reached when, over a period of time the pupil looks *at human life in the world through the eyes of a student of religion*' (my emphasis). (Naylor, 1975, p. 125)

I can almost rest my case. Although there are broader and more dynamic meanings to the term 'student of religion', in the context it seems to mean an adept in religious studies, western academic style, in which the distinction between the student of religion and the religious person is especially wide. If so, this ultimate level of attainment embodies a dangerous weakness of RE, which is that religion functions in it only as a component in religious education. This is not how it functions in the world at large. Very few real people use religion solely for this purpose. Only a very small minority of school pupils is likely to find such religion attractive and, if I am correct, those who seem to be that way inclined will often have extra-curricular reasons for their preference, which they will have acquired in activities aiming to produce the religious person rather than the student of religion.

I contend that this perceived distancing of mature religious studies from personal life in its totality is precisely why RE teachers *cannot* produce a school full of students of religion. To take the whole of Naylor's example, which related to Bloom's cognitive approach as well as Krathwohl's work on affective attainment, we may seriously wonder how well this set of learning experiences *alone* would equip a student not merely for paper-and-pencil tests of measurable religious learning and attitude formation, but for the formative pressures after school of economic inequality, of adult relationships in religiously plural communities with the need for self-esteem and of fear of the harrowing mysteries of love and loss. It is experiences like these, with their warnings of finiteness and imperfection, for which many people need religion.

Experience, Please Come In

The recent classroom work of John Hammond and others (1990) is attempting to help pupils within school to relate to their total experience. This work takes account of findings by David Hay (1982), Edward Robinson (1977) and Sir Alister Hardy (1966) which show that 'religious experiences' of some sort are extremely common in the population at large. Despite the risks, schools would do well to acknowledge this amongst those whom they teach.

Whether classroom work of this kind will overcome professional inhibitions remains to be seen at the time of writing. Its intention is to compensate for most children's lack of a religious framework to life. Quite rightly, advocates of these methods of RE maintain that children are *indoctrinated* by secularism so that they cannot conceive of the possibility of personal religious experience; therefore they cannot empathize with the religious experiences of mankind. Or, if they have had their own 'peak' experiences, they are *intimidated* by secularism, so that they cannot acknowledge these experiences for their own benefit or those of their fellow-learners.

If this 'professionalization' of religious experience in the classroom were to be achieved, and if the skin of what is 'educational' could be stretched to contain it, the priority for RE to acknowledge its dependence on 'non-educational' religious factors would be greatly diminished. This approach has the enormous merit of addressing that sector of the school population (by far the largest) which I have so far mostly ignored. These are the young people whose background is entirely secular and who have no contact with a living and supportive faith community.

The reservations that might be expressed on conventional professional grounds are, however, most important. They tell us much about the challenges that RE is facing. My previous review of evidence would suggest that we can do most in RE, of whatever kind, with young people who bring their own religious experience to school. The introduction of experiential approaches to RE indicates that the more we are dealing with young people whose spiritual experience is either nil or unstructured, the more we will incline to a confessional, even an *evangelistic* posture in the classroom. There is no alternative to these shocking words when considering an approach which aims to invite secularized young people to sample experiences of transcendence.

It would be a mistake, for example, to think that RE organized round 'numinous' or 'peak' experiences is non-confessional. Encouragement of meditation techniques likely to lead children to pray to an imaginary ancestor (Hammond, 1990, p. 147)[3] excites my serious concern as a parent, and my awe-struck sense of irony as an evangelical Christian. As ex-Cabinet Minister Sydney Webb said when his successors took the pound off the gold standard, 'Nobody told us we could do that'.

At the same time, we should welcome the objective of actually making RE possible for many pupils by countering the indoctrination which is already inflicted on them by a secular culture (*ibid*, p. 15). Permission to provide an encouraging learning environment in which children can feel more secure in describing their special experiences is an enormous step forward in enabling RE to achieve anything. The news, for example, that people who have had these experiences tend to be in better psychological health than those who have not had them would be a salutary reversal of most pupil's opinions, if you could get them to believe it.

Three developments of these ideas need to be stressed. Firstly, it is essential to note that educationalists' rather belated utilization of these experiences should not mean that their function and interpretation can be monopolized by schools. As regards the function of transcendent experiences, it is not exhausted by their usefulness in religious education. In other words, those who have these experiences in educational surroundings must not be railroaded into a belief that they always happen so that those who have them can understand *other people's* faith.

Similarly, it would not be correct to interpret such experiences as wholly subjective, and entirely validated by the cultural background, personality types and life experiences of the individual people who have them (*ibid*, p. 22). Nor for such reasons can they be translated as ultimately congruent with each other. When Rabindranath R. Maharaj experienced the presence of Jesus it was not for him a mere variant of the experiences he had had as a Hindu (1978, p. 137). Unless such eclipsing of previous religious experience is recognized the new experience is insufficiently supported and the person is demeaned. There is, in many such experiences, a sense of reality which relativizes a person's previous experiences or other people's accounts of their quite different experiences. While there may certainly be enhanced empathy, there may also be dissatisfaction. Those whose inner eyes are opened to the God of Moses and Mount Sinai certainly do not regard as equally truthful an experience of Brahman as the all-inclusive deity. Similarly, the Hindu or Buddhist experience can only regard as illusion the ethical monotheist's transcendent awareness of the radical, irreconcilable difference between good and evil. These negative certainties would often be absent were it not for experienced insight which eclipses other insights. The experiences of Moses and Muhammad generated intolerance as a corollary of religious progress. If educational spirituality minimizes this, with the best intentions, its posture will, paradoxically, be confessional in the worst sense.

I mention this 'strife of visions' because the new interest in spirituality can be interpreted to mean that discord can be avoided altogether. It is sometimes said that experiences of the spiritual dimension are ultimately complementary, and apparent difference is due to the destructive effect of words, logic, dogma, the left-hemisphere of the brain and all things rational. Such a view may make glimpsing the spiritual seem safe and soothing, but that is in itself a highly sectarian view. It is identifiable in the spectrum of world religions. Insistence by teachers that it is the way to interpret peak experiences is indoctrinatory.

That is why I welcome to some degree John Wilson's concern elsewhere in this volume that RE should encourage reasonableness. Spiritual experience may transcend everyday rationalism, but it does not banish rationality. It merely adds to its data while teaching it its place. A spirituality which excludes distinction and discrimination amongst contradictory concepts brings problems for schools and society. A case for it may be argued; it should not be assumed. Moreover, the spiritual quality of discernment, distinguishing good and evil in the spiritual realm, is important, indeed vital, in these experiential times.

I labour this point because RE does have a very important role in helping children to appreciate the force of religious differences which have been felt in their intensity, and to live with them. Multi-faith RE is more than letting young people know that religious beliefs are different. The real challenge to the subject is preparing many young people for harmonious adult life together while believing that each other's beliefs are wrong. That is what it really means to live in a religiously plural society. Schools would be guilty of insular cowardice if they tried to evade the force of this in the hopeless belief that schools could or should shut out the realities of life.

Whether RE has the time and resources and whether teachers have the wisdom and maturity for this I do not know. But if RE assists harmonious, mundane cooperation amongst deeply held religious differences, no one need ask what RE achieves. It will have achieved something outstandingly important. Life in the world has to go on as a continuous process of bargains between people who say in effect:

We disagree deeply about the things that ultimately matter most, the nature of God and humanity and the destiny of the universe; but for now we must together, as human beings all valued by our separate religions and ideologies, measure this playground, carry out this experiment, act in this play, play this football match, compile this report, dig up this road, govern this country or cleanse this environment.

The Importance of Encouraging Dialogue

My argument has been that many, perhaps most, pupils who are highly motivated in RE receive their motivation from extra-curricular religious experience. If this is so, it means that factors other than school RE contribute to genuinely educational attainment by pupils. These factors, and the people involved in them, work by means which, if practised in school, would probably be condemned as indoctrinatory.

We saw that modern developments in RE, responding to the impotence of older and safer methods, propose the taking of far greater risks with 'indoctrination' than seemed possible a few years ago. I have asserted that these proposals, while showing welcome release from former frigidity about experience, could, unless very great care is taken, become guilty of trying to put over something confessional whereby some religions are misrepresented and some children's faith might be illegitimately reinterpreted.

I have further cautioned that the inclusion of first-hand experience in classroom RE may, by adapting the experiential to the currently educational, misinterpret such experience, denaturing it and inhibiting it from serving its centuries-old purpose of creating commitment and focusing life's loyalties. Schools may be able to go no further with young people than 'learning from religion' (see especially Grimmitt 1987). Moses, Jesus, Muhammad and Guru Nanak expected more than that and it is their faiths, not that of the county council, for which martyrs have shed their blood.

Education is always a dialogue between life as seen by adults and life as seen by young people. Both must be taken into account if education is to happen. Teachers must, therefore, allow religion to meet the pupils where they are in the classroom, and this may give rise to some kind of 'religious experience'. They must also enable pupils to see that religions make claims to objective truth about the world beyond individual experience, because the dialogue is also between human perceptions and the reality of what exists beyond the solipsistic mind. Theological statements do not have to answer for their whole authenticity at the bar of each pupil's spiritual capacity. Contrary to the dogma of the New Age Movement, the individual does not 'create his or her own reality' in religion, let alone anything else.

This dialogue is essential if the pupil's freedom is to be preserved. Such freedom may be overridden by the dogmatic delivery of unquestionable 'truth'. Teachers have been warned repeatedly that this style is indoctrinatory, and therefore illegitimate. It is also generally ineffective and counter-productive. Teachers may ask themselves how often they have met a 15-year-old who has been successfully indoctrinated in this way.

The dialogue, and therefore the freedom, may also be curtailed, however, by another approach which seems to be much less often questioned. This is one that sees truth about religions, and indeed religious truth, not as that which speaks to the pupil and waits for the pupil to speak back, but rather as a process of mutual interpenetration in which 'meaning' is alternately absorbed by the pupil's spiritual consciousness while itself absorbing the pupil's personality.

It is not experiences like that which have, in my experience, liberated young people for dialogue with faiths other than their own. It is, rather, extra-curricular encounters with a faith which makes sweeping and dogmatic claims to be exclusively true while respecting the individual's right to assess such claims, and giving time and space for them to be tested by reason and experience; these encounters can initiate the pupil into an appreciation of a religious frame of reference.

Such encounters provide training in patience with those who find the incomprehensible aspects of a religion obstructive to understanding; it is, after all, God-like to wait for pennies to drop in others' minds. Such encounters, while providing a standard for discriminating amongst religious truth-claims also, by that very provision, require a dialogue to be opened with such claims so that discrimination can take place. This dialogue with evidence is precisely what is required at least by the cognitive side of all education in the Western tradition.

My evidence for this view is drawn exclusively from young people whose extra-curricular encounters have been with traditional, orthodox Christianity. It may well be that encounters with other faiths have the same effect. Or perhaps there is a special quality about devotion to Him who stands at the door of the human personality, knocks and waits to be admitted, that opens minds, encourages questions, responds to evidence and argument and so makes possible the education in religion for which RE teachers hope and strive.

Religious educators need, therefore, to recognize three facts which may be unpalatable. Firstly, religious experience and nurture provided by faith communities may have a uniquely dynamic and enabling effect on young people's religious education in school. To put it in graphically extreme terms, a fundamentalist background might in practice be an excellent preparation for multi-faith religious studies. Secondly, a dialogue has to be maintained between the immediate experiential relevance of religion to the pupil, and the universal purpose which the religion claims for itself. Religious experience in classroom conditions may help with adolescent struggles over personal identity. But if a religion claims that humanity will be separated as sheep and goats according to allegiance or defiance of its messianic prophet; or if its central affirmation is the ultimate reconciliation of Adolf Hitler and Mahatma Gandhi, these priorities should have priority in the educational presentation of the faiths. This again means taking faith traditions and communities seriously. Thirdly, and most delicate of all, is the fact that in a truly plural society, the individual can freely choose amongst religious and non-religious life-stances; therefore, faiths are in competition. The pupil should know how to evaluate the truth-claims of a faith, and to know not only what it says and who believes it, but how it functions. The teacher needs to encourage the question whether or not a faith stands up intellectually, culturally and morally in the modern world. Does it actually meet the needs of those who profess it in modern secular society? That is a severe test for any faith, not least secular humanism, and teachers who help pupils with it need extra-ordinary and flexible knowledge and acute pastoral skills.

Notes

1   Notable examples are the Westhill Project, based at Westhill College, Birmingham; the FARE (Forms of Assessment in Religious Education) Project based at the University of Exeter School of Education; a Working Party of the Association of Religious Education Advisers and Inspectors; a Working Party of the Religious Education Council of England and Wale, and working parties of LEA SACREs.

2   A survey carried out for the National Curriculum Council by Michael Grimmitt in 1990 showed that 70 per cent of SACREs (Standing Advisory Councils on Religious Education — under the 1988 Education Reform Act every local education authority has to appoint one) were planning assessment of RE on lines similar to those for National Curriculum subjects; only 3 per cent declared themselves to be opposed to assessment RE, a surprisingly low figure for a potentially strong and popular position (Report for National Curriculum Council, 1990).

3   To be fair, the authors place early stress on the need for teachers to be positive towards 'opting out' by a pupil. Yet the step-at-a-time methods described would given even a theologically sophisticated child little advance notice of where an activity was leading.

References

BLOOM, B.S. (Ed.) (1956) *Taxonomy of Educational Objectives Handbook 1: 'Cognitive Domain'*, London, Longmans.

FRANCIS, L.J. (1989) 'The drift from the churches: Secondary school pupils' attitudes towards Christianity', *British Journal of Religious Education*, **11**, 2, Spring.

GOLDMAN, R. (1964) *Religious Thinking from Childhood to Adolescence*, London, Routledge & Kegan Paul.

GRIMMITT, M. (1987) *Religious Education and Human Development*, Southend, McCrimmon.

HAMMOND, J. et al. (1990) *New Methods in RE Teaching: An Experiential Approach*, Harlow, Oliver & Boyd.

HARDY, A.C. (1966) *The Divine Flame*, London, Collins.

HAY, D. (1982) *Exploring Inner Space*, London, Penguin.

HOWKINS, K. (1966) *Religious Thinking and Religious Education, A Critique of the Research and Conclusions of Goldman*, Bristol, Tyndale Press.

HUDDLESTON, T. (1956) *Naught for Your Comfort*, London, Fontana.

KAY, W.K. (1981) 'Religious thinking, attitudes and personality amongst secondary pupils in England and Ireland', an unpublished PhD thesis, University of Reading.

KRATHWOHL, R. (1964) *Taxonomy of Educational Objectives Handbook 2: 'Affective Domain'*, London, Longmans.

Richard Wilkins

NAYLOR, D. (1975) 'Curriculum development' in SMART, N. and HORDER, D. (Eds) *New Movements in Religious Education*, Aldershot, Temple Smith.

NORCROSS, P. (1989) 'Effects of cultural conditioning of multifaith religious education in the monocultural primary school', *British Journal of Religious Education*, **11**, 2, Spring.

RABINDRANATH, R.M. (1978) *Death of a Guru*, London, Hodder.

ROBINSON, E. (1977) *The Original Vision*, Oxford, Religious Experience Research Unit, Manchester College.

WILKINS, R. (1989) 'What does RE do to children?', *Digest*, **15**, 3, Summer.

Chapter 5

The Religious Approach to Religious Education: The Methodology of Awakening and Disciplining the Religious Sensibility

---

Syed Ali Ashraf

On Defining Religious Sensibility

Education is a process through which the total personality of an individual is developed and refined in a balanced way. This concept of education thus assumes a concept of human nature: 'spiritual', 'moral', 'intellectual', 'imaginative', 'emotional', 'physical', are the different terms used to signify different aspects of that personality. The cultivation of these aspects are achieved through the cultivation of the different 'sensibilities' of an individual. Of these sensibilities the educationalists speak of the moral sensibility, the rational or the logical sensibility, the aesthetic sensibility and the social sensibility.

The 'religious sensibility' is always neglected or branded as something which a person may 'privately' cultivate. Education, it is generally assumed, may inform pupils about religions but it should not try to cultivate, discipline or refine the religious sensibility. Education is not allowed to be *neutral* about cultivating the social sense of the aesthetic sense or the scientific approach. But 'religious sense' appears to them to be too personal. If a person cannot appreciate a well-known painting or a novel, or music, that person is declared to be deficient in some vital element in the human personality. But the same educationalists would like to avoid discussing the deficiency in the spiritual realization of the God-human being relationship, or for Buddhists the spiritual realization of a Transcendental Reality, and for those who believe in God, the joy of submitting their own Will to the Will of God. Thus aesthetic sensibility and need of it for the growth and development of humanity have been explored and discussed and the methods of imparting, refining and increasing its efficacy among pupils, have been advocated by eminent educational thinkers like Matthew Arnold, Leavis and Herbert Read. When the Harvard Report was prepared by twelve presidents of American universities — a report which revolutionized curriculum designing — they explained the need to cultivate the social sense through the study of social subjects, 'imaginative thinking' through the study of fine arts, and 'logical thinking'[1] through the study of natural sciences. But these very scholars failed to see the need for cultivation of a moral and spiritual sense through the study of the religious traditions of humanity.[2]

Educational planners have also refrained from analyzing what is meant by this religious sensibility and what would be the best method or strategy of cultivating it. This is because of the prevalence of the secularist assumption in education, namely, the idea that there is no God anyway and that religion is fundamentally, and at a deep level, based on a lie. That is why, though religious education is obligatory for all pupils in the United Kingdom, it has in most schools degenerated into teaching about different religions. Even when Christianity and other religions are taught, the teacher is afraid of stimulating the religious sensibility of children for fear of indoctrinating children. The margin between indoctrination and rousing religious sensibility, they think, is too thin to be meddled with. As a result religious sensibility goes by default, and a vital element in the human personality is ignored. Education becomes not merely partial, but defective.

It becomes defective because religious sensibility is an integral part of human consciousness. Educationalists can appreciate this fact only when they approach human nature with an open mind and notice how inborn is the sense of basic values in every child irrespective of the child's colour, race, or community. A child is born with a sense of Justice, Truth, Love, Mercy and Compassion. Hence children can, and do, transcend subjective selfishness in the interest of the norm of Justice, Truth or Righteousness. Even a three-year-old child responds unfavourably to an injustice done to it and acknowledges justice even if it hurts its pride or interests. A child also trusts a person when it realizes that he/she is truthful, but it can never trust a person who may show affection to it but whom it has found out to be telling lies. Love of Truth and Justice are thus inborn in every child. This *moral sense* is intrinsic. It has not been taught by society though its application to society may vary from time to time and from place to place.

This sense has a transcendent and a universal character. In view of the fact that the physical self of an individual could not have produced this moral consciousness it is but logical for us to conclude that there is within each child some other self that transcends the physical, mundane, earthly self, a self that must have received from some transcendent source this consciousness of the abstract principles of Justice, Truth, Righteousness, Love, Mercy and Compassion, the principles, in other words of the *Virtues*, a term that was at one time commonly used in religious metaphysics. All great religions of the world speak of the impingement of the Transcendent Divine on the physical self of the human being.

That is why this higher self of a human being enables the person to transcend subjective interests and provide a norm of conduct for the society that derives its principles from the immutable, transcendent absolutes of justice, truth and the other virtues.

There is thus a constant conflict within the heart of each individual between the self that is guided by subjective selfish interests and the self that tries to establish the transcendent norm. This is the struggle that many great souls such as the Buddha passed through in order to reach enlightenment. By religious sensibility I mean, therefore, that element in human nature that makes human beings aware of the transcendent *selfless* norms of Justice, Truth and all such values that pull the heart away from selfishness towards selflessness, strengthen it and compel the heart to transcend subjective interests and establish that which is just and true.

Biological or physiological evolution can never create this pull towards selflessness; instead it leads us to selfishness through the principle of the survival of the fittest. Similarly social change leading to the evolution of society or social values can never demand compassion for a particular individual. On the other hand this process of change compels the society to let the good of the individual be sacrificed to the greater good of the whole. As a result the belief in the inevitability of social change destroys the belief that there is a basic human value-structure which transcends social change and upholds the good of each and every individual on the basis of an immutable norm of justice, truth and compassion.[3]

When this consciousness of the norm of Virtue is appreciated, the door then opens for the realization of the Supreme Transcendent Reality, and this turns the application of high moral standards into love for the ultimate good of each individual. This realization is not just an intellectual phenomenon arrived at through logical calculation. It requires the uplifting of the heart beyond the narrow confines of the material worldly self, an expansion of the heart beyond all calculations, a transcendence which for Muslims, Christians, Hindus and Jews cannot occur without the presence of the Supreme Being-God, so there is a direct relationship between the transcendent and the human being. For Muslims the means of this relationship is the heart (*qalb* in Arabic) which is the spiritual organ through which intuitive cognition is achieved, affecting the whole self. Thus spiritual cognition is intimately related to the affective process.[4] Knowledge that we have a spiritual existence creates faith in the immortality of the human soul and the sense of being accountable for our actions, good and bad, in this life and after death.

The question may be raised as to the method of enabling pupils to become conscious of the religious sensibility, of arousing it and refining it. What particular methodology should be adopted to achieve this most important aspect of religious education without at the same time making religious education a means of indoctrinating children into a particular faith or making them feel that they are tasting a syncretic form of a new religion?

Teaching Methodology: The Strategy of Presentation

The Qualifications of a Teacher who Teaches Religious Education

The most important thing needed is that the teacher should have a religious faith and a belief in the spiritual nature of human beings. A religious sensibility is something that a person may also have though the person may not belong to a particular faith in any formal sense. A person who has no religious faith in any transcendent Reality, such as a person who is an atheist or a person who believes they can explain every phenomena from a secularist empirical or rational stance alone, can never teach religious education; it becomes an anachronism and a farce. Would a headteacher ask a teacher who cannot appreciate poetry to teach poetry in a class? Would the head ever ask a person who does not have any sense of colour or any appreciation of the aesthetics of art and painting to teach painting in a class? Why then are atheists and people without any faith even in the spiritual nature of human beings or without any experience and knowledge of this sensibility, asked to teach religious education? The idea of Jean Holm, that a person can suspend his or her own ideas and be in the shoes of a believer and thus understand what religious sensibility is has not proved to be true. Nor can it be true. How can you have spiritual experience if you do not believe in it at all? One cannot be an atheist and suddenly imagine oneself to be a religious person and then again return to one's atheism with magic alacrity. Religious sensibility is not an intellectual mechanism which can be understood and conveyed or roused or disciplined through a neutral intellectual process. It is not a reasoned theory, nor is it a matter-of-fact object. It is that which only a person spiritually alive and intellectually trained to receive and transmit this knowledge can appreciate, organize teaching and teach.

In other words the very teaching of religious sensibility and the very planning and organization of this teaching require both some spiritual awareness of it and an intellectual assessment of the techniques to be employed to teach it in the classroom. Teaching of religious education implies therefore the necessity of having teachers who have faith in the basic dimensions of the religious sensibility and who are trained to adopt a proper teaching methodology. A methodology that seems appropriate and adequate is given below. Religious education can be greatly encouraged or totally marred because of its methodology; methodology indeed plays the dominant role in religious education.

A Methodology

1   The teaching of religious education should begin by helping children to be conscious of the joy of performing virtuous deeds. Every single child has a sense of justice and truth and can be encouraged to feel the joy of doing acts of charity and showing compassion. The joy of giving something, the sense of sympathy for someone suffering and the sense of surrendering one's immediate interest and being ready to listen to something better than what one is doing — all these should be explored.

I am asking teachers to start with the 'joy' of doing something virtuous for three reasons.
(a)   All teachers who deal with small children do discipline the moral sense through the disciplining of their behaviour and conduct, how

to talk, walk or sit, how to share toys with other children, how to sympathize and help another child in difficulty, how not to be arrogant and rude, and how to be sorry for being so, and so on. This is something that the child knows and understands. I am not therefore asking teachers to do anything new. What I am trying to do is to help them see this training as part and parcel of religious education.

(b)   The teacher can do so if he/she sees the intrinsic nature of these virtues. This is the second reason for starting with virtues. It is necessary for the teacher to understand and appreciate the fact that every single child has an inborn sense of justice and an inborn love for truth. Even before socialization, that sense is seen operative. If a 2-year-old child is slapped wrongly, it protests. Unless that sense of justice is built in its inner nature it could not have done so. Similarly the child may fictionalize and imagine strange things, but its inner love for truth becomes obvious in a social situation. If its father is strict but gives the child what he promises, but if an uncle is profusely affectionate but hardly ever fulfils his promises, whom is the child going to trust? Each virtue can thus be tested by the teacher if the teacher doubts the veracity of what I am saying. Sometimes in order to be truthful it may be necessary for the child to suffer. But once the child can be persuaded to overcome this fear and dare the consequences of speaking the truth, will the child feel a kind of 'joy' in standing up for what is right? Similarly, the sense of charity is inborn but it sometimes means giving up something one likes to have. How are we to be charitable? Is it not possible for the teacher to tell stories in which there is a conflict between charitableness and miserliness and allow the child to give its own conclusion? All these indicate that virtues are inborn but they need awakening. They also need the strengthening of the will of the child to be virtuous.

(c)   It is here that the third reason comes. There is in each child another force which may be broadly characterized as 'selfishness'. Christianity presents it as the consequence of original sin, Man's fall and the stain in human nature. Islam explains it as the impact of the worldly forces in the 'self' that pulls a human being towards personal gain in this world and is also a result of the whisperings of the satanic forces of the world into the soul. There is thus a continuous struggle in every soul between the 'good' and the 'evil'. Hindus and Buddhists explain this as a continuous conflict between immortal truth and the evanescent illusion (*maya*). What the teacher has to do is to get fully acquainted with the essential principle common to all religions. Then it becomes easy for the teacher not to bother about subtle doctrinal and even metaphysical differences in their theories and concentrate on the child, be that child a Hindu or a Buddhist or a Jew or a Christian or a Muslim. The teacher is here engaged in dealing practically with the conduct of the child. He/she has to think of all the possible situations which the child at its age may possibly encounter and draw up a programme of activity relating to such conflicts. Even a multiracial situation can be utilized in different age-groups in order to show that racist activities are unjust. The higher the age-group the more complex should be the investigation. Even the communal attitudes of different religious groups can be taken up as something wrong from a religious point of view. Thus the children can realize that if they want to be just and good there is a norm higher than the racialist or communalist norm. It is this sense of transcendence of the norm that children should be made to cultivate. This transcendence must be felt and understood not intellectually discussed at lower levels. Selfishness can be wide-ranging: from 'narrow self' to 'family interest', 'group interests' or 'race or community interests', 'national interests' and even 'international worldly interests'. It is for the teacher to extend the range gradually according to the age-range of the children. It is, however, true that even a little child with little education can understand and respond to the transcendent mainly because it is supported by its own innermost virtuous self without its becoming fully conscious of that 'self'.

2   The next step in this methodology is to help children to become conscious of the sense of the worship of God. Brenda Watson (1987) rightly places this consciousness in the heart of religious education. She says, 'Genuinely religious people worship not themselves but God. If we wish to understand what religion is about, we must concentrate on what religious people themselves see as the heart of religion. To attend only to what *religious people* do and think is to attend to what is peripheral' (p. 122). Distinction must be drawn between the *practices* of religious people and *faith* in God. The teacher should avoid dogmatic argument with students and discourage premature intellectual discussion about faith in God and worship. As the teacher's intention is to stir and refine the religious sensibility, it is better to proceed to show how the moral sensibility that the teacher has made pupils aware of is invariably part and parcel of religious sensibility. All genuinely religious people are morally 'good'. The notion of the 'good' is by far the most common notion among all religious people.

One cannot be good just by making a formal external profession of one's faith. That person alone is genuinely religious who not only declares his/her faith or religious feelings but also tries to follow in thought and action the moral and religious code of their religion. This does not mean that a religious person cannot make mistakes or be selfish etc., from time to time, but the genuineness of a person's commitment to religious belief comes out when the person's contrite heart compels them to feel sorry and to try harder to overcome whatever it was that made them do what their conscience tells them was wrong. In Judaism, Christianity and Islam this genuineness of a person's *faith* is thus supposed to be established through that person's *good deeds*. Deeds are only 'good' when the intention of the person is to obey the selfless transcendent norm and not act for the sake of fulfilling selfish ends at the expense of others. Intention can be selfless when the heart is selfless and personal passions and desires do not control and guide the person's heart. Most religious traditions have a concept of punishment for bad deeds and reward for good deeds, and the fear of punishment, whether in this world or the next, is also instrumental in helping us to maintain the moral norms or virtues of religious faiths.

It is here that examples of faith transforming bad people into good people becomes necessary. The teacher will, I think, find the teaching of religious education highly interesting, enjoyable and fruitful, if he/she gets the students involved in finding out what happened to these people and how this transformation was not just an intellectual change but a radically emotional and attitudinal change towards that which the children have already come to know and appreciate as the sign of a 'good' human being. This recognition and realization of the impact of faith on individuals and society needs historical examples and analysis which can be planned by teachers in graded stages.

It is also necessary for pupils to become aware of the common belief of all great world religions in a Transcendent Reality whom Hindus, Muslims, Christians, Jews and Sikhs call God and whom Buddhists regard as the Transcendent. It is here that some knowledge or understanding of a Transcendent moral norm which is there and waiting to be developed in each individual, of which pupils may have already become conscious, becomes extremely helpful.

The claim of most world religions that the Supreme Being, God, is the Transcendent Reality and faith in Him means a bond of unity between Him and the human being can then be analyzed. How far children who have come from homes where they never hear or learn about God or worship or faith will be able to understand it even intellectually is a question that cannot be answered so easily. But once a child can realize that the essence of the moral norm, the norm of *Virtue* or the *Good*, is latent within us and can be developed and which at the same time transcends each individual and community, it becomes comparatively easy to understand the need for some Supreme Reality that provides that transcendent norm within human beings. All great religions explain these moral qualities to have been granted by God and their roots are in God's own qualities. Buddhists also explain their origin in the Eternal, the Absolute, the Transcendent.[5] Hence the intimate relationship between the human soul and God (or the Divine).

How worship or having a religious faith can remove pride and arrogance so that a person may be humble, self-critical, good and compassionate can then be investigated through the use of examples from the lives of great religious people and from literature that deals with the subject. Great literature, both poetry and prose, from different parts of the world by great religious and mystical poets can then be used to rouse that consciousness and that feeling of humility, self-effacement and self-realization that can be gained through worship. Jalal Uddin-Rumi's *Masnavi*, the Noh plays of Japan, T.S. Eliot's *Four Quartets*, the *Gita*, some of Eckhardt's writings and many more can be used to convey this feeling generated through religious faith and worship. It is only when this method is adopted that religious sensibility can be roused and deeper feelings stirred within the souls of pupils. The feelings associated with deeper realizations of religion can never be appreciated through simply showing a mosque, a church, a synagogue, a temple or a gurdwara, or through intellectual information about forms of worship or religious activities. If my definition of the purpose of religious education is accepted, that is, that it should strir, rouse and refine and deepen the religious sensibility of pupils, then the methodology suggested so far cannot be ignored.

3   As we have already seen, religious sensibility includes some consciousness of the immortality of the soul and human beings' accountability for their actions after death. At present religious education teaches about the last 'rite of passage', that is, death of the physical body and how religious people deal with the dead body. But it never tries to convey what response to this event religious people have within themselves because of their belief in the immortality of the soul: for Buddhists (if the dead person's soul has not attained Nirvana) judgment on their Karma, and their rebirth; and for other religions, the Judgement after death by God and the reward or punishment in either Heaven or Hell. All these can be taught for information, but this information by itself cannot stir the religious sensibility if the pupils have no understanding of the spiritual aspect of human beings.

Here I think two dimensions ought to be tackled, one metaphysical and the other emotional. From the metaphysical point of view, I believe, as the children grow up, it is possible to help them to realize that there is something called the Spirit of a human being which transcends physical existence. This idea is generated by the experience of the spiritual norm that I have termed the norm of Virtue which transcends the self altogether. Death brings about a dissociation between the two entities. Muslims believe that the spirit and consciousness — both spiritual and physical — leave the body though the matter that the body is composed of remains. It is also necessary for pupils to know what writers with religious consciousness have written about their response to this dissociation and death, this realization of our worldly existence, the immortality of the soul and of accountability after death for our actions in life. Here again one has to depend on the great moral and religious literature of the world irrespective of particular religious doctrines. Thus the knowledge of the religious sensibility will be conveyed to pupils.

4   The last aspect of religious sensibility is the feeling that we have a need for divine guidance, or guidance from the great religious teachers. Most great religions were preached by individuals who claimed to have received some divine guidance for themselves and whose life and character became important models for their followers. Religious sensibility can never be properly understood without understanding this aspect of religion. Love of God is central to most religions and the great preachers or teachers of religions are generally held to be the finest examples of what a religious person should be — people who live up to the high ideals and display

all the virtues in the course of their lives and activities. This aspect can be conveyed to pupils by focusing their attention on the following:

(a)   In incidents and situations which illustrate how the virtues which children have become aware of are seen fully manifested through the character and conduct of these religious leaders and teachers.

(b)   The history of those different religious groups who accepted divine guidance through their leaders and Prophets and were transformed; and other great religious teachers such as Buddha and the history of Buddhist people.

The main objective is to show the historical fact of the transformation and the means of achieving this end so that the pupils realize that throughout human history the same need was felt and repeatedly fulfilled by religious leaders and teachers and especially those who claimed prophethood. The self-analysis recommended earlier and the process of self-examination indicate the shortcomings of most of us and the need for some help and guidance in order to strengthen our attempts to become more virtuous. The intellectual and emotional search for guidance thus becomes an important element in religious consciousness.

It is necessary here for religious education to be a means of uprooting from the heart of people narrow sectarianism and prejudices and helping them to realize that, for example, those who follow Jesus Christ or Muhammad should not condemn each other. If religious education cannot succeed in doing this, then education and its methodology must be seriously defective. It is through the historical analysis of the condition of people before and after the acceptance of these preachers as their guides to the path of God, or of teachers who teach a way towards a Transcendent Reality, that pupils may gain a greater understanding of themselves and other religious and ethnic groups. That is why I suggest that only by rousing respect and reverence in pupils' hearts for these preachers and teachers will it be possible to eliminate the narrowness and prejudices which are entirely contrary to that feeling which we characterize as 'religious'.

The Religious Tradition

If the strategy given above for the presentation of religious education is followed, the informative aspect which is already to the fore in current RE practice will be seen to fall into place. It will include:

(i)   the beliefs and practices of different major world religions (the six religions now present in the UK);

(ii)   their historical emergence;

(iii) the way of life that the followers of these religions are expected to maintain.

This informative side is more or less looked after by teachers nowadays. But I wonder whether any attempt has been made by teachers to indicate and explore the great tradition which we should term 'the Religious Tradition'. This is a common tradition to which all the great religions of the world belong. It is common practice in schools to treat each religion separately. It is true that their rites and practices are mostly unique, but most religions have some common denominators of beliefs, with God in the centre and the spiritual-cum-moral dimension of the human personality as the basic contextual area to work upon. In this tradition, behind the facade of different rituals, there are common beliefs in a Transcendent Reality, the spiritual essence of human nature, the common unchanging moral values and the need for Divine Guidance. This tradition is completely opposed to the new scientific tradition with a world-view that ignores life-after-death, the transcendent, God and Divine Guidance and considers moral values as social products or as something which is somehow needed for human beings or which has somehow evolved through human effort. Are we going to teach religious education in the context of this scientific world-view or in the context of the religious tradition of the world? I opt for the latter. It is a very strange phenomenon today that just because there are atheists or agnostics in modern society we who believe in religious consciousness should bow down to them and accept their world-view. This, as I have said earlier, is an anachronism and a farce. Religious education should encourage children to be aware of the religious view of life and hence it must be taught in the context of the religious tradition of the world, however varied may be its expression.

Religious Education and Religious Instruction

We have so far kept religious instruction and religious education in two separate categories. Religious education is the training of religious sensibility of all pupils irrespective of their particular faiths, and religious instruction means an analysis of the expression of that sensibility through a particular religious form. Students should be allowed to choose one of the six religions and enter into detailed knowledge of that religion and its relevance for human beings in the world today. It may be a form of catechesis, hence it assumes that children attending these lessons would like to follow that religious path or are already in that path and would like to know more about it. Whereas religious education is given without any assumption of faith and without any doctrinal discussions, initiations or catechesis, religious instruction is planned to help children practise a particular faith correctly.

From the above discussion it is thus obvious that religious education, as explained above, has retained the critical openness as explained in Brenda Watson's book *Education and Belief* but it is expected that students should try to suspend their disbelief in order to gain the experience. What Coleridge says about understanding and enjoying poetry may to some extent be applicable here. What we need is a 'willing suspension of disbelief'. We need this as the first step but we need more. We need 'willing adventure' into the experience of religious sensibility.

Notes

1 *General Education in a Free Society* (1946) Report of the Harvard Committee, London, Oxford University Press.
2 See my comments on it in chapter 2 of Ashraf, 1985.
3 Utilitarianism and logical positivism both lead to the pragmatization which Dewey advocated according to which there is no ultimate truth. That is what Bertrand Russell protested against in the chapter on 'science and values' in his book *The Impact of Science on Society*.
4 An attempt to show the common but different versions of the same approach in different religions has been made by Schuun (1975). See also his *Logic and Transcendence* (1975) Harper & Row and Newman's *Grammar of Assent*, (1870) Various editions.
5 The above uses terminology which Buddhists do not use, such as God and worship of God. At the same time it assumes that the religious sensibility is basically a realization of the importance of spiritual transcendence and of the Transcendent Reality and also of the conflict between the baser and the higher selves. This Buddhists also believe in. They also believe in this higher love (Compassion) which is not just an intellectual phenomenon but is also a spiritual one. Hence it is possible to use the concept of Transcendence and spiritual love to explain their concept of religious sensibility and thus find correspondence between what I have stated above and what they believe in.

References

ASHRAF, S.A. (1985) *New Horizons in Muslim Education,* London, Hodder & Stoughton.
SCHUUN, F. (1975) *The Transcendent Unity of Religions* (rev), London, Harper & Row.
WATSON, B. (1987) *Education and Belief,* Oxford, Blackwell.

Chapter 6

A Look at the Christian Schools Movement

Bernadette O'Keeffe

A New Movement

There has been a renewal of interest in Christian education in recent years. For the past two decades a number of different factors, directly and indirectly, have gradually come together so that it is now possible to talk of a new Christian initiative in education. Since 1979 between three and eight new Christian schools have been founded each year. Today, there are approximately eighty such schools with more due to open later this year. In this chapter I share with readers some of the results of a research project.[1] I explore the ways in which these schools are working towards an appropriate reorganization of education in which religion will be given a central place.

Since 1870 schools with a Christian foundation have played an important part in educational provision in Britain. However, these new Christian schools are significantly different in a number of respects. They are non-denominational in character. They are sponsored and controlled by local church fellowships, Christian communities and parents. In contrast to a denominational constituency, they were founded in response to the 'secular drift' in state schools by Christians who wish their children to have an education which is in accord with their 'deepest religious and philosophical convictions'.

The House Church Movement has been significant in the steady growth of these new independent Christian schools.[2] Generally, schools have opened with a small number of pupils, some with less than thirty pupils. The trend so far has been for a rapid growth in pupil numbers. The majority of schools have long waiting lists and require larger premises and additional financial resources to meet the increasing demand for places. The quality of school buildings vary considerably. Some pupils are accommodated in purpose-built buildings which are well-equipped, while others make use of church halls with fewer amenities. All are day schools and the majority provide continuing education through primary and secondary levels. As schools are an integral part of their Christian fellowships, the composition of governing bodies reflect this link.

Schools are financed in different ways. A minority of schools charge set fees substantially lower than the per capita cost of state-maintained education. A few rely entirely on donations from parents and church members while others adopt ability-to-pay schemes. However, the majority of schools are financed by a combination of standard fees, ability-to-pay schemes and voluntary donations. Compared with state-maintained schools, these schools are considerably under-resourced financially. Many schools would like to expand their buildings but they do not have the necessary finance to do so. In some schools teachers are prepared to accept salaries well below the government's pay scales.

Why Has It Arisen?

Secularism and Pluralism in Education

Britain today is both secular and pluralist and therefore we can no longer assume a wide social acceptance of a Christian way of life. The terms secularization and its derivative, 'secularism', have been employed in numerous ways. Sometimes, the terms are used in a purely descriptive and non-evaluative way or as ideological concepts charged with evaluative resonances. Without taking an evaluative stance, Berger (1969) provides a straightforward definition of secularisation which provides a useful starting-point for the discussion which follows:

> By secularization we mean the process by which sectors of society and culture are removed from the domination of religious institutions and symbols. (p. 107)

As a result of this process, religion has been pushed to the periphery of modern life and, in this respect, the maintenance of religious belief systems becomes a subjective and privatized enterprise. Not only have we seen a secularization of society and culture, but also a secularization of consciousness, 'Put simply, this means that the modern West has produced an increasing number of individuals who look upon the world and their own lives without the benefit of religious interpretations'. As a result, the impact of the secularization process has resulted in 'a widespread collapse of the plausibility of traditional religious definitions of reality' (*ibid*, pp. 150–1).

Accompanying the growth of autonomous secular areas is an increasing pluralism in the areas of religious beliefs. Instead of one religious tradition maintaining a monopoly, religious groups compete not only with each other but also with non-religious groups. Consequently, pluralism makes it increasingly difficult for religion to maintain its plausibility because society as a whole can no longer be enlisted to give social confirmation. To quote Berger again:

> the pluralist context multiplies the number of plausibility structures competing with each other: Ipso facto, it relativizes their religious

contents and deprives them of their taken-for-granted reality and the self-evident plausibility is lost. (*ibid*, p. 151)

Reflecting the wider society, religion no longer provides the source of value-consensus in our educational system. The dominant philosophies of education owe little, if anything, to a Christian world view of the nature and destiny of the individual. The dominant educational model, it would appear, is the property of experts and experts operating from secular assumptions. Reflecting the concerns of Christians and the shift away from any kind of Christian consensus, Cooling and Oliver (1989) observe that pupils:

> are given fewer and fewer points of spiritual contact and possibilities of Christian understanding at school. Many of our schools, especially secondary schools, do not even offer the possibility of serious en-counter with the ideas and beliefs of Christianity as a vigorous, modern and relevant world view. (p. 6)

Increasingly, Christians have challenged this essentially secular model. They believe that their children are being given a false account of the world and human life in the majority of state-maintained schools.

Thus, the Christian Schools Movement has sought to provide a structure within which the group's world view is plausible. A sound plausibility struc-ture allows the meaning system to be held as a common, taken-for-granted entity. Likewise, it has the potential to strengthen the beliefs of individuals, to provide mutual protection of their view of reality and to give the necessary social support. Serving this purpose are locally-sponsored new Christian schools exhibiting a high level of group commitment and consensus. In this context, primary group relationships provide a structure within which the believers' distinctive world view is plausible, whereas outside the group that world is disconfirmed.

The Privatization of Religion

In November 1990 a Private Member's Bill was introduced into the House of Lords to amend the 1980 Education Act and the 1988 Education Reform Act. The purpose of the Bill was to make it possible for new independent Christian schools to receive government funding.[3] Although the Bill mentioned the word 'Christian', it was designed to include schools 'which provide an alternative religious or philosophical ethos'. However, new inde-pendent Christian schools are by far the largest group of schools involved. The proposed amendments would have enabled these schools to move out of their current isolation. It would also have signalled an acceptance of a faith-based education within the framework of equal opportunity in a pluralist society. The majority of schools hoped to benefit if the proposed amendments had come into effect, provided that they were not required to compromise their religious ethos.

Although the Private Member's Bill had the support of the major political parties in the House of Lords and the House of Commons, it faced strong
opposition during its second reading in the House of Lords from those who
did not wish to see freedom of choice extended to religious groups who are
unwilling to accept the dominant model of education.[4] For opponents of the
Bill, a single education model is assumed to provide the best means of building a unified social fabric where individuals can focus on what binds them
together. Representing this viewpoint, Baroness Blackstone states:

> There is a good case to make all publicly maintained schools secular
> schools, as in the United States of America and many European
> countries. Religious teaching is then left to the churches and other
> religious bodies and takes place outside schools rather than within
> them ... children can receive their secular education together without
> being segregated into separate schools according to their parents'
> religious faith. That has much to recommend it in a multi-racial,
> multi-faith society. (Hansard, 4 March 1991, col. 1255)

Also opposing the Bill and placing materialistic and utilitarian values high
on the agenda, Baroness Flather takes the view that parental rights are sub-
ordinate to the good of the wider society. Thus the view emerges that in
serving well the needs of the wider society, the educational system is able also
to serve well the needs of pupils:

> Parental choice cannot be paramount. It must be balanced with the
> needs of society and those real consumers, the children themselves. It
> is their future and ability to compete and function alongside their
> peers that we should be most concerned about. (*ibid*, col. 1265)

Once again, Baroness Flather confirms the view that parents and not state
schools are responsible for the religious dimension: we cannot absolve the
parents from their own responsibility for the nurture of their children (*ibid*).
Thus religion is made private.

Many supporters of the Bill reject the idea that religious beliefs can be
confined to the private sphere, emphasizing instead that religious beliefs
provide a framework for living — a vision for life, and they cannot, therefore, be confined to the private domain. The following quotation provides a
clear example of such a standpoint:

> The growth of Christian schools is driven by two convictions. The
> first is that we are commanded by God to raise our children in the
> ways and knowledge of the Lord: 'You shall teach these ways
> diligently to your children.' (Deut 6:7). This applies not only to
> religious 'education' but to every aspect of home and school: ... The
> second conviction is that learning for life in this way cannot be done
> in the present state schools. So one of our concerns is to shift
> education from government and to Christian parents and other
> members of Christ's body.' (Marshall, 1990, p. 4)

These new Christian schools are endeavouring to provide a school environment akin to an 'absorbing ambition' of Thomas Arnold — where education was not based on religion, but was itself religious. Arnold was making a distinction between schools which through Church affiliation have a veneer of Christianity and those where religion is the very fibre or 'heart beat' of education (Arnold, 1946).

To this end, strong links are maintained between three socializing institutions — the family, the school and the Christian community so that a greater coherence may be achieved for pupils, parents and teachers than is often the case in state maintained schools. In other words, the home, school and Christian community provide a unified education direction.

On a most fundamental level, the issue of government funding for religiously based schools is one of contrasting world views. These differing world views give rise to contrasting views of education. It raises important issues including questions on the social location of religion in our society and whether parents rather than the government should be the primary bearers of responsibility for education. On the one hand, opposers of religiously based schools regard religion as a private matter and highlight religion's potential to divide people. On the other hand, for the supporters of the Bill, religion belongs to the public domain and they highlight the capacity of religion to provide an integrating world view or meaning system.

Balancing Tradition and Relevance Today

In their different endeavours, those seeking to provide a distinctly Christian education see it as a summons to return to a position that is old and at the same time new. The call to education is a call back to the Bible and Christ; it is a return to an education which promotes the view that Christ and the Bible have relevance for our time and context. It is at the same time a challenge to 'go forward with Him' in a society which exhibits a whole range of competing values and alternative world views. The challenge is to go forward in a climate where the taken-for-granted quality of religion is no longer an important source of legitimacy for the majority.

Approach to the Curriculum

What is Knowledge?

Thinking through a Christian approach in all subjects has been developed to varying degrees by schools in the study. The following is an example of how one school gives the whole curriculum a specifically biblical perspective. The approach adopted is one which relates the whole context of learning to developing pupils' knowledge of God (see appendix 3).[5] The following extract outlines the thinking behind this approach:

Unlike most of the current education thinking, knowledge in the Biblical sense is more than simply intellectual understanding, which in our culture is itself deified; it is always the knowledge of God. Wisdom, or a deep desire to be obedient to God and His principles for life, will teach us to practise and understand God's norms and values and this in turn leads us to know God, in whom is all wisdom. This is not a vertical line which takes us out of our relationship to nature and culture, into a higher realm of 'spirituality', nor is it knowledge first leading to wisdom and understanding, which tends towards the Greek deification of knowledge, but rather it is a mystery and a unity of these principles.

The focal point of all the teaching material involves the following:

1 Knowing God personally and having a personal, meaningful relationship with him.
2 Knowing God's laws and principles for life and being obedient to them. This includes the areas of personal relationships in the family and the schools etc., as well as issues of broader significance, such as public justice and a godly stewardship of the created world.
3 Knowing the created world: through understanding sciences and maths.
4 Knowing God as the Creator: imaging Him, by being creative in all aspects of life.
5 Knowing God's plan for His Creation — the story of Man, creation fall and redemption.
6 Knowing God's calling — each person's sense of identity and purpose in life.

Thus, apart from the basic skills of numeracy and literacy, all teaching material is approached in an integrated manner, with the focal point being the knowledge of God. This working curriculum model acknowledges that all truth, wherever it is found, is of God. Thus every lesson is potentially an opportunity for acquiring knowledge of what God has revealed through Christ.

There are those who continue to use the term 'Christian education' primarily in connection with some kind of religious education as a subject offered in schools. When teachers in the study use the term religious education they have a much broader view insofar as they see religious education happening all the time in a Christian environment. Nevertheless, the majority of schools see the need to have formal religious education classes.

Religious Education

We now turn to look at the kind of formal religious education provided in Christian schools. The overall conception of the teaching of religion conveyed by teachers is one that is concerned to transmit the Judaeo-Christian heritage including the Bible as the Word of God and His plan for redemption. In the majority of schools the content of religious education is based on the authority and authenticity of the Bible as God's revelation concerning matters of faith, truth and practice. What is taught is planned around the concept of progressive revelation through history. Starting from the premise that God has spoken in history it is an aim of religious education to inform pupils about, to have a knowledge of, and to understand what God has said.

The most frequently stated aims express the intention of providing the knowledge to enable pupils to appreciate the Judaeo-Christian heritage and help them to be informed about the life and teachings of Christ. The following extracts illustrate such aims:

> We aim to develop a good knowledge of the Bible and a real love of God's word.

> In Biblical studies our aim is to help pupils to develop the necessary skills to undertake an objective and critical study of the origins and development of the Christian religion. We seek to help pupils to understand the nature of Christian beliefs and practices and their importance and influence on the lives of believers.

These aims are pursued through direct study of the Bible. This involves a study of the Bible itself, in its books of history, poetry, prophecy and doctrine. In addition, Church history, Christian doctrine and traditions of the Church are taught.

Preparation for Christian Commitment

Schools seek to provide the context for pupils to become aware of a spiritual interpretation of life in order to provide them with a sense of purpose and fulfilment in life. This aim is asserted positively from a Christian point of view:

> An important aim is to help pupils to become aware of a spiritual interpretation of life from a Christian perspective.

> Our aim is to assist pupils in their search for answers to the fundamental questions about the meaning and purpose of life and help them understand the relevance and challenges of the Christian religion.

Another stated priority of Christian schools is that of leading pupils on in continuing nurture 'to increasing stature in Christian character'. A sample of these explicitly stated confessional aims include:

> RE is concerned with the whole child and its aim is to enable pupils to encounter Jesus Christ in their lives.

> We aim to develop a good knowledge of the Bible and a real love of God's word as a blueprint for their own lives.

> We are teaching a life style not a theory of life. Our aim is that pupils understand the Biblical principles of this life style.

Training in approach to God through Christian worship is another stated priority. Worship is intended to help children enter into and appreciate a basic religious and spiritual dimension. All schools 'instruct' pupils in the ways of prayer and worship. Teachers stress the importance of celebrative ritual as an important means of communicating religious faith. School assemblies involving acts of worship bind pupils and staff together as a religious community. They become a source of shared values and beliefs reinforcing group solidarity and cohesiveness.

Nurture in schools also involves preparing pupils for personal decision-making. Questions dealing with the aims of Christian schools and replies relating to priorities for religious education highlight the importance of training in discipleship as the following extracts illustrate.

> We are seeking to raise a generation of believers in, and ultimately disciples of, Jesus Christ.

> We hope pupils will understand that as Christians a call to discipleship is a call to the imitation of Christ. (Jn. 13.15)

A Christian Perspective on Moral Issues

Adopting the view that the moral judgments of pupils do not arise out of a vacuum and therefore have to be based on something, Christian schools teach specific moral principles. Without resorting to systematic indoctrination of the oppressive type, teachers make markedly familiar to their pupils a Christian perspective on moral issues. Pupils are encouraged to look to Christ as the norm for the moral life. Gustafson (1968) captures well the message teachers wish to convey to their pupils:

> Christ gives insight and direction; he shows something of the way in which his disciples are to follow. He helps them to see what options are more in conformity with the human good as it is understood in and through God's work and disclosure in him. He helps them see what choices about ends to be sought and means to be used are in accord with trust in the goodness of God who gives and sustains life, and who acts to redeem it. (pp. 269–70)

Thus, pupils are encouraged to consider how Christian beliefs and commitments can be brought to bear on the interpretation of moral situations and the choice of alternatives for moral actions. In one school, for example, in helping pupils see contemporary issues from a Christian standpoint, teachers offer a range of topics and the relevant material to stimulate discussion. For instance, under the heading of sexual ethics and love, material is used to get pupils to think about Roy Jenkin's statement that we are living in a 'permissive society'. Pupils study what the Bible has to say about sexuality and how it should be used. Other topics covered from a Christian standpoint require pupils to think through responses to questions such as: if a Christian couple are in love and plan to get married, having made the commitment of engagement, why should they not begin a sexual relationship? Other contemporary issues include the family, the world of work, employment, racism, prejudice and equality.

It thus follows that religious education in Christian schools does not isolate the doctrinal and moral dimensions of the Christian faith but treats both dimensions together as it initiates pupils into an informed understanding of their faith.

In short, biblical studies have moved beyond a traditional factual approach associated with many of the earlier Agreed Syllabuses. In addition to an academic orientation to the Bible, Christian schools have opted for an approach which highlights personal and social relevance.

The Linking of Cognitive and Effective Learning

All schools have a vision of what they hope to achieve for their pupils by the time they leave school. With regard to religious education the following extracts reflect the dominant vision of schools in the study:

> We hope that when they leave school they will have an understanding of the Judaeo-Christian heritage, that they are informed about the life and teachings of Christ and the history of the Christian Church.

> We hope pupils will have sufficient knowledge to understand a Christian world view.

> We hope that they have a framework of understanding that enables them to make sense of reality from a biblical perspective.

The above objectives are largely intellectual in emphasis and are concerned with knowledge and understanding. Yet the nature of religious education is such that in communicating knowledge and understanding of the Christian faith the affective dimension is also given a prominent place. Indeed, teachers acknowledge attitude-change as an important aim of religious education. Affective (emotional) objectives were expressed in the following way:

Hopefully they will be equipped for life in the kingdom of God and life in the world.

That they are keen to do the will of God for the rest of their lives.

As a result of their education if pupils have a living faith in Jesus Christ that will be central to their endeavours and a guide to their relationships we will have succeeded as Christian educators.

Drawing on educational objectives devised by Bloom, Lupton (1982) makes a useful distinction between affective objectives, where the teacher is aiming at *developing a sensitivity* to what is being taught and affective objectives, where the teacher is aiming to *encourage a willingness* to relate what is taught to daily life (p. 138). In Christian schools both these components are clearly illustrated in their objectives. For teachers, it is the person of Jesus Christ that is the true object of faith; whereas the object of belief are things concerning that person. Teachers frequently make the distinction between intellectual assent to doctrine and its acceptance by the heart. For teachers, faith, knowing God, is infinitely more important than knowing about Him. Clearly such an approach is a significant departure from the dominant one found in most county schools which demonstrates a stance outside of religion from which other religions are understood and evaluated.

The Parallel Between Educational Vision and Christian Vision

We can sum up at this point by saying that the study of religion is conducted in 'a climate of belief', in contrast to a climate of unbelief. It is based on a Christian vision of a good life as a source of belief and value in our contemporary society. 'To be educated', writes Peters (1965), 'is not to have arrived at a destination: but to have travelled with a different view' (p. 110). There is an unmistakable resemblance between the concept of education possessing a humanizing and person-building dimension which enables a person to travel the journey of life 'with a different view', and the concept of a 'Christian vision of life', which draws upon and interprets the experiences of life in a way that is specifically Christian. For Peters (1966), the ideal of 'the educated person' is one in whom there is an ongoing cognitive transformation which affects every aspect of life and enables a more effective perspective on the world as understanding grows. Hence, knowledge is transforming in its effects, enabling a kind of understanding which discerns the 'reason-why' of things (p. 4). In Christian schools, forms of knowledge and experiences are sought with reference to overarching religious principles. The quotation, 'Build up your whole lives on Christ and become stronger in your faith as you were taught' (Col. 2–6) is frequently used by teachers to illustrate this point.

Bernadette O'Keeffe

World Religions and Other Stances for Living

The content of religious education in six schools is broadened to include the study of world religions and other stances for living. While there is a growing recognition of their responsibility to help pupils question and explore the claims of different religious groups, schools adopt different methods of teaching. In four of these schools the introduction of world religions and other stances for living are generally brought into integrated topic work, project work and life skills programmes. In the remaining two schools alternative perspectives are introduced and studied in depth at secondary level. What is clear, however, is that the study of world religions begins firmly with Christian faith having taken-for-granted the finality of the Christian faith.

Research on Pupil Attitudes

What patterns of religious behaviour do pupils have? What are their attitudes to Jesus, God, the Bible and personal prayer? I now turn to provide answers to these questions on the basis of my research with pupils. Before doing so, it would be useful to outline briefly dimensions of religious behaviour.

Since the 1960s, researchers in the sociology of religion have been developing classifications for looking at dimensions of religious behaviour. The most influential of these is the classification developed by Glock and Stark (1965) who distinguish five dimensions.

(i) the **experiential** dimension concerns the subjective religious experiences and emotions. For example, it refers to a feeling of intimacy with the 'divine';
(ii) the **ritualistic** dimension includes religious practices such as worship, prayer, the sacraments and church services;
(iii) the **ideological** dimension refers to the content of beliefs for the members of a religious group;
(iv) the **intellectual** dimension refers to a knowledge and understanding of the basic tenets of the group's beliefs and sacred scriptures;
(v) the **consequential** dimension includes the effects of religious belief, practice, experience and knowledge upon the individual's behaviour in all areas of involvement. 'In the language of Christian belief, the consequential dimension deals with man's relationship to man' (*ibid*, p. 18). The implication here is that definite consequences should follow from religious commitments in institutional settings, for example, family, employment and leisure-time activities.

Christian schools endeavour to incorporate all five dimensions in their Christian education programmes. Indeed these dimensions are considered to be an integral part of their educational endeavours regarding the religious development of pupils. Adapting Glock's multi-dimensional model of religious experience, research was undertaken among pupils to explore their

102

Table 6.1:   Religious Values of Pupils

	Positive response	% responses Negative response	Not certain
I know that Jesus helps me	92	3	5
I want to love Jesus	93	3	4
God helps me lead a better life	89	4	6
I know that Jesus is very close to me	87	5	8
God is very real to me	88	5	7
I know that God helps me	92	3	5

attitudes towards God, Jesus, Church attendance, the Bible, prayer and religion in schools. This chapter touches upon two dimensions — the experiential and the ritualistic.[6]

Attitudes to God and Jesus

Table 6.1 brings together a number of sentences to which pupils were asked to respond to. The religious values expressed in this table correspond to the experiential dimension of the Glock model. The responses of pupils illustrate that for the majority of pupils, Jesus holds a very significant and meaningful place in their lives. They accept the reality that Jesus helps them in their day to day activities. They are, however, marginally more uncertain about God's influence in their lives. Whether this slightly lower percentage of positive responses can be attributed to the unrealistic expectations of religious experience is difficult to quantify.

Attitudes to Church Attendance

Regular church attendance is extremely high among pupils. Eighty-two per cent of pupils attend church once a week. Overall, 97 per cent of all pupils in the study have some experience of participating as a member of a believing community.

The research undertaken provides evidence to suggest that parental church attendance has a very strong influence on whether their children attend regularly. The majority of pupils (88 per cent) come from homes where at least one parent attends church on a weekly basis. Eighty-two per cent of pupils whose mothers attend church weekly also go to church weekly. These research findings give support to other research undertaken, in confirming that the religious practices of parents have a strong influence on the religious behaviour of the younger generation (Francis, 1987).

While 70 per cent of pupils said their church community was important, not all enjoyed participating in their services — 20 per cent of pupils found the actual experience of Church services boring. It would appear that more needs to be done to meet the needs of their younger members.

Bernadette O'Keeffe

Table 6.2:   *Religious Values and Personal Prayer*

	% responses		
	Positive response	*Negative response*	*Not certain*
I think prayer is a good thing	92	2	5
Saying my prayers helps me a lot	79	6	15
I believe God listens to my prayers	94	2	3

Attitudes to Personal Prayer

Although church attendance is the most frequently used index of religiosity, it provides only a partial picture as it fails to reflect other dimensions of religious experience. In order to tap the dimension of free, personal commitment, pupils were asked to respond to a number of statements. Their responses to personal prayer provide an indication of the place of private religion in their lives in contrast to the public place of religion which finds expression in church attendance. The responses of pupils are given in table 6.2. The statistics in it illustrate the overall positive attitudes of pupils to personal prayer. For 92 per cent of pupils prayer is an important activity in their lives. The responses of a slightly higher percentage of pupils (94 per cent) illustrate the importance of the subjective religious feelings containing a personal dynamism involving faith and trust in the divine. However, whilst the majority of pupils confirm the general importance and value of personal prayer, 13 per cent are less confident that prayer helps them individually.

Over half (59 per cent) of pupils in the study pray daily at home. For another 10 per cent, prayer is part of a weekly routine. Only a small percentage (6 per cent) of all the pupils said that they never prayed. The overall responses of pupils regarding the benefits of school prayer are also very positive. Eighty-five per cent of pupils disagreed with the statement: 'I think saying prayers in school is a waste of time'. For 8 per cent of the pupils there was uncertainty about its benefit and the remaining 6 per cent agreed with the statement.

Attitudes Towards the Bible

In order to discover pupils' attitudes towards the Bible, the following two statements were included in the questionnaire and pupils were asked to indicate whether they agreed or disagreed with them.

> I think the Bible is old fashioned and out of date.
> I find it boring to listen to the Bible.

Their responses illustrate that for the majority of pupils, the Bible continues to be relevant in their lives. Eighty-six per cent of pupils reject the suggestion that the Bible is out of date. While 6 per cent were uncertain about its relevance, 6 per cent held a negative attitude towards the Bible. Pupils' responses show however, that there is less enthusiasm for listening to the Bible being read to them. While 73 per cent of pupils enjoyed listening to the Bible, 15 per cent were uncertain and another 13 per cent actually found the activity boring.

On the basis of these findings, it would appear that Christian schools have proved successful in making the Bible relevant for their pupils. The case put forward by Goldman that very little of the Bible is suitable before adolescence and that it is often regarded by children as remote, irrelevant and boring has not been borne out by my own research in schools.[7] This may well be due to the fact that children in the study are, from an early age, socialized within a world view where religion is a guiding force and where children are encouraged to see the relevance of the Bible in their lives. What Goldman failed to recognize was the complementary roles of the home, the school and religious community in the religious understanding and development of the child.

Conclusion

The main conclusion to emerge from this study is that schools are exercising a positive influence on their pupils' attitudes towards Christianity. The responses of pupils demonstrate that the majority of pupils hold positive attitudes towards God, Jesus, the Bible and personal prayer. It is clear that the overwhelming majority of pupils have a high regard for personal religion.

Whatever the outcome of the controversy concerning the role of nurture in education and whether it will ever be resolved, religious nurture in Christian schools is accepted as essential to Christian growth. I have shown that one of their first tasks as educators is to bring about conditions where the pupil may be presumed to be informed and have a prepared predisposition to understand and respond according to the level of maturity from a Christian basis. It is that idea of preparation, and the fostering and promoting of a receptivity and capacity for responding that may become stepping-stones upon which further ends can be reached.

The Wider Context

A Sociological Comment

Like all institutions, schools are organic and undergo constant adaptations and adjustments. They absorb change and incorporate experience. This is not to say that they are shaped entirely by the learning process, because they already possess a semi-determinate character. We have seen that Christian schools have carved out a 'determinate' education of the full arc of educational and social possibilities.

The socialization process in schools involves selections out of the overall range of options in order to provide a degree of coherence. However, some of the options selected contain more potential for alternatives than others. There is always the possibility that in providing a firm social base in the pursuit of stability, the pattern may become one of reproduction rather than development. Some options selected by schools in their task of socialization contain more potential for alternatives than others. The direction of some schools ensures stability but inhibits creativity. In such instances no contrary vision of society is allowed to disturb or disrupt patterns of reproduction. In contrast, other schools are attempting to strike a balance between necessary stability and destructive openness.

The Needs of Society

No matter how successful schools are in helping pupils to develop positive attitudes to Christianity or helping pupils to seek meaning and fulfilment in life in response to a religious ideal, the context in which they find themselves is a secular and pluralist society. We have seen that Christian schools recognize the primacy of Christianity as a personal relationship with God in Christ manifest in and through one's relationships with others. The prime importance of people coming to terms with one another is fundamental in working towards a harmonious society. Reflecting on the responsibility of Christians in this area Hubery (1972) observes:

> If there is any validity in the Christian interpretation of the revelation of God's nature and purpose, it must surely point to the recognition that all people are equally important in the eyes of God, and that we must learn to treat them with respect as persons in their own right, whatever they may do and whoever they might be. (p. 41)

A Deeper Approach to the Study of World Religions

There is considerable scope in Christian schools to broaden their religious nurture in order to develop an approach in which the study of world religions is given a deeper and a more exciting meaning for pupils than is often the case with the phenomological approach. Such an approach would be concerned to help pupils recognize the applicability of their own methods of enquiry to new situations thus broadening and deepening their understanding of how others search for meaning and significance in their lives. Implicit within this approach is the avoidance of the kind of intellectual arrogance evident in the phenomological approach; an approach which is careful not to place undue emphasis on the superficial or on the externalities at the expense of the 'interiority of faith'; one which avoids relativizing or distorting religions by presenting them as no more than variants of a phenomenon called religion; one where pupils are not required to 'bracket out' their own presuppositions, religious beliefs and prior commitments (even if it is conceivable to do so) in order to enter into the experiences of the believer and see the world through his/her own eyes. In developing religious education from the basis of a particular religious tradition, schools would signal a faithfulness to their religious identity while at the same time giving their pupils a better understanding of the secular and pluralist nature of British society which they will encounter when they leave school.

The Need to Handle Diversity Creatively

Pupils need to be able to share the reality of their experience with others and find common ground. They must learn to differ from one another in the ways they interpret their faith and the grounds for holding it without disrupting the essential quality of relationships. Genuine conversation in ways of thought and behaviour is an essential element in working towards an unified, harmonious society. For as Aspin (1988) notes, in the final analysis, unity consists in what can be said —:

> For all there is, finally, is people talking together; insofar as we fail to help young people and children learn to be able to engage in conversation with the widest range of people, we fail to prepare them for the complexities of the world and the problems of all its denizens. (p. 41)

Pupils need to be ready for frank and searching discussion with those of other faiths and ideologies; to be ready for the kind of human conversation where, on a fundamental level there is a willingness to listen and to talk, to learn as well as to teach, to give as well as to receive.

A New Priority: Environmental Education

In the last part of this chapter I want to suggest an important area for curriculum development in Christian schools which is comparatively new and concerned with developing positive and responsible attitudes towards the environment. The importance of environmental education is summed up by the National Curriculum Council (1990) in the following way:

> In schools it aims to increase pupils' knowledge and understanding of the processes by which environments are shaped; to enable them to recognize both the quality and the vulnerability of different environments; and to help them identify opportunities for protecting and managing the environment. (p. 6)

A Need for Global Awareness

In shaping education which articulates purpose, coherence and meaning, educationalists and policy makers are tireless in their attempts to promote the concept of the common good. It is clear that the common good has more than a national or European dimension, it is planetary. As we approach the end of the twentieth century we face in unprecedented form the challenge of learning to live together in a world that is faced with almost insurmountable problems in such areas of ecology, energy, pollution, over-population, the wasteful use of non-renewal resource and human exploitation of nature.

Fortunately, an awareness of the increasing destruction of the natural world and what many see as the deepening ecological crisis is growing, and interest groups are calling for profound changes in the way human beings relate to the natural or created world. In recent years, many Christians and Christian leaders have begun to respond to environmental concerns. Increasingly, we are witnessing ecumenical and inter-religious cooperation in the promotion of ecological values and in the quest for a new solidarity among the 'earth community'.

Although there is a wide spectrum of beliefs, values and perspectives concerning environmental issues, there exists, nevertheless, much common ground among the different interest groups. For instance, the Christian Ecology link identifies a number of parallels which serve to illustrate how secular and religious groups, with their distinctive ways of viewing the world, share common concerns in working constructively to care for the planet.[8]

Science and Religion

Today, important steps are being taken to build bridges between science and religion in the growing recognition of their important contributions in responding to environmental concerns. There are hopeful signs of a new joint partnership between science and religion as scientists, religious leaders and theologians together scan new horizons to care for the planet.[9]

The way we relate to the environment is shaped and largely determined by what we hold to be true. It is shaped by our perception of reality and our understanding of where we humans stand in relation to the rest of creation or nature. It is therefore an important area for religious education to explore.

A Cross-curricular Approach

I am not advocating a response only in terms of adding new content to formal religious education classes. On the contrary, beliefs and values concerning the environment and care of the planet have distinctive implications for the whole curriculum. The National Curriculum Council includes it as one of five themes essential to the whole curriculum.[10] The religious perspective needs to be clear, not because it has all the answers, but because of the insights it can bring to caring for the created world. Any approach to environmental education which fails to incorporate the religious perspective will be incomplete. A source of weakness in the dominant secular humanist stance draws from its failure to acknowledge the legitimacy of viewpoints which are essentially religious in origin.

Towards a Balanced Christian Perspective on Environmentalism

As we have seen, the priorities for Christian schools include the development of a biblical perspective on a wide range of contemporary issues and also the nurturing of a value of discipleship. Although one or two schools are turning their attention to environmental concerns, the majority of schools have not developed this curriculum area. A key question for Christian schools to address is raised by McDonagh (1986) in his analysis of the progressive destruction of the natural world — 'How is a disciple of Jesus to respond to the rampant destruction and poisoning of the natural world which, if the current rate continues or increases, will threaten all life on Earth'? (p. 3) Approaches to religious education must necessarily avoid simplistic treatment when tackling this question. An exploration of the ways in which the Christian message has been interpreted and lived out over the centuries will provide material for much discussion, debate and reflection, increasing pupils' awareness that the Christian faith does not give its followers 'heaven-sent' answers to difficult and complex problems. In discussing the ways in which the Christian message has been lived out in the past, McDonagh shows how different approaches to the natural world have shaped Christian consciousness. He describes a 'bright' side of Christian caring, involving responsible stewardship, respect for the natural world and gratitude. However, he also discusses the 'dark' side which places human beings over and against nature, which is driven by utilitarian concerns to 'domesticate' nature and bring it under human control to satisfy human needs (*ibid*, p. 131).

Although the Christian understanding of history and God's actions, particularly through the person of Jesus Christ, has much to contribute to other religions and cultures, with its emphasis on the personal dimension, this vision is also incomplete, and, as McDonagh observes: 'like every other religious and non religious tradition is vulnerable and needs to engage in dialogue with other traditions' (*ibid*, p. 152). Starting from a Christian perspective, and exploring the values people derive from Christianity, teachers can help pupils to explore the teachings of other world religions. Biblical revelation and Christian tradition can be enriched with insights from other religious traditions which contain many appeals to individuals to show respect and compassion for all life. Christians have much to learn from the close relationship with nature and the importance given to the natural world which other religions have developed over the centuries. For McDonagh:

> Cosmic and Earth revelation is, after all, the primary revelation of God. It is also the common heritage of all human beings and so can provide a fruitful basis for dialogue between religious people. A new spirituality which sees the Earth as permeated with the divine presence would undoubtedly provide the basis for worldwide cooperation among religious people today in respect and care for the Earth. I believe this new religious sense, especially among Christians, must permeate our concern for the Earth. (*ibid*)

Recognizing the importance of interplay between science and religion for the benefit of the 'Earth community', McDonagh has this to say:

> Confronted with the ecological challenge we are challenged to open our minds and hearts to the wisdom of the scientific tradition and the creative vision of other religions in our efforts to respond adequately to the central problem of our time. (*ibid*, p. 153)

Mutually Enriching Dialogue

Indeed, an openness to interplay between religious and non-religious interpretations to environmental concerns leads to mutually enriching dialogue. In their turn, pupils stand to benefit from this discourse as it permeates the school curriculum. The school environment itself becomes an integral part of the wider environmentally-conscious world of which an American student observes:

> My generation's odd privilege is to have been inundated with images of dying rainforests, slaughtered whales, hazardous wastes, malnourished children, and now war.[11]

Aware that there are no easy answers, a minority of Christian schools have placed these concerns high on their agenda, in their case, working with their pupils to achieve greater self-understanding and global awareness from the basis of their Christian faith.

The inclusion of care of the planet in the school curriculum will assist tomorrow's world in the emergence of a more environmentally concerned citizen, a more socially responsible citizen and a more tolerant religious or humanist citizen. It is in their awareness of that possibly better world that pupils and teachers may find signposts pointing the way to a new kind of human solidarity, leading individuals with their different meaning systems to recognize they share much in common with their fellow citizens.

Notes

1   The material used in this chapter is based on research activities begun in 1988 in a sample of fifteen recently established independent schools. The research will be published shortly.
2   The term House Church Movement is used to describe a variety of Christian fellowships and independent groups which exist outside the mainstream denominations. The charismatic renewal played a significant part in the formation of the movement. The House Church Movement contains several hundred house churches. The English Church Census shows that independent Christian churches have increased their adult members by 43 per cent between 1975 and 1989 and that child attendance has risen by 30 per cent.
3   The Private Members Bill was introduced by Baroness Cox education (Amendment) Bill. The Bill was intended to make it easier for certain categories of inde-

pendent schools to obtain voluntary aided status. In addition, the Bill sought to extend eligibility to recently established independent schools to apply for grant maintained status. At the present time this is available only to existing state maintained status schools who wish to opt out of local authority controls.

4 At the commencement of the second reading, Baroness Cox informed the members of the House of Lords that the Bill would be withdrawn at the end of the debate.

5 I am grateful to Ruth Deakin for allowing me to reproduce this curriculum model and explanatory note in this chapter.

6 Dr. Leslie Francis kindly gave me permission to use a questionnaire which he has developed and used over a number of years to test the attitudes of pupils in state maintained schools. The questionnaire is a twenty-four Likert-type scale of attitudes towards religion. It contained twenty-four unambiguous sentences which were indicative of the attitude areas under review. Pupils were asked to rate their level of agreement or disagreement with the individual sentences on a five-point scale, ranging from 'agree strongly', 'agree', 'not certain' and 'disagree', 'disagree strongly'. The statistics in this chapter are based on the first stage of my research involving 439 pupils between the ages of 8 and 16 in six schools. To ensure confidentiality pupils were not asked to put their names on the questionnaire.

7 Goldman (1964) and (1965). On the basis of his own research in the early 1960s directed at the intellectual aspects of children's religious understanding, Goldman concluded that the Bible is not suitable for young children and it should not, therefore, hold a central place in religious education. He maintained that the Bible is often regarded by children as remote, irrelevant and boring.

8 The Christian Ecology Link founded in 1981 (formerly the Christian Ecology Group) has the following aims: first, to spread ecological insights among Christian people and churches; second, to spread Christian insights into the Green Movement. *Christians and the Planet: How Green is Our Church* (1990–91). Further details, from the Secretary, 17, Burns Gardens, Lincoln, LN2 4LJ.

9 In 1990 thirty-two world scientists made an appeal for science and religion to work hand in hand to preserve the earth's environment. The appeal was organised by Carl Sagan, the astronomer, at the Moscow meeting of the Global Forum of Spiritual and Parliamentary Leaders.

10 The four remaining themes are: economic and industrial understanding: careers education and guidance; health education (National Curriculum Council 3, 1990–91, pp. 3–4).

11 Extracts from speeches at the IIED/Observer meeting where world leaders joined youth to address environmental challenges quoted in *The Guardian*, 22 March 1991.

References

ARNOLD, T. (1946) quoted in PATTERSON, H. (Ed.) *Great Teachers*, New Brunswick.

ASPIN, D.N. (1988) 'Critical openness as a platform for diversity — Towards an ethic of belonging' in O'KEEFFE, B. (Ed.) *Schools for Tomorrow: Building Walls or Building Bridges*, Lewes, Falmer Press.

BERGER, P.L. (1969) *The Sacred Canopy*, New York, Anchor Books.

COOLING, T. and OLIVER, G. (1989) *Church and School: The Contemporary Challenge*, Grove Pastoral Series, 39.

Bernadette O'Keeffe

FRANCIS, L.J. (1987) *Religion in the Primary School*, London, Collins.
GLOCK, C.Y. and STARK, R.N. (1965) *Religion and Society in Tension*, Chicago, IL, Aldine.
GOLDMAN, R.J. (1964) *Religious Thinking from Childhood to Adolescence*, London, Routledge & Kegan Paul.
GOLDMAN, R.J. (1965) *Readiness for Religion*, London, Routledge & Kegan Paul.
GUSTAFSON, J.M. (1968) *Christ and the Moral Life*, New York, Harper & Row.
HUBERY, D.S. (1972) *Christian Education in State and Church*, London, Denholm House Press.
LUPTON, H.E. (1982) 'Checklists for study of the religious education syllabus' in HULL, J. (Ed.) *New Directions in Religious Education*, Lewes, Falmer Press.
McDONAGH, S. (1986) *To Care for the Earth: A Call for a New Theology*, London, Geoffrey Chapman.
MARSHALL, P. (1990) *The Christian Schools Newsletter*, **4**.
NATIONAL CURRICULUM COUNCIL (1990) *The Whole Curriculum 3*, London, NCC.
PETERS, R.S. (1965) 'Education as initiation' in ARCHAMBAULT, E. (Ed.) *Philosophical Analysis and Education*, London, Routledge & Kegan Paul.
PETERS, R.S. (1966) *Ethics and Education*, London, Routledge & Kegan Paul.

Chapter 7

Roots in Religious Education

Kevin Nichols

Current Trends

Advancing the Conceptual Understanding of Religion

Educational thought today, though abundant and varied, often seems, to the interested, though uninvolved, observer such as the present writer, to be seeking an effective means of 'disowning the past' as T.S. Eliot put it. The educational philosophy of thirty or forty years ago consisted of reflection on the work and writings of 'the great educators'. This is now greatly, indeed excessively, scorned. Its place is filled by a more technical professional philosophy which seeks to base education on a network of tested and timeless concepts. Such logical clarity will generate purposefulness. It will rid education of contradictions and confusions, making it timeless, streamlined and effective. So, in the field of religion, good teaching will depend, first of all on a clear idea of religion: it is characterized centrally by the feeling of awe or by the concept of the holy; or it is 'morality touched by emotion', or a tradition with mythic, doctrinal, ritual, social, experiential and ethical dimensions. Secondly the concept of education must be clearly analyzed and expressed. It must initiate students into a form of knowledge so that they come to move freely in it. It must promote autonomy and critical openness, avoiding indoctrination. To develop an effective and defensible curriculum, the material organised in the first set of concepts must be fitted into the processes determined by the second set.

Obviously these analyses and clarifications have been of great service to religious education and have challenged many teachers to think more effectively about it. However we should beware of falling into a clarity-neurosis. This network, though of tough logical filagree, is not strong enough to take the whole weight of so complex and many-sided an enterprise; a little too abstractly logical and timeless to be manageable in the flesh. It was, Newman observed, the weakness of some philosophers that they 'consult their own idea of how the mind should work'. They would do better to give more attention to how, in the real world, human minds actually reach conclusions in complex and important questions.

Promoting Social Harmony

If one way of approaching religious education is characterized by ahistorical and rather fleshless logic, there are others which seem too much under the sway of present actualities. So some see religious education at the service of social harmony. Our society is often said to be pluralist. The word is something of a chameleon. I take it here to mean a society that contains several substantial groups of people whose lives are organized and given meaning by different systems of religious belief. Social cohesion depends on the growth of mutual understanding and sympathy between these groups, and religious education should address itself to that. It should be multi-faith. It should go beyond knowledge, even understanding (we are not concerned with comparative religion). It should ensure that children grow up not only knowledgeable about, but sensitive, empathetic towards the experience of those who live within a different religious system. With the growth of these sympathies, social discord will evaporate.

Such social purposes in education are legitimate and important. The early history of education in the USA shows how it was shaped by the need to develop some degree of social cohesion in the bewildering diversity of its immigrant population. It should aim, in the words of a Maryland School Code, at 'sufficient like-mindedness to ensure the survival and progress of the American people'. It would be strange and contradictory if any form of religious education did not promote respect for persons and their faiths, and willingness to appreciate and learn from other traditions; similarly, if it did not include in the ethical dimensions of religion, tolerance, fairness and social cooperation.

While these social aims in education must be taken seriously, they should not be overriding; they should not become the context into which other purposes must be fitted. Personal and liberal purposes also have their rightful claims; the development of religious understanding; spiritual growth; the search for or the maturing in a tradition of faith.

Sampling the Traditions

Both of these two ideas of religious education envisage and encourage a multi-faith approach which will draw its materials not from one but from a number of different religious traditions. For, they argue, if an 'initiation into the world of religion' is what is wanted, then the similarities and differences between the various traditions must be studied. Only thus will the categorial concepts, the logical and imaginative geography of religion be learned.

Although I can see the force of this approach in the modern world, this process of selective and sympathetic sampling is not without its weaknesses, even dangers. First such an exploration of the 'world of religion', of religion as a realm of meaning in a way which is accurate, fair, balanced, sensitive and sympathetic, is a task which makes enormous demands on teachers; demands which, given the time available, add up to an impossibility.

Secondly, to lay side by side, however intelligently, elements from the mythic or the doctrinal or the ritual dimensions of say, Christianity, Judaism and Islam opens up the prospect of serious misunderstanding. Elements which have a place in a unified system look different when they are extracted from it. Their meaning depends on their interconnections and on their place in the whole. Newman (1889) makes this point in his discussion of religious assents and certitudes:

> The same doctrines, as held in different religions, may be and often are held very differently, as belonging to distinct wholes or forms, as they are called, and exposed to the influence and the bias of the teaching, perhaps false, with which they are associated. Thus, for instance, whatever be the resemblance between St. Augustine's doctrine of Predestination and the tenet of Calvin upon it, the two really differ from each other *toto coelo* in significance and effect, in consequence of the place they hold in the systems in which they are respectively incorporated, just as shades and tints show so differently in a painting according to the masses of colour to which they are attached. (p. 251)

The whole is greater than the sum of its parts. Truly to understand the part requires an appreciation of its place in the system and a grasp of the whole within which it has its meaning.

Encouraging Spiritual Development

These difficulties in sampling techniques, this necessity for inhabiting religious systems as wholes, brings to prominence another approach to religious education. This argues for an 'initiation into the world of religion' in which the word 'initiation' conveys the notion of deliberate nurture. The starting point here is not the understanding of the religious world or religious systems; nor the need in a pluralist world for responsible and caring citizens. The starting point is the reality of a spiritual dimension to life to which pupils need to be awakened. Such a spiritual awakening, such spiritual nourishment will make possible a deeper understanding of religious realities; it will also promote the growth of spiritually mature persons likely to be socially responsible, caring and tolerant. It is an approach which does not exclude so vigorously a religious education based within a single tradition. I began by suggesting that these various recent developments or lines of thought (each of which certainly expresses some truth or contains some value) agree in being ahistorical. They rest upon pure logic or they focus largely on contemporary concerns. This gives to them a certain fleshless air, a character of rootlessness. They have a vivid foreground but little depth. I suggest that something different and quite important may be learned by considering the story of religious education within a particular tradition of faith. No doubt all such traditions have their educational stories. But the Christian tradition serves this purpose unusually well; because of its historical developing character; because of its long effort to come to and remain on terms with human reason; and because of its peculiar but persistent relationship with education. In the course of this discussion I shall try to show that the distinction often drawn between nurture or catechesis (a private dialogue) and education (an enterprise in the public forum) is not a clear-cut one; that between them exists a variety of similarities and differences, rather than a definitive line.

Education Within Christian Tradition

Catechesis in the Early Church

In its early days, Christianity stood apart from the Hellenic culture by which it was quickly surrounded in its expansion westwards. It developed elaborate procedures for initiating new members; a long and highly structured Catechumenate. But these procedures owed nothing to the principles or methods of the Greek Schools. The title they were given 'Initiation into the mysteries of faith' set them against systematic reason and critical reflection so that they resembled more the mystery-cults of those days. It made great use of sermons, symbols and ritual gestures designed to solemnize and fortify choice and commitment. We look in vain in the great Catechetical sermons of Augustine and Ambrose for any whiff of the noble humanism of Greece. On the whole they were opposed to it, thinking it harmful to souls. Even the urbane and erudite Jerome rumbled in his crusty ways about the incompatibility of Athens and Jerusalem.

The Alliance between Faith and Education

But this radical chasm between humane learning and Christian truth, this sharp demarcation of a world of 'nurture' or 'Catechesis' quite separate from education, left some of the church fathers uneasy. 'There came to me' wrote Origen, 'adherents of the various schools of thought and men conversant with Greek learning, particularly with philosophy. It seemed therefore necessary that I should examine the doctrines of the schools and see what the philosophers had said concerning the truth'. Origen's problem was, at the first level an educational one; can liberal education and Christian catechesis coexist, even fuse? At a deeper level, it was a theological one; is there one 'river of truth' into which the twin streams of humane learning and the Word of God, equally fall? A positive answer to this question would imply that Christian faith is not an arcane mystery totally inaccessible to reason but rather a word, a doctrine, a 'gnosis' which has a legitimate and necessary place in the world of education.

Origen set up his school in Alexandria to exemplify this positive answer. A born teacher, he turned to the methods of the Greek schools primarily to respond to the concerns of his students. His curriculum was not exactly a synthesis of faith and reason. It was based on the 'circle of the sciences' which constituted the Greek 'paideia' broadened to include the knowledge embodied in God's Word. That knowledge was not to be a strait-jacket distorting the other sciences. It was to provide a perspective and a principle of intellectual order. In a panegyric on Origen, one of his disciples describes the approach and the atmosphere of that school.

> Nothing was forbidden us, nothing hidden from us, nothing in-accessible to us. We were to learn all manner of doctrine — barbarian or Greek, mystical or political, divine or human. We went into and examined with entire freedom all sorts of ideas, in order to satisfy ourselves and enjoy to the full these goods of the mind. When an ancient thought was true, it belonged to us and was at our dispo-sition with all its marvellous possibilities of delightful contem-plations. (quoted in Fuller, 1957, p. 157)

The writer of this passage (Gregory of Neocaesaria) gives us a whiff of the creative excitement inherent in genuine (and good) education; its critical openness of mind, the search for truth and for intellectual order and the mental energy this releases. It is true that in the course of history the admir-able virtue of this Christian *paideia* has often been eclipsed. Faced alike with the constricting over-confidence of power and the stress of failure and division, it has often been replaced by flat rote-learning or by crippling indoc-trination. Yet it has never died. It has been constantly recovered and has flowered in the work of Vittorino da Feltre, Erasmus, Colet and Thomas More. It is the ideal of which Newman wrote; that 'perfection of the intellect ... the clean, calm, accurate vision and comprehension of all things as far as the finite mind can embrace them, each in its place, and with its own characteristics upon it. It is almost prophetic from its knowledge of history; it is almost heart-searching from its knowledge of human nature; it has almost supernatural charity from its freedom from littleness and prejudice; it has almost the repose of faith, because nothing can startle it' (Newman, 1915, p. 131).

Two Objections

True education then, can thrive perfectly well within a tradition of faith. Nothing disqualifies it from that accolade except for abstract logical dis-tinctions. Faith traditions certainly engage in nurture, communicating their beliefs and principles in informal ways and settings. They are also prepared to launch out into the riskier waters of education and have made substantial contributions to its development. However, what is logically acceptable may not be practically desirable. Two arguments are often brought against the idea of religious education within a setting of commitment. The first is that what is possible within a religious culture in a society which is largely homogeneous, is neither practicable nor morally acceptable in a pluralist world. For the imposition of a majority faith or a traditional one would be offensive to minority groups. It would be educationally ineffective and socially divisive. I will discuss this argument further on in this chapter; observing for the moment only that while it rightly points to major problems, practical and moral, it does not necessarily exclude the deployment of commitment in *some* form within the processes of religious education.

The second argument is that a neutral but sympathetic approach to the world of religion, intelligent, fair and honest, is a perfectly adequate and suitable basis for a programme of religious education. For what can commitment *educationally* add? What difference can it make except in the selection of material? Is not the 'neutral' teacher who explores the religious dimensions in a well-informed and tactful way doing the same thing as a Christian teacher, say, who is exploring the idioms of faith — given that the latter is professionally bound to honesty, to the promotion of autonomy and to sympathetic openness to the world of religion outside the tradition? It is the conviction that commitment does add something, does make a difference to the quality of religious understanding that I wish to argue next.

The Need for Commitment

What is Commitment?

Commitment is a different reality from the knowledge we have of verifiable facts or the belief we have in specific principles. We attach the word most readily to persons or values or causes. We would not easily speak of being committed to the Second Law of Thermodynamics. Commitment involves certainly an acceptance that something is the case. But also, and definitively, a declaration of commitment asserts that its object is not only true but also important and beloved. Commitment differs from holding a belief because of our personal investment in its object. We are prepared to abide the consequences of it, to suffer for it, to enact in our own lives its moral principles and ideals. Faith is often distinguished from belief as being a 'fundamental existential commitment', perhaps precognitive and preconceptual; whereas 'beliefs' describe those elements, unpacked from this global commitment which make claims about what is the case. So the word does not envisage as its object (except secondarily) the acceptance of specific beliefs. It is primarily a personal investment in a religious tradition as a whole; for example in what Newman called the Christian 'idea' existing in history and developing there.

Newman's distinction between notional and real assents illustrates this difference. Notional assents acknowledge inferences and conclusions. They are concerned with surfaces and aspects, with 'notions neatly turned out of the laboratory of the mind and sufficiently tame and subdued, because existing only in a definition'. They have their importance, being the conservative principle of knowledge and the principle of its growth. But real assents, not to conclusions but to realities, are what really count in life and especially in religion. Though their groundwork is subtle and complex, they lead to action and 'life is for action. If we insist on proofs for everything, we shall never come to action'. True religious life and understanding takes place at the level of real assent or faith. 'It is the whole man that moves. Paper logic is but the record of it. You might as well say that the quicksilver in the barometer changes the weather'. (Newman, 1912, p. 28) Is it possible in religious education to deal with real assents so that they are not emasculated, and how is this to be done?

Commitment to Truth Alone?

It is sometimes said that in religious (as in all) education, truth itself is the only necessary and legitimate commitment. Loyalty to a particular tradition only serves to narrow and blunt that supreme loyalty. This argument though unexceptionable is over-simple. Against it stands this striking sentence of Newman. 'In the schools of this world, the ways towards truth are considered open to all men, however disposed, at all times. Truth is to be approached without homage'. Truth indeed is not attended by a set of simple and uniform tests.

> On a huge hill Cragged and steep, truth stands and he that will
> Reach her, about must and about must go;
> And what the hill's suddenness resists, win so. (Donne 1931, p. 116)

The image of the search for truth as a demanding climb, rather than a logical exercise, sets religious education in a different perspective. Newman's phrase, 'approaching truth with homage', contains two requirements. The first is that the search goes beyond the submission of the mind to a submission of the heart. It is a willingness to be open to, to acknowledge and be humble before the mystery at the heart of things, that

> love which moves the sun and the other stars

Such a view of religious education, far from viewing commitment as a hazard to be circumnavigated, would set it at the heart of the enterprise. True learning 'begins in wonder, goes on in humility and ends in gratitude'.

Moral Commitment

It is when we speak of education in the register of morality that the place commitment may hold in it appears most clearly. It is the point at which the notion of a sympathetic but detached participation appears at its weakest. To me the language of striving and virtue suggests that the moral dimension of religion cannot be sympathetically sampled. It is in the world of real assents and real demands and its true nature can only be known in meeting these demands or in failing to meet them. It may be true as Newman claimed that 'you do but play a kind of hunt-the-slipper with the fault in our nature till you come to Christianity'. But it is also true that you will not come to Christianity in any profound way without the effort to meet its moral demands. For the different dimensions of a religious tradition interact within a single whole and affect each other. Moral life strengthens or weakens doctrinal belief, faith itself and the quality of religious understanding. As Plato wrote many centuries ago, the truth and the form of the good converge. Truth and virtue spring from a single root.

Commitment to Comprehensive Meaning

John Stuart Mill in his Essay on Bentham and Coleridge, characterizes these two 'seminal minds of the eighteenth century' in two typical questions. Bentham asks: is it true? He wishes to apply to whatever is at issue, objective and external tests for truth. Coleridge asks: what does it mean? He wishes to burrow inside the idea so as to view it from within, believing that only in this way will he be able to appreciate right its true character and scope. The Coleridgean approach seems to me the right one for religious education. Nor, I think, is the religious insider the interested and congenial visitor. The insider has a commitment to the idea (maybe an imperfect and questioning one). This commitment gives him a comprehensive view and enables him to see by participating, how the different dimensions interact within a single whole, how the different languages of faith complement each other in a single way of life. He has a firm stance, though an open-minded one. This stance, far from invalidating such a person as an educator, provides a source of strength.

The central problem of hermeneutics — of how to understand a text or a tradition which is historically or culturally distant from us — is, what do we do about our presuppositions and prejudices in attempting this understanding. Demythologizers suggest that, by stripping away the cultural facade of the alien text, we shall be able to come to a kind of common humanity, universally comprehensible. Others, Gadamer for instance, argue that cultural foreignness need not altogether be an obstacle to understanding. There may be an interaction between the text and the interpreter which brings about a 'fusion of horizons'. To stand within a tradition of faith, provided we are aware of it and open-minded, may be a help to understanding both our own tradition and those of others. It will be a stronger base, give a better foothold than the Western, liberal and agnostic stance which it is often recommended should — even though tactfully, even though for purely procedural reasons — be adopted.

Pluralism and Wholeness

Religion as a Unifying Force

Origen's vision of the single river of truth into which there fall from one side and the other the two streams of humane learning and the Word of God, implies that religious education may have purposes beyond spiritual nourishment and social harmony. These, sometimes described as 'architectonic', cast religion in a constructive, directive or unifying role. One of the effects of religious faith is the unifying of life. The believer's understanding of the world, perception of the meaning of events, and moral experience and effort are held together in a single perspective. It is true that this perspective is patchy and spasmodic. Difficulties and conflicts exist and may continue long unresolved. But a unifying principle of meaning exists and, if faith remains dynamic, it will strengthen its hold as life goes on. Such talk causes alarm if it is misunderstood to mean a kind of curricular imperialism. Talk of Christian maths, even more of Christian history sets alarm bells ringing (though 'black history' or 'feminist history' causes less offence.) The problem set in a Victorian textbook, 'There are seven sacraments, ten commandments and twelve apostles; multiply the sacraments by the commandments and take away the apostles', exposes the folly of such a misunderstanding. If religion does have a unifying role, it is certainly not that of imposing on other subjects a constricting and distorting straitjacket.

The Interconnectedness of Knowledge

What is meant rather is what Newman understood by the 'circle of the sciences'. They 'are one and all connected together; as they are but aspects of things, they are severally incomplete in relation to the things themselves, though complete in their own idea and for their own respective purposes' (1915, p. 42). Forms and fields of knowledge have their own autonomy which must not be violated. But their various ways of looking at reality, their methodologies and also their moral excellences, only reveal their true meaning when seen as part of a larger pattern. Thus science discerns the order of the physical world and also promotes both scrupulous exactness in investigation and the bold search for larger meanings. Literature and the other arts embody the imaginative logic of experience and encourage senitivity to its nuances. These insights and these virtues lose themselves if they are not seen together; or worse may become distorted and breed 'one-issue fanatics' — the part mistaken for the whole. In an intellectual world marked by specialization, complexity and fragmentation, the search for unity in education is more than usually important. Religious education has good qualifications (though not the only ones) for this task.

I do not mean to say that religion can or should attempt to provide an outside cognitive framework within which other fields of knowledge can be contained, knocked about and reshaped. The long relationship between Christianity and liberal education — often damaged, never destroyed — depends for its survival on respect for the integrity and particular genius of the several fields of knowledge. Trouble arises when religion (or usually the Church) tries to exercise a kind of intellectual imperialism, to decree what books should be read and what ideas might be accepted.

> God us keep
> from single vision and Newton's sleep
> (Blake, 1935, p. 137)

What religious education can offer is certainly not such a monocular vision. What it can be is a potentially unifying principle, a witness to the possibility that the mind can achieve an intellectual order (simple or complex), a possibility based on a conviction of the radical unity of truth. Religious education committed but searching, ought, alongside its own inner concerns, to be in relationship with other disciplines, probing the wider significance of their insights, their vision and their tactics. Encouraging interdisciplinary enquiry, formal or informal, can be its greatest contribution to education generally. Such a vision of education may be thought appropriate to the Middle Ages or perhaps to an Islamic country. But has it any bearing on a society like ours, in some sense pluralist, in some sense secularized; with religion privatized and marginal? Certainly RE has to address the realistics of the times. But I believe the educational ideal I have outlined retains some relevance and some vigour.

Practical Issues

In our system, voluntary-aided schools, though under some pressure, remain. Their survival, I think, testifies to a general recognition that these schools embody certain educational values which, though eclipsed in these days, continue to be distantly reverenced. They offer the particular kind of religious understanding and religious nourishment which, as I have argued, can only be achieved within a tradition of commitment. Secondly, they can provide a style of education which, though open and searching, promotes in principle unity within the spectrum of understanding and in the various levels and phases of life. It is up to these schools to understand better their particular character, and to demonstrate the ideals around which they are constructed to be both achievable and educationally worthwhile.

Within the state system generally, emphases and hopes will be different. I have agreed that a style of religious education based on sympathetic insights into the world of religion generally has its limitations. Yet it undoubtedly has its virtues; both in the degree of religious understanding it can offer and in the social understanding it can promote. Although the institution and the curriculum must remain uncommitted, the personal commitment of teachers can, it seems to me, be positively deployed. Needless to say this deployment must not lead to efforts to indoctrinate or evangelize. A good and scrupulous teacher knows how to express personal convictions while respecting the vulnerability of children. What is needed is not the psychological gymnastics involved in becoming a neutral chairman. What is needed are the virtues of tolerance, sensitivity, open-mindedness and tact.

References

BLAKE, W. (1935) *Poems*, London, Dent.
DONNE, J. (1931) *Satire III*, London, Dent.
Fuller, ?. (Ed.) (1957) *The Christian Idea of Education*, London, Yale University Press.
NEWMAN, J.H. (1889) *The Grammar of Assent*, London, Longmans Green.
NEWMAN, J.H. (1912) *Apologia Pro Vita Sua*, Walter Scott Publications.
NEWMAN, J.H. (1915) *On the Scope and Nature of University Education*, London, Dent.

Chapter 8

Unity and Diversity:
The Search for Common Identity

Edward Hulmes

At bottom all the movements and uprising (in India) revolve around a single issue: identity. It is for this reason that neither Indians nor the rest of the world can afford to undervalue the events in India. In one way or another, the majority of the world's population will have to figure out how diverse groups of people are to come together under common political structures. (Ghosh, 1990, p. A19)

The Problem of Integrity

In many parts of the world besides India — not least in Britain and the United States — it is the *integrity* of society which is at stake. By the word 'integrity' I mean the organic unity of society, a unity that may as certainly be disrupted as enriched by religious and cultural diversity, especially if the educational implications of such diversity are not understood, or if understood, simply ignored. The *educational* importance of studying world religions — not in place of, but in addition to, the continuing study of Christianity — was correctly identified as a new priority for religious education in Britain twenty five years ago. One of the results of this broadening of the field of study is a growing realization on the part of many that the coherence of a 'pluralist' society, as of any other society, ultimately depends upon the *readiness* as well as the *willingness* of individuals to cooperate in the common interest. What part has religious education to play in preparing students to cope with the complexities of a divided society?

The Search for Shared Values and Beliefs

Are shared values and commonly-held beliefs to be *dis*-covered beneath the outward expressions of the apparently different, and even conflicting, world-views which are represented in Britain today? The question suggests a priority for religious education. It may not be a new priority but it is still worth reconsidering in the light of present circumstances and needs. I would describe it as the obligation to keep in mind the question just raised, at successive stages of education in such ways as to encourage teachers as well as students to formulate (and to reformulate) their answers — however tentatively and provisionally — with the help of new knowledge, understanding and experience.

The purpose of this is three-fold: (i) to enable students to discover a sense of their religious and cultural identity; (ii) to encourage them to appreciate the merits of alternative systems of belief and action; (iii) to help them as they mature to acquire the capacity to review, and if necessary, to modify or change their own convictions in later life.

At every stage, teachers and students confront the possibility of failure in that, individually as well as collectively, their immediate responses to each other may lead to actions which might compromise the fragile integrity of the wider society to which they all now belong. Not for the first time, perhaps, education in general may have to serve an *explicitly* instrumental purpose whilst religious education, in particular, assumes more and more the characteristics of a *risk* venture.

In educational terms, however, the risks are worth taking. The willingness of individuals to become personally involved in the search for common identity cannot be assumed. Nor would it be sufficient for the immediate task if it could be assumed. In any case, to be *willing* to participate in the search is not necessarily to be *ready*. Willingness may indicate an intention, or a preliminary disposition, but readiness signifies preparedness, and requires preparation.

Limits of Tolerance

The phrase 'unity and diversity' presents a unique opportunity as well as a special difficulty for teachers of religious education at all levels of education. The practical difficulty which faces many teachers in their efforts to control the potentially explosive effects of bigotry and ignorance raises legitimate educational questions about the limits of tolerance and about the role of education in helping students to distinguish between freedom and licence.

In theory, a pluralist society is one in which different cultural, religious and non-religious, traditions can be accommodated without passing negative judgments about any of them. In practice the limits of tolerance in a pluralist society have to be firmly drawn. They may not always be explicitly stated, in which case there may be misunderstandings among minority groups who, not surprisingly, take the promises of pluralism at face value. Yet the limits of tolerance must be set if that society is not to degenerate into anarchy created by conflicting convictions about the way in which civilized life is to be organized. The problem is one of achieving and of maintaining equilibrium, without destroying diversity.

The sobering fact is that it is *students*, young and old, who are likely to suffer most from the effects of the revolutionary experiments of their elders, not least in education. Experiments in education are not repeatable. The temptation is for teachers to experiment where it is unnecessary and disruptive. This has left many teachers as well as students uncertain not only about what should be included in the curriculum, about the best methods to be adopted in teaching and assessment, but also about the purpose of education in what is increasingly (and misleadingly, in my view) called a 'pluralist' society. (Hulmes, 1989, especially chapter 1).

Towards Inclusiveness

Religious education has gained rather than lost its importance in the curriculum, despite all the criticisms that can be levelled against its present theory and practice. Its importance is unquestionable, not because it can be used as an instrument for inculcating specific religious beliefs, or even for describing the bewildering multiplicity of such beliefs which are to be found. It is important because it offers, uniquely in my opinion, opportunities for a systematic consideration of a universal need. Religion has been described as a biological necessity (see, for example, Hardy, 1978). The point can be overlooked. Spiritual malnutrition is a condition which can become endemic.

The Language of Affirmation

When confronted by evidence of different kinds and forms of personal belief, students are apt to dismiss what they do not understand, or what cannot be explained and interpreted in terms of their existing but limited knowledge. What is needed is a form of discourse which is inclusive, which enables its users to be mindful of particularity without prejudicing what is universal.

In many cases, perhaps in most, this will require a shift in personal attitudes. It is easier to deny what (at first sight) may be strange, than to allow that it may possibly contribute to our self-knowledge. The ability to affirm — not necessarily to agree with, or to tolerate — the different beliefs that others hold is not a natural endowment but an acquired skill. The development of this ability may fairly be described as a further task in dealing with the priority for religious education identified earlier. In a culturally diverse society *religious* education may best serve the common interest by helping individuals to acquire some degree of fluency in the language of affirmation. Its acquisition marks an important stage in the development of religious literacy. Like any other language it has its vocabulary, its grammar, its nuances and its idioms. In considering questions of personal beliefs, values, and experience, this language has an important part to play in facilitating intercommunication.

Engagement with Controversy

It may not be long before teachers will have to acquire the skill of practising their profession defensively. The knowledge that not only their failures and

partial successes, but also their better efforts and more imaginative experiments, might be cited in the course of litigation by dissatisfied 'consumers'
may induce still greater caution in a profession which is often criticized for its
natural conservatism. At a time when it looks as if a readiness to acknowledge *uncertainty* is the surest proof of personal maturity in matters of belief
and action, it may be morally preferable (as well as professionally prudent)
for teachers to avoid controversial and potentially divisive topics. There may
be calls for the further removal of elements of controversy from the curriculum in order to minimize the possibility that the religious, moral and
cultural, susceptibilities of individuals and groups be offended.

Yet these elements are vital for sharpening the critical faculty and for
enabling students to think for themselves. Religious education, which thrives
in an atmosphere of open and critical enquiry, will be one of the first cas-
ualties in any campaign to eliminate controversy from the classroom, rather
than to explore its causes and consequences educationally in a controlled
environment. Yet it is just in this situation of uncertainty and confusion that
teachers can demonstrate the usefulness of inclusive and affirmative language
as an instrument of mediation, explanation and interpretation.

How Real Are Differences?

In practice most teachers, whatever subject they teach, are confronted by
groups of individuals who may hold *apparently* different religious beliefs,
who may try to defend *potentially* conflicting cultural norms, and who may
strive to achieve *ostensibly* exclusive social goals. The adverbs in the last
sentence are deliberately chosen, in order to suggest that it is the exploration
of these 'differences' which, far from consolidating existing social divisions,
may reveal hitherto unsuspected sources of shared experience and common
aspiration. Such shared experience and aspiration can be expressed in
language which is expressly affirmative and inclusive. Intuition, imagination
and emotion, are not excluded either, provided that teachers are aware that
the language of affirmation and inclusiveness is not always verbal (Buber,
1961, p. 24).

The Essential Functions of Religious Education

I would name three. The first is the *descriptive* function. The second is the
evaluative. The third is the *integrative*. The first challenges every kind of
cultural provincialism, not least in education, by describing alternative ways
of understanding the human predicament and of making sense of the world.
The second enables students to develop a clearer understanding of the ways in
which their own assumptions, prejudices and beliefs, influence their decisions
in every aspect of life. The third provides students with the means, however
rudimentary to begin with, of discerning possible links between the separate
subject courses which they take in school and the lives they have to live

127

outside. This integrative, mediating, function is important because education as a whole, and not just *religious* education, will have to provide for the social as well as the intellectual needs of an increasingly complex society as the full implications of cultural diversity become more apparent.

Neglect of the Evaluative Function

In recent years the emphasis in religious education has been on the descriptive and informative aspect of teaching. Religious beliefs and practices of many different kinds have been presented as accurately and as objectively as possible. The art of evaluating the claims of the various beliefs put forward has been steadfastly discouraged for several reasons. It is said that children are too immature and inexperienced to do anything of the sort; that parents would object to attempts to discriminate between the validity of different expressions of sincerely held 'Truth'; that there has not *yet* been sufficient time to consider the information available. Despite this latter point, true enough in the obvious sense that if we are to await all the necessary data our decisions will always be indefinitely postponed, students are somehow to *choose* for themselves in questions which are essentially matters of private opinion. In education, however, it cannot be as arbitrary as that. If informed choice is desirable it is essential that a spirit of critical inquiry, of critical *self-inquiry*, be developed and nurtured. As often as not the rejection of religious beliefs and values (whether theistic or not) is irrational, ill-informed, and frequently abusive. The educational task is to challenge the irrationality in order to elicit a more reasoned response based on the information considered *so far*.

An Integrative Function which Avoids Indoctrination

Education (and hence religious education, as an important constituent of the whole enterprise) should assume a prescriptive and, where necessary, a corrective function, delegating to teachers an explicit, rather than as at present a vaguely implicit, responsibility for *enabling* students to understand the importance of discovering the values they must learn to share, if the society in which they live is not to disintegrate. Does this amount to indoctrination? Has indoctrination merely re-emerged in a different guise? Not necessarily, for what protects the student from indoctrination is the development of the critical faculty to which reference has just been made. Not even the encouragement of tolerance as a desirable social goal can, therefore, be conducted stealthily or subliminally, because the process is monitored for ill-considered opinions and bias at each successive stage. The lessons to be learned are explicit and open to question in an educational programme which is constantly under review. Individuals are prepared for, not inducted into, the wider adult community. The specific task of religious education is to respond to the needs of the community as a whole, without neglecting legitimate sectional interests, but always questioning the legitimacy of rights and privileges — from whatever quarter — which are simply demanded or assumed.

A New Approach to Confessionalism

If religious education is to play a constructive, and a conceivably mediating, role in reducing the tensions between groups which are divided from each other by religious and cultural differences, there will need to be a shift in attitude to the whole question of confessionalism. Fear that the mere charge of indoctrination might further damage the claims of their subject to respectability has had an inhibiting, not to say a baleful, effect on the work of many teachers of religious education during the past two decades (Hulmes, 1979, pp. 5–18). When the charge amounts to one of unprofessionalism, that is to say, of imposing beliefs and values on students, it is not surprising to find that teachers respond in self-defence by trying to eliminate, so far as they are able, all traces of personal bias from their work. But teachers of religious education have never held a monopoly on questionable educational methods. Nor is it fair to identify them as the teachers uniquely tempted, by the nature of the subject they teach, to indoctrinate rather than to educate.

The Descriptive Function: The Need for a More Inclusive Approach

The range of religious education is already well established in practice and there is a wealth of published material available to teachers about many important belief systems. Much of this material can readily be adapted to suit local needs. An important, but sometimes overlooked, aspect of this descriptive work is the extent of diversity *within* a particular tradition. The assumption that religions are monolithic in character is not difficult to question, but what follows depends to a large degree on the professional skill of the teacher in devising ways of stimulating a constructively critical response from students. For obvious reasons it is easier to confine the descriptive exercise to the less controversial aspects of different ways of life. When the subject-matter is strange and new, a careful selection of the topics to be described may suffice to introduce students to exotic and possibly bewildering new ideas, but the changing situation calls for a bolder course. *Description*, if it is to be balanced and accurate, has to be more inclusive and less selective. This is because in every culture there are darker sides to human activity and experience in the name of one belief system or another. The destructive aspects of religious commitment, especially when personal beliefs are expressed in fundamentalist or nationalistic terms, also have to be considered if a fair and balanced evaluation is to be made. Students can be encouraged to learn to distinguish thoughtfully between what is acceptable in the common interest and what is not.

A Bogus Pluralism?

Is 'Multi'-cultural Education 'Mono'-cultural

Further questions begin to emerge, each of them raising practical as well as theoretical issues. How realistic is it for parents and other interested parties to expect, or demand, that a universal system of state education shall provide for special sectional interests? What is meant by 'multicultural' education, and why is it becoming less attractive to members of the ethnic minorities whose interests it is designed to serve? Would it not be better to discourage individuals from attempts to preserve their minority cultural identities? Each of these questions may sound crude, but they are being asked by increasing numbers of people, and not only in Britain. In India, for instance, the last question has recently assumed a powerful political significance. India, I have heard it said, cannot *afford* the luxury of cultural diversity when minority groups continue to press for special sectional recognition and for what they consider to be a fair share of scarce resources. The aim should therefore be to work towards a situation in which the emphasis is more on unity than on diversity, a situation in which education has a crucial role to play. Given the scale of the problem in India, a country of almost unimaginable diversity, the idea may be unrealistic, but it does no service to education to praise the sub-continent for its ideals of non-violence and tolerance whilst ignoring the scale of its continuing history of violence and intolerance. Here again the reader is reminded of the quotation which appears at the head of this chapter.

It may be tempting to ignore the differing views (convictions would not be too strong a word) about the ways in which state education is to be provided for the members of a society that is divided by religion and culture. The problem of the future integrity of society tends to be disregarded amid the welter of theoretical analysis which only serves to confirm the *mono-cultural* assumptions of accepted educational theory and practice. This means that alternative views about what is to count as knowledge, as well as about the ways in which such knowledge is to be acquired, are ignored in the pursuit of educational aims and objectives which are objectionable in principle to the beliefs of sizeable minority groups. In default of agreement about the limits of tolerance in a pluralist society, and about the role of education in helping to preserve a measure of social cohesion and integrity, it must be asked if unity, in all but a superficial sense, is possible.

On a recent visit to the United States I heard an expert on demographic trends state that before the end of the century '85 per cent of the working population in the USA would consist of minorities'. What struck me at the time was not the unconscious humour of the percentage figure, which may or may not be accurate, but the idea of a 'society' consisting of discrete groups united by nothing so important as their need for employment and their capacity for labour. What is becoming clearer to minority groups in Britain and in the United States, for instance, is that diversity is tolerated in the educational system only up to a point. That point is seldom publicly admitted and rarely discussed. The dominant philosophy of education ensures that even when 'new' data *about* other cultures and different ways of life are introduced in religious education, the manner in which the facts are presented derives from the European tradition of critical enquiry. Islam, for example, may feature as an important constituent element in a world-religions course, but not in a way which satisfies Muslims that an Islamic approach to knowledge, and to its acquisition in education, is being fairly presented as an independently coherent *alternative*. In practice, therefore, education proceeds, relatively unchallenged by the claims of diversity, on the basis of a set of principles which are effectively *monocultural* rather than *multicultural*, despite protestations to the contrary.

The ideology of pluralism is already exercising a dominant influence on the theory and practice of education in Western societies. The neo-confessional consequence of this influence has not gone without notice. By drawing attention to the extent of *religious* pluralism and to the need for an objective approach to different systems of belief, teachers may give the impression — consciously or not — that it matters little which 'option', if any, is to be preferred, or that it is somehow improper to declare a preference at all. The question of student 'choice' is thereby pre-empted. The implication that all the 'options' are, at best, relatively true reinforces the conviction that it may be wiser to ignore them all.

Unity and Exclusiveness: The Example of Islam

The clearest contemporary example of the challenge present to the ideology of pluralism by a coherent world-view is provided by Islam. Muslims not only reject the separation of church and state as an aberration, but insist that Islam is the *true* religion for all mankind. This belief obliges the Islamic community, especially that part of it which forms a minority in a non-Islamic whole, to engage in *daʿwah*. By this Arabic word is meant a *call*, or more accurately, a *summons*, in the name of God, to non-believers to submit to the will of God as it is revealed in the teachings of Islam. In *any* society in which they find themselves, therefore, Muslims share a responsibility not only for preserving the integrity of the *ummah* (the Islamic community), but also for extending its influence by means of systematic advocacy. Muslims often claim that there are no Islamic 'missionaries', no missionary cadres. By this they mean that the responsibility for propagating the Islamic way of life devolves upon all Muslims, and not just on a specially trained group. This responsibility extends to the provision of appropriate educational facilities for members of the Islamic community. In order to meet this responsibility younger as well as older Muslims must be educated according to Islamic principles.

Muslims believe that society can only be ordered legitimately in conformity with the revealed will and purposes of God (*Alláh*). All that it is necessary for human creatures to know about God's will is contained in *al-Qur'án*. From the same divine source comes all that Muslims will ever need to know, in every conceivable circumstance. The exemplary life of the Prophet Muhammad (570–632 CE), recorded for posterity in the authenticated collections of Islamic Tradition (*hadīth*), and the emerging consensus of religious practice, faith, ethics, which succeeding generations of competent *Islamic* scholars have produced, set the guidelines for present and future action, interpretation and exegesis. This is an edifice of belief and practice, a household of faith, which must be kept inviolate and in good repair from an

Islamic point of view. No orthodox Muslim is in a position to allow what pluralism demands, namely, the concession that different religious traditions (Islam included) are all merely *relatively* true.

Clearly, this has important consequences for education. From an Islamic standpoint education — as everything else — must proceed in accordance with Islamic principles. If the sizeable Islamic minorities in Britain and the United States, for example, concede that their right to practise Islam is subject to *un-Islamic* limitations, they will not consider themselves free to be Muslims. The unity which they would otherwise detect in every aspect of human existence is seriously compromised. If they do not concede this, however, their presence in a non-Islamic society will always constitute a challenge to the basic assumptions of a 'pluralist' society.

What begins as an understandable human concern for the needs of disadvantaged minorities in a host-country may have to be modified in the course of time. Are the members of an Islamic minority to be permitted to live in accordance with their own customs and laws, using education as the indispensable means for inducting their children into the adult Islamic community? If not, it is clear that the adjectives 'pluralist' and 'multicultural', as applied to education, are ambiguous. They are being used in a limited sense which may provoke dissension in minority communities, sooner rather than later. And there may come a time when the unsatisfied needs of an immigrant community begin to be expressed more confidently in the language of its own cultural tradition, and to come into conflict with the different needs of other groups. The attitude of Muslims is summed up in the Arabic word *islām*, a word which signals a consciously made decision to submit personal desires to the incomparably supreme external authority that is God. By means of this act of self-surrender to what God requires of his human creatures, the Muslim (that is, one who submits himself or herself to God) enters into a state of peace and inner harmony. Muslims insist that there is no other way than that of submission to God for any human being to experience a sense of inner harmony and peace. Human beings are free to accept Islam or to reject it, yet the freedom which is permitted to them is limited in time. This is because the sovereignty of God is ultimately irresistible.

Muslims are not free *as Muslims* to speculate about the existence of God, about their religious duties and beliefs, or about the correct way for society to be regulated, in ways which non-Muslims assume to be both a right and a responsibility. There is a regulating conservatism in Islam which is both characteristic and distinctive. This conservatism is reflected, for example, in Islamic exegesis (*tafsír*) of their holy book, the Qur'ān. Their interpretation of the Qur'ān is quite different from the study of the Bible to which many Christians have become accustomed since the beginnings of historical-critical studies in the West. The faithful transmission of the text and of its interpretations are the responsibilities of all Muslims so far as they are capable of meeting them. The text of the Qur'ān has been established in every particular. There can be no change.

There is another aspect of its preservation, however, which has far-reaching educational implications. The preservation of the Qur'ān is a feature of the interior life of a devout Muslim. It begins with the first attempts of a child to memorize passages from the holy book, and ends when the whole book has been committed to memory. The Arabic word *qur'ān* means 'that which is to be recited' or 'that which is to be read aloud'. The act of recital gives immediacy to the word which comes from God. The process of memorizing and the response to what is being memorized ensure that the Word of God is not merely preserved in an objective and inaccessible way between the covers of another unread book. It is preserved where it should be, readily accessible in the minds of those who profess Islam. This is misunderstood if it is regarded as a kind of Islamic biblicism or fundamentalism. It is neither. It is essentially Islamic. The Qur'ānic petition, 'O my Lord, increase me in knowledge' (20, 114), is also a confession that God is the only source of all that is worth knowing. He it is who discloses knowledge to whomsoever he wills, though it is still the responsibility of the student to seek for that knowledge wherever it is to be found. The value of memory-training in education, of rote-learning as an educational method, is, incidentally, consistently underestimated in non-Islamic circles, as if it had been conclusively demonstrated that those with trained memories are incapable of thinking for themselves.

Personal effort is required if human beings are to know what God's will is. The learning process begins, as it ends, with obedience. The Arabic word *jihād* is often translated as 'holy war'. It cannot be denied that at different times throughout the course of history Muslim leaders have called upon the faithful to fight to extend as well as to defend Islamic interests. But the root meaning of *jihād* takes us beyond the idea of 'holy war' in a narrow sense. The root suggests personal effort in a general sense, directed towards serving the highest cause, namely, that of Islam, 'the Straight Path' (*ibid*, 1, 6). In this sense every Muslim is a *mujāhid*[1], that is, one who strives to his utmost ability to be obedient to the will of God. Every occupation provides opportunities for the faithful to engage in *jihād*. The purpose of Islamic education is, therefore, to enable individuals to direct their best efforts towards this goal, and to understand how faith finds its truest expression in action. Faith and works cannot be separated, any more than faith and reason, without doing violence to the spirit of Islam. All that is worth knowing, all that is worth striving to understand, comes from God. And what can be known in this way is not opposed to reason. Indeed, that which is *certain* is that which God has *revealed*, and we may accept it with confidence.

> Of all religions Islam is the only one that blames those who believe without having proofs and rebukes those who follow opinions without having any certainty ... Whenever Islam speaks, it speaks to reason, and the holy texts proclaim that happiness consists in the right use of reason. (Amin, 1958, p. 64)

Continuing Tensions in a Pluralist Society

In 1990 CE, a few days before Jews in the United States began to celebrate the Jewish New Year (*Rosh ha-Shanah*), there were several anti-Semitic incidents in some American cities. This 'day of Judgement' (*Yom ha-Din*) calls Jews to special acts of remembrance at the sound of the blowing of the *shofar* (the ram's horn trumpet). During the feast on this important day sweetmeats are savoured and bread is dipped in honey as those gathered round the table pray for a good and sweet year. The most important day of the penitential season at this time is *Yom Kippur* ('day of atonement'), on which reconciliation between God and his creatures and between human beings is solemnly effected. The twelfth century Jewish Talmudist, philosopher, and physician, Moses Maimonides wrote,

> Awake from your slumbers, you who have fallen asleep in life, and reflect on your deeds. Remember your Creator. Be not of those who miss reality in the pursuit of shadows, who waste their years seeking vain things that neither profit nor deliver. Look well to your souls, and improve your actions. Let each of you forsake his evil ways and thoughts. ('Repentance', Code of Law 3, 4)

In Madison, Wisconsin — 800 miles West of the place where this chapter was written — Jewish children, as the custom is, asked their parents about the meaning of *Rosh ha-Shanah*. In 1990 CE some of them asked an additional question in Madison, 'Why are there armed guards posted outside the synagogue?' A report about an increase in racial attacks on Jews and other minority groups, published in *The New York Times* read, in part, as follows.

> Madison, a city known for its liberal tradition and appreciation of diversity, has been shaken by hate crimes in recent weeks. 'People are in disbelief that these kinds of things could happen in Madison, with the liberalism, education and high level of culture', said Rabbi Jan Brahms of Beth El, who has hired off-duty police officers as guards for the holidays ...

Further newspaper reports from the same area of the United States described what happened at Hillel, the Jewish student centre at the University of Wisconsin. Rocks were thrown at buildings and individuals. Jewish student clubs were vandalized and daubed with racial graffiti. One student added, 'There has always been an assumption that prejudice was the result of ignorance, and that education would solve the problem. One of the most troubling things about all of this, it seems to me, is that it shows that even people who are educated are capable of anti-Semitism'. Another student, whose family left the Soviet Union for the United States in 1974, spoke of the betrayal of America's promise. 'In order to escape the anti-Semitism of the Soviet Union, mother was willing to take a job opening envelopes in Montgomery Ward in Chicago. It is disconcerting, to say the least, to find that we have not altogether escaped it'.[2]

The rights of ethnic minorities cannot be guaranteed, however, not even within a 'pluralist' country like the United States, which seeks to protect such rights by legislation. Indeed, the adjective 'pluralist' is misleading because it promises a social reality which, as this former Soviet citizen discovered, simply fails expectation. Pluralism, defined in all but the most superficial sense, remains an ideal towards which many (though not everyone, from all accounts) are prepared to strive. The result of this is that education is given a specific directional thrust, even a confessional tendency. If the pursuit of pluralism is approved as a social end it becomes necessary to consider the *concept* of a pluralist society systematically, not just to assume its validity, and to do this as an integral part of the educational process. Amongst other things, the intention will be to discover the educational implications of pluralism. The search for common identity, as a practical and continuing task within the confines of formal education, can encourage the transformation of attitudes. Law, however enlightened, cannot solve the problems of discrimination without the active cooperation of those who are bound by its provisions. Responsibilities, as well as rights, have to be considered if society is not to disintegrate for want of balance. But neither rights nor responsibilities are easily understood in a complex modern society. For this reason a neutral, objective, approach to either is now increasingly suspect morally. The re-assessment of the moral basis of education in a religiously and culturally diverse society emerges as an important new priority.

There are some things which cannot be changed, though the situations in which they present themselves may be transformed by the introduction of a new spirit of tolerance and of acceptance. *Attitudes* can be transformed. Education — at least in part — can help to enable those involved to understand the nature of the transformation required. Thus, for instance, it can be shown that the victims of various kinds of persecution in one set of social circumstances are themselves capable, in different circumstances, of disregarding the human rights of others. The present tension between Palestinians and Jews in what, for different reasons is *holy* land to all of them, is a case in point. Meron Benvenisti lives in the city of Jerusalem. He is a *Sabra*, that is, a Jew born in Israel. He acknowledges the suffering endured by his people in Europe, especially during the period from 1933–1945, but notes the paradox that in the State of Israel the rights and aspirations of the Palestinian minority have been consistently disregarded by the very people who ought to have understood the problems of a disadvantaged (if not persecuted) minority from their own history and experience (Benvenisti, 1986, p. 4).

One of the chief difficulties today in discussing these issues is that the debate has grown stale. The relative stability of society in a country such as Britain contributes to the blandness of our response to fresh challenges from other parts of the world. Societies with a longer history of cultural diversity than ours have much to teach. Take, for instance, the recent developments in the USSR. Not all the voices, to be heard after seventy years of state capitalism and centralization (in what is each day less accurately described as the Soviet Union) speak of the mutually enriching effects of cultural diversity. On the contrary, it is asserted that an empire, even a federation, of heterogeneous peoples must be divided into its constituent entities if any are to prosper. Russification, it is charged, has stilled the expression of cultural diversity, from language to religion. The prospect of separate development, rather than of integration, presents a growing threat to what is felt by some to have been at best a spurious social unity. Separate development may be coming to an end in South Africa but it is a notion which finds powerful support in some quarters of the world where the imposition of cultural uniformity in the service of a political ideology has left a bitter legacy of hate and distrust. It has been my experience in recent months[3] that there has been a significant shift in opinion among the leaders of minority groups in Britain and the United States to questions of assimilation and integration. Part of the reason for this is undoubtedly the dissatisfaction among minority groups with a well-intentioned ideology of accommodation which employs the rhetoric of multiculturalism whilst ignoring all but the cosmetic aspects of cultural diversity. Paradoxically, this characteristically Western philosophy of education, which ignores — as it may well have to in the common interest — the discrete ways in which knowledge is defined in other cultures, not to speak of the different ways in which such knowledge is to be acquired, is perceived by ethnic and cultural minorities to be an imposition and a denial of the promises of pluralism.

There is, in short, plenty of new material available from a wide variety of cultural traditions to reinvigorate the debate about aims and objectives in education generally, and about the role of religious education in particular. Here is where the distinctive role of *religious* education may be identified as that of serving the special needs of the contemporary world in which human beings, either denied or bereft of spiritual understanding, endure separation whilst searching for (or at least talking about) the need for reconciliation and unity.

The objection may be raised that to require of students in schools an attempt to understand the significance of these matters is unrealistic. I am not so sure that our expectations of students are always as high as they might reasonably be, but even if it be true that the young are too immature to understand these issues, it cannot be held that this is so for their teachers. Earlier I mentioned an approach to cultural diversity in education which, self-conscious or not, is misleadingly selective. A less selective, and thus a more balanced, presentation of information, which includes rather than excludes what may be considered to be negative in the first instance, will place students in a better position to formulate their own opinions. To take this case as an example would be to move beyond description towards evaluation, in a way which I would encourage.

Adapting Method to Purpose: Some Practical Suggestions

Martin Buber was not given to providing tips for teachers, but he often challenged them to think for themselves about the relationship between the teacher and the taught — a relationship which can release a spirit of cooperation in the class-room, as elsewhere. In his own unique way he spoke the language of inclusiveness and affirmation, providing teachers of religious education with several clues about adapting method to purpose in reconciling apparently conflicting sectional interests by resort to a unifying spiritual principle.

The Underlying Purpose of Religion

The underlying purpose of all great religions and religious movements is to beget a life of elation, of fervour which cannot be stifled by any experience which, therefore, must spring from a relationship to the eternal, above and beyond all individual experiences.

By identifying 'the underlying purpose' of the great religions in this way Buber provides teachers with a clear aim. The word 'elation' gives a strong signal concerning the way in which this aim should inform teaching. It must be stimulating, imaginative and creative in its impact. He here touches on something which many teachers will instantly recognize. It is not that students are incapable of understanding different, even opposing, views of life. In practice *teaching*, as opposed to education, tends to consume more time and effort in tedious repetition which alienates rather than attracts those to whom it is directed. There is simply neither time nor space left for innovation, for exploration, for risk, for genuine *pluralism*.

Buber goes on to hint at a priority for teachers to consider. Within the context of the sense of disappointment with life which is the common experience of people across religious and cultural barriers, he identifies the special role of religion as providing people with concepts which can make real for them the world of the spirit. He expresses it like this:

> Since the contacts a man makes with the world and with himself are frequently not calculated to rouse him to fervour, religious concepts refer him to another form of being, to a world of perfection in which his soul may also grow perfect. Compared to this state of perfect being, life on earth seems either only an ante-chamber, or mere illusion, and the prospect of a higher life has the task of creating fervour in the face of disappointing outer and inner experiences, of creating the fervent conviction that there is such a higher life, and that it is, or can gradually become, accessible to the human soul under certain conditions beyond the bounds of earthly existence. (Buber, 1947, p. 2)

Buber's reference to religious concepts is interesting because it suggests that without them we are far less capable of searching for any meaning in life —

still less of finding any sense of common identity behind our differences. In the first place we have to learn what these fundamental concepts are. In religious education, in particular, they have to be described and explained. They introduce us to ideas of which we are not naturally aware and remind us of realities which it is too easy to overlook. Here one might mention several important concepts such as *God* (the reality manifested in so many subtle and puzzling ways); submission (of the individual will to that of the Creator); obedience (and the personal freedom which, paradoxically, flows from it); revelation (of the Divine purpose in the scriptures and traditions preserved by the believing community); reconciliation (of conflicting or potentially conflicting claims); integrity (the health and the wholeness of individuals and communities). Differences of interpretation and experience do begin to emerge when these, and other, concepts are considered in greater detail. Such differences are not readily explained in school, but the foundations for subsequent exploration can at least be laid. In some of the great religions the links between the world in which we live and 'the higher life' of which Buber speaks are established from the godward side, not by speculative human concepts. In Christian terms, for instance, there is a divine initiative which ensures that the link between the Creator and the creation is more than a symbolical projection from the human side.

The Search for Unity in Diversity

In dealing with differences, Buber's analysis of religion is important. He identifies the place at which the search for unity in diversity may begin. In doing so he allows for the *possibility* that this underlying unity may be discovered beneath the variety of names and forms which *apparently* divide human beings from each other. It may be no more than a possibility, but the attempt is worth making, for even if his analysis is considered to be idiosyncratic, to be too subjective, or to be no more than a personal opinion, it cannot be ignored without damaging still further the reputation of a 'pluralistic' approach to education which is already under suspicion for being too selective.

The *explicit* search for common identity in a society divided by sectional and sectarian minority interests, by intolerance, and by competitive pressures from many different sources, can become a new priority for religious education in the coming decade. There can be no guarantee that what is sought is to be found, but even if unity in diversity turns out to be a chimera it will have been worth the seeking, if only to expose the practical limitations of pluralist rhetoric.

Notes

1 The Arabic word **mujáhid**, like the word **jihád** to which it is related, has a more menacing connotation in non-Islamic societies. The words have come to be associated with the violence of terror, an association that is far removed from the kind of spiritual warfare for which the concept still stands.

2   From a report by Johnson, D (1990) printed in *The New York Times*, 17 September, p A16.
3   This chapter was written towards the end of 1990.

References

AMIN, O. (1958) *Lights of Contemporary Moslem Philosophy*, Cairo.

BENVENISTI, M. (1986) *Conflicts and Contradictions*, New York, Villard Books.

BUBER, M. (1947) *Tales of the Hasidim: The Early Masters* (trans by O. Marx), New York, Schocken Books.

BUBER, M. (1961) *Between Man and Man* (trans by R.G. Smith), London Fontana Books.

GHOSH, A. (1990) 'In India, death and democracy', *The New York Times*, 26 November.

HARDY, A.C. (1978) *The Divine Flame*, Oxford, Religious Experience Research Unit (R.E.R.U.).

HULMES, E. (1979) *Commitment and Neutrality in Religious Education*, London, Geoffrey Chapman.

HULMES, E. (1989) *Education and Cultural Diversity*, London, Longman.

Part 3
Focus on the Classroom

Editorial Introduction

The three chapters forming this part are different in style from the rest of the book, and from each other. They are written much more directly from the perspective of the classroom.

Michael Poole vigorously addresses a major obstacle preventing pupils from taking religious education seriously: the pervasiveness of scientism and relativism — the view that only science can lead us to reliable knowledge and all else is just opinion, subjective and related to a person's particular situation. Scientists themselves can effectively draw attention to the faulty thinking involved in such a view, as Capra (1983) has noted: 'In a culture dominated by science, it will be much easier to convince people that fundamental changes are necessary if we can give our arguments a scientific basis. That is what physicists can now provide' (p. 32).

This is what Poole provides in this chapter: carefully thought-out units of work which are realistic in terms of fitting into actual syllabuses and schools as they are. For those concerned with questions of assessment in RE, they provide some sound material which could be used for that purpose. It provides something important in helping pupils to move forward towards a less fragmented understanding of knowledge and of life, and it relates to what is common to all the great religions.

The eight units give valuable background material for teachers and suggestions as to how each topic might start. There are many helpful suggestions and analogies for communicating the necessary concepts involved. Although written primarily with the upper forms of secondary schools in mind, there is much here which can be adapted for use with younger students and with children in primary schools.

Work with younger children is the focal-point of Elizabeth Ashton's chapter. An experienced primary school teacher, she takes as her starting-point the importance of helping pupils to address what is fundamentally involved in any stance which can be termed religious — an awareness that there is, in our experience of reality, something more than what can be understood and explained in scientific terms. She wants to direct children's attention to that which requires the word 'spiritual' to denote it.

All the great world religions either focus attention on this, or imply that this spiritual reality is at the 'heart and root of existence' (quoted by Slee p. 45). In most religions this central concept is given a name: God, Allah, Brahman, Nam, even though this concept is understood to be beyond any kind of adequate description in words, ritual or any other means. Ashton sees the major priority in religious education as seeking to engage children's authentic interest and attention with regard to this concept behind concepts, so that they are able to think about it in a way which is meaningful to them personally and ask the questions about how this concept can be understood and expressed, and whether it is basically true or a delusion.

In order to do this it is necessary to help children to move beyond the naive literalism which serves to prevent them (and many adults too) from thinking any further about religion, or developing more sophisticated concepts. She therefore wants religious education to help children appreciate the metaphorical and symbolic nature of language so that they learn how to interpret it and begin to relate to theology.

A major part of her chapter is a sharing of work about symbolism from her own teaching experience in an [urban environment] which is in part an educationally deprived area; [a high percentage] of the children come from de-religionized homes. What she achieves is impressive. Readers may be able to see many ways in which this kind of work could be developed, thus breaking the stranglehold imposed by the now discredited Piagetian notion of children's incapacity to handle abstract concepts or think metaphorically.

The final chapter in this part specifically relates to the book as a whole. Michael Donley, a secondary school teacher, has given his own impressions of the priorities argued for by the other contributors. He sees a considerable measure of convergence relating especially to the importance of spirituality, the need to focus on the truth-claims made by religion, and the way in which RE can contribute to personal development (and as a result also to social harmony, if it is allowed to be true to itself). This means it must be centred on helping pupils to come to a real understanding of the basis of religion, accepting its controversial nature. Maximum discussion and reflection should be promoted in which the teacher also participates at a genuine level, very far from that of a neutral chairman. He points out that such engagement is in fact de-indoctrinatory, and enables pupils to find the subject exciting and meaningful.

He would like to see more attention paid to the way in which religion can succumb to forces of evil. As a member of the Russian Orthodox tradition he is not impressed by the assumption which he finds all too common today, that human nature is fundamentally good and trustworthy, and that the answer to the unsatisfactoriness, intolerance and violence present in our world lies simply in human endeavour and thinking. It may be that in this respect he stands farthest away from our opening contributor, Wilson, and yet like him he argues strongly for the use of reason. He also wishes to deepen understanding of the word 'spiritual' and on that basis to look further at the relationship between religion and the arts. As a keen musician, his comments on this deserve consideration.

The title of the chapter suggests what I, as editor, think he might have chosen as his priority for RE if he had been asked to develop one. All that he writes is calling for a quality of discernment which is something which can be encouraged in all pupils. He notes that often it is those who might be termed of lower ability who ask the most searching questions and can engage in discussion with real involvement.

Reference

CAPRA, F. (1983) *The Turning Point: Science, Society and the Rising Culture*, London, Flamingo.

Chapter 9

Teaching About Issues of Science and Religion

Michael Poole

Why Do It?

It is a matter of priority that school pupils should be given adequate help in relating their religious studies to their science studies (Poole, 1990). For there are many misunderstandings about the interplay between the two disciplines, prominent among which is a widely-held view that science and religion are at war — even though such a view has long been regarded as simplistic in academic circles. The reasons people give for holding a warfare model include particular perceptions of historic episodes associated with Galileo and Darwin, and explanations of the origins of the universe. Furthermore, science has been variously held to 'prove' things, to be the ultimate test of all beliefs, and to be able to pass verdict on miracles. Among other misunderstandings are found the ubiquitous 'distinctions': 'science is facts', 'religion is faith'; 'science is objective', 'religion is subjective'.

Difficulties to Overcome

The breadth and complexity of some of the subject-matter, and the fragmented nature of the curriculum, particularly at secondary level, present challenges to be overcome. Recent emphases on cross-curricular work and the relating of subject specialisms in the National Curriculum deserve a cautious welcome. Until recently, any school-based attempts to relate scientific and religious perspectives on the world tended to fall to the religious education department. That reflected the asymmetry between the two subjects: science can easily be taught without reference to religion; but the converse is not so simple, since pupils frequently ask how religion fits in with a scientific world-view. A recognition of the need for religious perspectives on the world to take account of science is evidenced by about half of a random sample of fifty-five Agreed Syllabuses specifying some treatment of the topic.

The National Curriculum for science significantly changes the traditional preoccupation of science with subject content. It encapsulates emphases, which were already coming in, on the processes, skills, theories and models of science and it stipulates that pupils should be given opportunities to

> develop their knowledge and understanding of the ways in which scientific ideas change through time and how the nature of these ideas and the uses to which they are put are affected by the social, moral, spiritual and cultural contexts in which they are developed; in doing so, they should begin to recognize that while science is an important way of thinking about experience, it is not the only way.

Also, pupils should 'explore the nature of scientific evidence and proof', 'appreciate the inherent uncertainty of evidence and the tentative nature of the resulting theories' and 'distinguish between claims and arguments based on scientific considerations and those which are not'. They 'should examine ideas that have been used, historically and more recently, to explain the character and origin of the Earth, other planets, stars and the universe itself'.

Science teachers, many of whom have little or no background in history and philosophy of science or in the social, ethical and religious dimensions of science, are encountering the same kinds of difficulties in addressing the new requirements which many religious education specialists find in grappling with scientific issues. So there is considerable scope for interdepartmental co-operation in the task of helping pupils relate the two areas of study.

Some Ways Forward?

I have outlined eight teaching units on science and religion, each of which could occupy a single half-hour period. In each case, I have indicated several key points to be made, various ideas for introducing the topic, and some suggested resources for teaching. Not all the material could be used in half-an-hour; some could be used for homework, some omitted, or more periods could be devoted to the work. Not everything is suitable for every age group, and much of the language needs simplifying for class use; but teachers can select and adapt, from the 'Meccano-set' of ideas, ones appropriate to their pupils, as well as using examples of their own.

I have already tried to present some of these complex ideas in simplified, illustrated format, for senior school pupils and students, in *A Guide to Science and Belief* (1990, Oxford, Lion). For those who might wish to use the *Guide* with classes, alongside the teaching suggestions set out below, appropriate pages are indicated, for example, (G 28).

Topic 1: Friends or Enemies?

Points to be Made

(i) The perception of science and religion as at war is a nineteenth century phenomenon. Attempts to propagate this view were remarkably successful and, although regarded by academics as simplistic, the view is still widely etched into popular folklore.

(ii)   The development of science owes a debt to religion.

Introductory Suggestions

Discussion

The group could be asked — giving reasons for their views — whether they think the relationship between science and religion is best described as:

(i)   a conflict;
(ii)   an 'uneasy truce';
(iii) a partnership.

The reasons given are likely to include many issues raised in Topics 2–8, so this could be a useful place to outline any course you may plan to give, or to let the class set the agenda of topics they would like treated in future lessons. Examples of views held by scientists about science-and-religion could be included (G 8–11, 26).

An introductory talk could then be given, based on the background material and further reading given below.

Background

For 300 years after modern science began its rapid growth, science and (Christian) religion enjoyed a fruitful partnership (G 26–8). Any idea of separating between scientists and religious believers would have been a non-starter, because, largely speaking, they were one and the same. Science and religion were seen as going hand in hand. Even before Francis Bacon (1561–1626) and the beginning of the development of modern science, God was regarded as having revealed himself through two great 'Books', of which he was the author. There was the Book of Nature, 'read' by scientists and there was the Book of Scripture, the Bible. One was the 'Book of God's Works', the other was the 'Book of God's Words'. One was about the creation, the other about the Creator (G 12–25). The 'Two Books' metaphor is not currently so prominent, because science does not now concern itself with First Causes. Science, by deliberately choosing to confine itself to the study of the natural world, is not able to tell us whether there is anything other than nature, i.e. God.

The 'Two Books' metaphor emphasizes a distinction between God and creation. Such a distinction was not always made and, in ancient Greece (c.600BCE–200CE), 'nature' was regarded as semi-divine — a tendency which is creeping back in 'New Age' ideas. This pantheistic view had repercussions on Greek science because, if nature was semi-divine, it seemed impertinent to interrogate 'her' by performing experiments; so science slowly ground to a halt. The distinction between Creator and creation, prevalent in Christian Europe, removed this barrier to experimental science. Indeed, the Old Testament seemed to encourage science and technology by its mandate to have managerial responsibility over the earth. For, if one was to manage earth and its resources, presumably one needed to understand them, and science seemed helpful in doing the job. It is important to stress that the commands to 'rule over' and 'subdue' the earth are not a licence to exploit it, as some have suggested, but a commission to exercise responsible stewardship.

The popular image of conflict is largely the result of a sustained campaign, by a small but influential group of Victorian scientific naturalists, to 'liberate' science from what they saw as clerical control. Eight of the group of nine were Fellows of the Royal Society. Led by T.H. Huxley, they called themselves the X-Club. Part of the strategy of their campaign for the cultural supremacy of science lay in portraying the Darwinian controversies as typical of the general relationship between science and religion (G 30f). Details of their strategy, which had far-reaching consequences for public perception of the relationship, are given in C.A. Russell's, *The Conflict Metaphor and its Social Origins*, (reprints from 'Christians in Science', 38 De Montfort Street, Leicester LE1 7GP, — 30p).

Further reading

HODGSON, P.E. (1990) *Christianity and Science*, Oxford, Oxford University Press, 32pp, including discussion questions.
HOOYKAAS, R. (1972) *Religion and the Rise of Modern Science*, Edinburgh, Scottish Academic Press.
JAKI, S.L. (1980) *Cosmos and Creator*, Edinburgh, Scottish Academic Press.
RUSSELL, C.A. (1985) *Cross-currents: Interactions Between Science and Faith*, Leicester, Inter-Varsity Press.
RUSSELL, C.A. (1987) 'Some founding fathers of physics', *Physics Education*, **22**, 1, pp. 27–33 (probably available in the school science department; the issue is given over to science and faith and a reprint is available from the Institute of Physics, Publishing Division, Techno House, Redcliffe Way, Bristol BS1 6NX at £5).

Topic 2: 'In the Beginning ...'

Points to be Made

(i) Physical explanations of the origins of the universe are not alternatives (logically) to explanations of divine activity and purpose. They are of different types, and may in principle be compatible with each other.
(ii) To confuse types of explanations is to make a 'type error', the prime example of which is the 'god-of-the-gaps'.
(iii) The universe gives the appearance of being 'fine-tuned'.

Introductory Suggestions

Teaching about the origin of the universe lends itself to the dramatic. The lesson could begin with some commercially available slides of the heavens taken through large telescopes. A suitable slide set is S684 Our Home Galaxy, Folio 1, available from The Slide Centre Ltd., Ilton, Ilminster, Somerset TA19 9HS. Another resource is the slide set 'Exploring the Cosmos', available from The Farmington Institute, 4 Park Town, Oxford OX2 6SH.

Verses 1,3,4 and 5 of Psalm 8 could be used, to illustrate a Hebraic response to the majesty of the heavens and the feeling of smallness it generated, even though relatively few stars could be seen with the naked eye. The theme of size could be revisited by using information from the background notes about the need, on current theorizing, for the universe to be as old and as large as it is, if we are to be here.

Discussion

Giving reasons for your answers, do you think the current picture of the universe makes it:

  (i)   more difficult to believe in God?;
  (ii) easier to believe in God?;
  (iii) leaves the issue unchanged?

(Our galaxy — the Milky Way — contains about a hundred, thousand, million stars; and there is likely to be a similar number of galaxies. Sir James Jeans, the astronomer, once said 'the total number of stars in the universe is probably something like the total number of grains of sand on all the sea-shores of the world' [cf Genesis 22:17].)

Psalm 19 could also be used, briefly, as a link with Topic 1. The first six verses are about the created order and the laws of nature; verses 3 and 4 are of particular note and could be compared with Romans 1:20ff. The rest of the Psalm is devoted, not to the laws of nature, but to the law of the Lord, hence the 'Two Books' metaphor.

By way of contrast with the two Old Testament psalms, here are the first two verses of a modern one, written by a scientist: Professor Sir Robert Boyd was, until recently, Professor of Physics at University College London, Professor of Astronomy at the Royal Institution and Director of the Mullard Space Research Laboratory.

> 'In the beginning', long before all worlds
>   Or flaming stars or whirling galaxies,
> Before that first 'big bang', if such it was,
>   Or earlier contraction; back and back
> Beyond all time or co-related space
>   And all that is and all that ever was
> And all that yet will be; Source of the whole,
>   'In the beginning was the Word' of God.
>
> The Word of God; Reason, Design and Form,
>   Intelligence, Whose workshop spans the stars

            Expressed within the Cosmos and alike
               In what seems chaos; He Who works as much
            In randomness as order, Who to make
              Man in His image scorns not to create
            By patient evolution on a scale
              Of craft divine which dwarfs a million years.

(The other five verses are to be found in *Faith and Thought*, (1975) **102**, 3, pp. 182–3, available from the Victoria Institute, **185** Wickham Road, Croydon CR0 8TF.)

For young children, the imaginative parable of creation given in the eighth and ninth chapters of C.S. Lewis's *The Magician's Nephew* (Chronicles of Narnia, Penguin) might provide a starting point for thinking about origins.

Background

A simple scientific account of current thinking about the physical origins of the universe is given below. Such explanations can be complete in themselves, yet make no mention of God. This is because physical (scientific) explanations are of one *type*, while explanations of a creator's plan and purpose are of another (G 40f). To confuse the two is to make a *type error* in explanation. Perhaps the best known example of this is the 'god-of-the-gaps', in which gaps in scientific explanations are filled by saying, 'that's God'! The 'god-of-the-gaps' arose because some religious believers thought God's role as creator was threatened by scientific explanations, and sought 'room' for God by pointing to gaps in scientific knowledge. Some non-believers, conversely, have enthusiastically looked for new scientific explanations in the belief that this pushed God out of the picture. Both positions make an explanatory *type error*. The logical status of the muddle is more apparent if the reasoning is applied to a non-religious example which, although not identical, has certain parallels: if someone dismantled a television, to understand the scientific principles, it would seem very odd if they attempted to explain the parts they could not understand by saying, 'That's Baird' — an inventor of television! For in a non-physical sense, Baird is 'in' the whole thing — not just the parts we cannot currently understand. To take the comparison a stage further, it would be equally odd if, after taking the whole thing apart, the investigator said he had found no trace of Baird! Yet the comparison with the way some people talk about God is only too apparent.

The current picture of the origin of the universe is that it started with a Hot Big Bang, not at a particular time in empty space, but *spacetime* itself came into being. This is a difficult idea to grasp. Creation, said Augustine, was not *in* time, but *with* time. One way of looking at the idea might be to say it would have no meaning to talk about time in the absence of even one atom whose vibrations could be made the basis of an atomic clock.

As the temperature began to drop after the Big Bang, both matter and anti-matter were formed. Had there been equal quantities, they would have annihilated each other. But there was just one part in a thousand million more matter than anti-matter — otherwise we would not be here.

Matter moves outwards at enormous speeds — close to the fastest speed possible, that of light (three hundred million kilometres a second). The furthest galaxies appear to be moving away from us the fastest, because the frequency of their light drops most — like the frequency of the horn of the fastest car drops most as it goes past us. When the frequency of sound drops, the note sounds lower; when the frequency of light drops, it looks redder — the Red Shift.

According to currently accepted ideas, the moving matter is slowing down all the time as gravity tries to pull it together again. The outward expansion due to the Big Bang and the inward contraction due to gravity are so very close that it is a matter of constant debate as to which will win. If gravity wins, there will eventually be a Big Crunch. If gravity loses, the universe will go on expanding. If these two effects were not so very nearly equal, we would not be here to think about it, for the following reasons:

The element carbon is the basis of life and our bodies contain a lot of carbon and heavier elements. These elements were made as atoms of light elements like hydrogen and helium came together under gravity, getting very hot in the process, and formed stars like our sun. The enormous heat and pressure fused these light elements into heavier ones like carbon. This took a long time — as long as the time for a typical star to be born and die — and since the speed of recession of the galaxies is enormous, so is the size of the universe. Some stars end their lives by exploding (supernovæ), which scatters the carbon and other elements into space. So our bodies are made from the 'ashes' of distant stars. If gravity were too strong, the universe would collapse before there was time for this to take place: if too weak, the universe would expand too rapidly for stars and galaxies to form. If the outward effects of the Big Bang and the inward effects of gravity were different from what they are by an infinitesimal amount, we should not be here. All this places a very different perspective on how we might view our size and age in relation to the rest of spacetime, compared with the feelings of human insignificance expressed by the writer of Psalm 8.

The incredibly 'fine-tuning' that would be involved in this, in the ratio of matter to anti-matter, and other physical constants, without which humans would not exist, have been expressed in various versions of the so-called 'anthropic principle'. Older pupils might like to debate whether this provides a knock-down argument for the existence of God. As might be expected, other interpretations are possible. Nevertheless, the 'fine-tuning' of the physical constants of the universe is thoroughly consistent with the universe having been designed by God with humans in mind.

Further reading

BROOKS, J. (1985) *Origins of Life*, Oxford, Lion.

HAWKING, S. (1988) *A Brief History of Time*, London, Bantam Press. (Because of its large sales, many people are likely to be familiar with this book. I am not as enthusiastic about it as some are (see my review in *Science and Christian Belief,*

1990, **2**, 1, pp. 66f). There are many splendid examples of how to make complex ideas available to a non-technical audience; but the excursions into philosophy and theology are disappointing and, in my view, should be treated with caution.)

POOLE, M.W. (1987) 'Cosmogony and creation', *Physics Education*, **22**, 1, pp. 20–6.

WEINBERG, S. (1984) *The First Three Minutes*, London, Fontana.

WILKINSON, D.A. (1991) *In the Beginning God?*, Methodist Church Home Mission Division, 1 Central Buildings, Westminster SW1H 9NH (£1).

Topic 3: The Idea of Creation

Points to be Made

(i)   There is a distinction to be made between the way the word 'creation' is used in religion, and the derivative ways it is used in science and in everyday life.

(ii) The religious idea of creation is left untouched by any particular theory of origins, whether in cosmology or biology.

(iii) The *processes* of evolution cannot be treated as alternative to the *act* of creation.

(iv) There are important distinctions to be made between the ideas of 'creation', 'Special Creation' and 'creationism'.

Introductory Suggestions

A link with the previous lesson could be made by introducing some of the various theories of origins, using selections from the slide set S683, *Concepts of Time and Theories on the Origin of the Universe* (The Slide Centre).

The lesson could continue with a discussion of what is common about the way the word 'created' is being used when saying:

- a games manufacturer has created an entirely new kind of board game;
- information technology has created a new problem for individual privacy;
- Frank Whittle created an entirely new form of propulsion with his jet engine.

The following analogy might help generate discussion about the difference between 'creation' and 'evolution':

The manufacture of a new car is an act of creation, with a small 'c'. A new model is brought in to being. The processes of manufacture will almost certainly involve automation. But no-one would regard manufacture and automation as alternatives; they belong to different categories.

Background

The common factor in the ways 'created' is used in the three examples above is the bringing-into-being of something new — an idea, a problem, an artifact or, in the case of cosmogony, a universe. In religion, creation carries the additional idea of God's agency — bringing-into-being-by-God.

When scientists borrow the word 'creation', they are loosely using it to mean the physical origins of the universe. Problems arise when certain scientific popularizers go beyond the competence of science and claim that exhaustive scientific explanations of 'creation' displace God. This, as indicated in Topic 2, is a *type error* in explanation. 'Creation', instead of implying God, is being used to give the impression it is a *substitute* for him.

Before the Big Bang theory was generally accepted, Bondi, Gold and Hoyle put forward their Steady State, or Continuous Creation theory. According to this, as the matter in the universe expanded outwards, it was replaced by hydrogen appearing at an undetectably slow rate. They thought this avoided any idea of a creating God, but, as Professor Mascall commented, it simply replaced one Big Bang by a lot of 'Little Pops'.

But what about suggestions, although not currently in vogue, that the universe is infinitely old or even oscillating between Big Bangs and Big Crunches? Even here, the idea of creation-by-God is left untouched. For, if time is part of the created order, the creation of an infinitely old universe is the creation of a universe whose time component has no lower boundary.

The religious idea of creation is left untouched by any particular theory of origins — biological as well as cosmological. *Some* process or other has to be involved in 'bringing-into-being'. Evolution and creation belong to different categories — they are not logical alternatives. To treat them as such is to make some kind of a *category mistake* (G 110). 'Creationism' falls into this kind of a category mistake, when it tries to force a choice between them. Part of the confusion has arisen because 'creation' also gets used as shorthand for Special Creation — which claims that different kinds of living things were separately created — for then there *is* a conflict with evolution. The idea of the separate creation of 'kinds', a word which is often, without warrant, equated with the modern biological term 'species', is contradicted by evolutionary theory. But such an interpretation of 'kinds' is not demanded by a careful treatment of the text of Genesis 1. The writer's intention seems to be to stress that God is orderly and not capricious: cows breed calves, ducks have ducklings; not giraffes or mice.

Creationism comes in various forms, but the most widespread is the young-earth variety. Despite an extensive quasi-scientific literature, which I have reviewed elsewhere (see below), its position is contradicted by every major branch of the relevant sciences. Not that current science has the final word, but any textual interpretation which puts forward a view so widely at variance with what can be 'read off' from the 'Book of Nature' needs careful scrutiny.

The doctrine of creation, from the Judaeo-Christian perspective, represents much more than a deistic, one-off act in the past. It involves the continuing relationship of God with the world, sometimes referred to as his *sustaining* — but it is a dynamic relationship that is pictured, rather than a static holding-together.

Further reading

MASCALL, E.L. (1956) *Christian Theology and Natural Science*, chapter 4, London, Longmans.

POOLE, M.W. and WENHAM, G.J. (1987) *Creation or Evolution — A False Antithesis?*, Oxford, Latimer House.

SANKEY, D. SULLIVAN, D. and WATSON, B. (1988) *At Home on Planet Earth*, Oxford Blackwell.

Topic 4: Evolution

Points to be Made

(i) Evolution is a *process*, whereby something happens, not the *cause* of it happening — it is not an agent which 'does' things.
(ii) Evolution — a biological theory — needs carefully to be distinguished from Evolutionism, a system of beliefs and values which are claimed to follow from it.
(iii) The words *chance* and *random*, as used in science, do not imply absence of plan or purpose.
(iv) The idea of humans being made 'in the image of God' is not ruled out by lowly animal origins.

Introductory Suggestions

Discussion

● The class could be asked to think about ways in which words are being used in these two statements, made on BBC's HORIZON programme, *The Blind Watchmaker*, by Dr. Richard Dawkins:

> 'evolution, the blind designer, using cumulative trial and error, can search the vast space of possible structures';
> 'am I really trying to persuade you that a blind, unconscious process, evolution, can build animal optics that rival human technology?'

Q. Are there any hidden messages about God carried by phrases like:

> 'evolution ... can search' and 'evolution can build'? If you think there are, say what message you received.

Q. When does a figure of speech (personification, in this case) help in understanding and when might it be confusing?

- Capitalism in Victorian England; Nazism under the Third Reich; and Communism have all claimed that what evolution IS about tells us how we OUGHT to behave.
Q. What do these three ideologies say?
Q. Do they provide grounds for thinking OUGHT can be derived from IS?

- In Victorian England, also, there was much talk about *evolutionary progress*.
Q. What was meant by the phrase?
Q. What sorts of 'progress' are involved in evolution and what sorts are not?

- Pupils could be asked to look at, and comment on, the three sentences:
1 'They met their next-door-neighbours by chance, while they were on holiday'
2 'Any particular radioactive atom decays by chance'
3 'In evolution, genetic mutations happen by chance'
What does 'by chance' imply in 1, 2 and 3? Do they all have the same meaning?

- The meaning of being 'made in the image of God' could be explored in view of our lowly animal origins and, 'dust you are and to dust you will return' (Genesis 3:19).

Background

The nineteenth century tensions over evolution were complex, and deliberately exaggerated in the interests of controversy (Topic 1). Popular folklore says that a few scientists and many theologians dismissed evolution. This is nearly the opposite of what happened; while the legendary encounter of T.H. Huxley and Bishop Wilberforce draws more on imagination than on the sparse details available about what probably took place (G 102f).

Some of the felt difficulties over evolution have sprung, not from the biological theory, but from extravagant claims about what is supposed to follow from it. It has been held, variously, to justify Capitalist cut-throat competition in business, the breeding of a Master Race in Nazi Germany and the Communist vision of struggle. The disparate conclusions reached from the biology are perhaps the best indication of the 'logical Grand Canyon' between what IS and what OUGHT to be. The Victorian emphasis on progress fares no better in its claims to follow from evolution. 'Progress' in Darwinian evolution only relates to genetically transmitted characteristics which favour survival and reproduction. Other desirable characteristics, which do not contribute to these, are not involved. Less was heard about the automatic moral progress of the human race after two World Wars (G 112f).

Some people have been over-enthusiastic about evolution, as though it provided some kind of surrogate god. The philosopher, Mary Midgley, examines this phenomenon in *Evolution as a Religion: Strange Hopes and*

Stranger Fears (Methuen, 1985). Similarly, evolution, as well as getting *deified* is often *reified* (confusing a concept with a real object or cause). Evolution is spoken of as 'doing', 'causing', 'planning', 'building' and so forth. The *fallacy of reification* extends to other concepts, such as 'chance', which also gets vested with the power to 'do' and to 'make', as seems to be the case in the HORIZON programme — 'we evolutionists seem to be saying that it (the eye) was created by blind chance, by random mutation'.

Figures of speech can be helpful, but when the denial of divine action is followed by vesting *concepts* with the powers hitherto attributed to God, the language becomes odd. The scientific use of the word 'chance' is very different from that of popular speech, which denies any plan or purpose behind an event, as in (1) above (G 116–9). But science is not competent to pronounce whether there is plan and purpose in the universe. So 'by chance' in (2) amounts to a confession of ignorance as to which radioactive atom will decay next. There is a mathematical probability for any one atom being the next to decay, but no-one knows which it will be until it actually happens. In the biological example (3) ignorance is again indicated, together with the *assumption* that a 'chance' mutation is one which is independent of the needs of the particular organism (G 120–25).

Further reading

BERRY, R.J. (1988) *God and Evolution*, London, Hodder & Stoughton.
BLACKMORE, V. and PAGE, A. (1989) *Evolution the Great Debate*, Oxford, Lion.
FORSTER, R. and MARSTON, P. (1989) *Reason and Faith*, Eastbourne, Monarch Publications.
HUMPHREYS, C. (1985) *Creation and Evolution*, Oxford, Oxford University Press.
LUCAS, J.R. (1979) 'Wilberforce and Huxley: A legendary encounter', *The Historical Journal*, **22**, 2, pp. 313–30.
SCHOOLS COUNCIL INTEGRATED SCIENCE PROJECT (SCISP) (1974) *Darwin and Evolution*, Harlow, Longman (a simple account of the biology for pupils — a science department which has been involved with SCISP will probably have copies).
SPANNER, D.C. (1987) *Biblical Creation and the Theory of Evolution*, Exeter, Paternoster Press.

Topic 5: Language in Science and in Religion

Points to be Made

(i) *Literal* and *literary* styles of writing need to be distinguished, both in science and in religion.

(ii) Communicating difficult ideas in science and in religion often needs a non-literal *genre* because language is limited; hence analogies, metaphors and models are used.

(iii) Figures of speech have their uses and their pitfalls; they must be used with care.

Introductory Suggestions

The class could be given examples of religious texts which use some of the following forms:

history, jokes, letters, parables, paradoxes, poetry, prayers, prophecy, proverbs, revelation; and which employ similes, metaphors, analogies and models (G 16–19).

They could be asked to take a religious subject, say 'the love of God' and to write about it in several different forms. They could, for instance, make up a parable, write down some similes, write a letter to an individual or a group about the subject or try their hands at a simple poem or song.

They could then be asked to do something similar for a scientific topic, like the Big Bang. Suitable literary forms might be a poem, a racy account written for a popular newspaper — including a block insert explaining the science — a sober piece of writing for a scientific journal, an allegory such as *The Magician's Nephew*, mentioned in Topic 2, a collection of similes or metaphors, or a piece of creative writing, from the point of view of an atom of hydrogen created just after the Big Bang. If someone has written a poem, they might like to see Professor Boyd's psalm, or the poem, *Star Death*, composed by a physicist, Dr. John Martin, to preface his book on General Relativity:

> Birth'd they were and cradled on the height
> of furious Creation's blazing start.
> Held up by raging chaos at their heart
> and dancing on the radiant outflow bright.
>
> Not for ever can they win this fight.
> The dying fires will cease to act their part.
> The pressure fails. No longer held apart
> their day is over, giving place to night.
>
> > There lies a singularity in wait.
> > Past the horizon (which to pass is death)
> > with world lines jostling, fighting for each breath,
> > racked by the tide, they plunge toward their fate.
> > Nor is there any time to question how
> > the rest of space will fare: their end is now.

Background

Some tensions over science and religion arise from failing to appreciate the diverse uses of language. In religion, literary style has sometimes gone unrecognized and the text taken literally when that was not the author's intention. Reading scientific ideas out of — or rather into — religious texts prompted Galileo's comment to people who tried to extract astronomy from the Bible that, 'the intention of the Holy Ghost is to teach us how one goes to heaven, not how heaven goes' (G 82ff).

Taking *literary* forms *literally* sometimes results from uncertainty about the intended literary form, and sometimes from the erroneous belief that the text is being downgraded if not taken at face value. Recognizing the different ways language is used can present difficulties to children, for whom concrete operational thinking looms large — and to many adults too. James Thurber recalls his childhood puzzlement that someone who was 'brokenhearted' could still be alive. In contrast to religion, with its extensive imagery, science appears to offer clarity of expression. Yet a sizable literature belies this picture and reveals just how steeped in imagery science is, with its analogies of waves, fields, currents, particles, clouds, avalanches and clocks.

In every area of discourse, the 'it-is-as-if' language of similes, metaphors, and models (systematically developed analogies) is needed to communicate difficult and novel ideas, because thought forms may not yet have been developed, nor words coined, ... to do the job.

Imagery operates both in the *cognitive* and the *affective* domains. In science, the former probably predominates; in religion, the latter. In religion, the *affective* aspect of an apt figure of speech can be seen in the Old Testament confrontation, by Nathan the prophet, of King David, with his double offence of adultery and murder. The effectiveness of this literary device of a parable is that David is made to condemn himself out of his own mouth (II Samuel 12:1–24). The *cognitive* aspect, in science, of an apt figure of speech is illustrated by the analogy of electricity to water flowing in pipes, where the pipes are the wires, the taps the switches and the pumps, the batteries.

As well as being helpful, models can be a potential snare, because of a tendency to think all details of an analogy can be utilized. In religious education, the pupil who asks, 'if God is a father, who is the mother?', reflects this inclination. In science, too, there are limits to the use of analogies. For instance, there is no obvious comparison with electricity to emptying all the water out of pipes. Nevertheless, attempts to press the details of models should not be dismissed too readily, for a closer inspection of unlikely details sometimes opens up fruitful lines of thought. Pupils might like to try this out on the religious analogy of God to 'light' and the scientific analogy of gas molecules to billiard balls.

In science and religion, figures of speech like *personification* (for example, Mother Nature) and *reification* (Topic 4) may simply be poetic licence, but they can be misleading. They are most likely to be the latter when used as substitutes for divine activity. So strong does the sense of order and purpose in the universe seem to be that, if God is denied, something gets used instead. 'Nature', the sum of all physical things, is commonly referred to as though it were some kind of a surrogate god. As seen in Topic 4, concepts, like 'chance', and processes, like 'evolution', get reified and credited with 'doing' things! Popular science writings which venture into philosophy and theology, abound in examples of this kind.

Further reading
BARBOUR, I.G. (1975) *Myths, Models and Paradigms*, London, SCM Press.
DONOVAN, P. (1976) *Religious Language*, London, Sheldon Press.
SOSKICE, J.M. (1985) *Metaphor and Religious Language*, (chapter VI), Oxford, Clarendon Press.
SUTTON, C.R. (1992) *Words, Science and Learning*, Milton Keynes, Open University.

Michael Poole

Topic 6: Miracles

Points to be Made

(i) Science operates with working principles, like the Uniformity of Nature, which are useful, yet unprovable assumptions, leaving the possibility of miracles entirely open.

(ii) Scientific laws describe the normal behaviour of the natural world; they do not say that things could never be otherwise.

Introductory Suggestions

A preliminary discussion of some typical sentences containing 'miracle' might help pupils to think about the difference between everyday and religious uses of the word.

It was a miracle the police car came by just as she was being mugged.

It was nothing short of a miracle that he survived when his tank hit a landmine.

The feeding of the five thousand was a miracle.

A smart card is a miracle of ingenuity.

It was a miracle the money they needed came just after they prayed for it.

The new drug is a miracle cure.

The analogy of science with map-making can be used to make the point that it is the data (scientific/geological) gleaned from the world which determine the form of scientific laws/maps. If the scientific laws/maps do not fit what we observe, then it is the laws/maps which need revising. Scientific laws no more determine how the world must behave than maps determine where the rivers must run.

Background

'Miracles' is an extensive subject, one with which religious education specialists are familiar. The only aspect under review here is whether science has any light to throw on such events. The term 'miracle' is notoriously difficult to define but, for present purposes, the key aspect is an event not in accordance with the normal behaviour of the natural world, described by scientific laws. Can/do such events happen? The standard objections are pithily summarized by David Hume in his brief chapter *Of Miracles*. Able, senior pupils might scrutinize some of these, to practise distinguishing valid from invalid arguments. Common reasons offered for disbelief in miracles are that they are precluded by the Uniformity of Nature and would therefore be 'breaking' scientific laws. The Uniformity of Nature, however, is a methodological principle, a working assumption, without which science could not be carried on. For without the assumption that doing the same experiment gives the same results, science would be impossible. But any attempts to raise the Uniformity of Nature from a *methodological principle* to a *metaphysical belief* fall foul of the Problem of Induction — reasoning from particular instances to universal laws.

> The man who has fed the chicken every day throughout its life at last wrings its neck instead, showing that more refined views as to the uniformity of nature would have been more useful to the chicken.
>
> Bertrand Russell

Science provides no guarantees against the unexpected. So, although miracles are not *normally* expected, science provides no basis for dismissing them as impossible. The word *normally* is the key, for the very idea of miracles presupposes a norm, a uniformity from which they depart.

Scientific laws are concise descriptions of the normal behaviour of the natural world, made up to describe what normally happens; but they do not legislate that things could never be otherwise. The word 'law' has caused confusion because it is used so differently in its forensic sense and its scientific one. The laws of the land are *prescriptive*; they prescribe what those who pass legislation, decree should happen, and steps are taken to enforce them. They can be obeyed or broken. Scientific laws, on the other hand, are *descriptive*; they describe what does (normally) happen but have no powers to make it happen. Such laws can neither be 'obeyed' nor 'broken', only 'conformed to' or 'not conformed to'. The simple distinction that laws of the land are prescriptive and scientific laws are descriptive is of limited help, provided it is remembered that there *is* a prescriptive element to scientific laws — they prescribe our expectations on the basis of precedent (G 68f).

Further reading
BROWN, C. (1984) *Miracles and the Critical Mind*, Exeter, Paternoster Press.
CHURCHILL, J. and JONES, D.V. (1979) *An Introductory Reader in the Philosophy of Religion*, section 4, pp. 104–39, London, SPCK.
HUME, D. (1748) 'Of miracles' in *Enquiry Concerning Human Understanding* (various editions).
POOLE, M.W (forthcoming) *Miracles: Science, the Bible and Experience*, London, Scripture Union (chapter 7 looks particularly at Hume's arguments).

Michael Poole

Topic 7: Religious Beliefs and Values in Science, Technology and Medicine

Points to be Made

(i)   Beliefs and values are bound up with science, technology and medicine.
(ii) Beliefs and values make open or hidden appeals to some standard.
(iii) Although not all moral codes are based on religion, moral judgments often do have a religious basis.
(iv) Education in beliefs and values presents a range of problems of which those undergoing formal education should be made aware.

Introductory Suggestions

Discussion

Pupils could be asked to say whether they think it is right or wrong to:

(a)   prohibit genetic engineering;
(b)   make expensive space-probes;
(c)   switch off a life-support machine when a person's quality of life has almost vanished;
(d)   experiment on animals.

The inevitable disagreements during discussion can be used to highlight how moral decisions appeal, either explicitly or implicitly, to some standard, and how there are differing views about these standards. This raises particular problems for education in beliefs and values, which older pupils could try to identify, outlining practical courses of action to cope with them.

Background

The educational value of discussions includes helping pupils to use and interpret data, to distinguish between valid and invalid arguments and to be aware of standard fallacies, widely used for persuasion in public debate. The potential weakness of discussions is that participants often come unprepared, so the activity becomes little more than a rearrangement of prejudices. Furthermore, in a society so wedded to relativism (G 56), the impression may be left that it does not matter what you believe as long as you have your own 'autonomous' opinion. The philosophical difficulties of such a view are examined in detail in Trigg, R. (1982) *Reason and Commitment*, Cambridge, Cambridge University Press.

Some of the problems confronting anyone who teaches about beliefs and values can be summarized thus:

●   even among those who are not thoroughgoing relativists, there is no universal agreement about what beliefs and values are normative;

160

- even among those who *do* agree on common beliefs and values, there is considerable diversity about the practical outworkings, for example, concerning birth-control and therapeutic abortion within particular religious traditions;
- if attempts to avoid the first two difficulties are sought in *phenomenalism* and *descriptivism* the impression may be left that the individual's free choice is all that matters. Of course, individuals' choices *are* important and they will make them anyway, whether we consider individual choice important or not! But ultimately, if there *are* choices which are right or wrong in an absolute sense, and for which we shall be held accountable, is a broad-brush picture of 'this is what people do', an adequate exercise of responsibility? Do young people have a right to expect more guidance than this; and is guidance possible without indoctrination? Values clarification is necessary, but is it sufficient?

Thorny issues of this kind regularly exercise the consciences of religious education specialists. The broadening of the science and technology curricula means that teachers of science, and of design and technology, will also be wrestling with such problems, so there could usefully be liaison between departments. It is of key importance, not simply that issues of beliefs and values should be raised, but that pupils should be taken into the confidence of the teacher and enabled to share in the dilemmas of teaching in this area — thus '*meta*beliefs and values' should also be part of the programme of study.

Further reading
COOK, D. (1983) *The Moral Maze*, London, SPCK.
WATSON, B. (1987) *Education and Belief*, Oxford, Blackwell.

Topic 8: 'Facts' and 'Faith'

Points to be Made

(i) Facts, interpretations and beliefs arise within both science and religion, making the popular view, 'science is facts; religion is faith', simplistic.
(ii) 'Interpretation' does not licence just *any* view; it must be consistent with the data.
(iii) As in religion, some evidence in science may be indirect and cumulative.

Introductory Suggestions

The medium of a detective story — such as Agatha Christie's *Sleeping Murder* — can be used to highlight the relationships between facts, their interpretation, and beliefs. It can also be used to show how conclusions are drawn from direct and indirect evidence, and how the cumulative effects of many small and separately unconvincing pieces of evidence may combine to produce a convincing whole.

Furthermore, the story can be used to make the point that, although different beliefs about the meanings of scientific and religious data may be possible in the incomplete state of our knowledge, in the end some beliefs will turn out to be true and others false — a point further illustrated by Hick's parable *The Road* in Hick, J. (1971) 'Theology and verification' in Mitchell, B. (Ed.) *The Philosophy of Religion*, Oxford, Oxford University Press, pp. 59f (also included in Churchill and Jones, op. cit., pp. 34f). An allied, and fashionable belief which could appropriately be discussed at this point is *relativism*, if it has not already been examined in Topic 7.

Discussion

The nature of belief could be explored by discussing some of the following quotations:

- 'Faith is when you believe, 'cos you want to, something which you know ain't true'.
- I wish I had your faith'.
- 'Faith is trust'.
- 'Preparedness to act upon what we affirm is admitted on all hands to be the sole, the genuine, the unmistakable criterion of belief' (A Bain, philosopher).
- 'Faith is a blind leap in the dark'.
- 'Unless I see the scars of the nails in his hands and put my finger on those scars and my hand in his side, I will not believe' (Thomas' comment about the resurrection of Jesus). 'Do you believe because you see me? How happy are those who believe without seeing me!' (Jesus' reply) (John 20:24–29, *Good News Bible*).

Background

Common distinctions made between science and religion are: science is objective, religion is subjective; science is about facts, religion is about faith — usually regarded as unevidenced belief. Science is seen as a public activity about which practitioners agree; religion is regarded as a private affair about which there is little agreement. There is, of course, enough truth in this caricature to give it plausibility and leave the impression that science 'proves' things, while religion is simply a matter of opinion!

But science, while striving for objectivity, involves many subjective factors which affect the choice and interpretation of the data collected. Social, cultural, spiritual and moral considerations influence the selection of research areas, the choice of models and decisions about funding.

Conversely, much of religion, while including subjective factors, involves factual bases which are not simply matters of personal preferences. Rather they are objective in the sense that they have to be taken into account, like it or not. Any idea of faith as 'unevidenced belief' would be abhorrent, for example, to Christianity, Islam and Judaism. Certainly the facts are interpreted, as in the credal statement 'Christ died for our sins', but they are still there. The fact of Christ's death is beyond reasonable historical doubt. The theological reason for his death is an interpretation, which is a cornerstone of Christianity.

But interpretations are not just free-for-alls, like some theological supermarket where 'you pays your money and you takes your choice'. There are hermeneutical principles to be applied; some interpretations are supported by the data, others are not. It is perverse to think that the word 'interpretation' can be used as a smoke-screen to imply that anything goes, and nothing remotely unpalatable need be faced up to. In the detective-story illustration, a principle of interpretation is that rational beings have motives for crimes, which favour some interpretations of the forensic evidence and rule out others. When these motives appear to be lacking, suspicions about the criminal's sanity may be entertained. In a detective story, as with science, social, moral, spiritual and cultural factors affect theories, and different interpretations of the data may be possible (see *Interpreting Evidence*, below). Indeed, one feature of a good story is the way in which it presents alternative conclusions drawn from the same evidence, conclusions which are reasonably, though incorrectly drawn, because the data are seen from different perspectives. Another feature of a good detective story is that the crime is not witnessed directly — that sort of *direct evidence* would take the fun out of the story by making the solution too simple. The skilled writer of detective fiction weaves a clever fabric, using *indirect evidence* and *cumulative evidence* to make a composite plot. Certain branches of the historico-observational sciences, such as geology, evolutionary biology and cosmogony (Topic 2), show parallels. They, too, concern events which were not witnessed and whose nature has to be deduced by attempting careful reconstructions from indirect and cumulative evidence. In a religious context, the way in which cumulative evidence is built up to make a convincing case for religious belief is developed in Mitchell, B. (1973) *The Justification of Religious Belief*, London Macmillan.

Topic 7 took an *inter*disciplinary look at some of the ways in which religious beliefs interact with scientific ones. Here we are concerned with *intra*disciplinary beliefs — those that occur *within* a discipline — in particular within science. There are, of course, differences in the beliefs involved in science from those encountered in religion, but there are some comparisons which can usefully be drawn. Both disciplines include beliefs about the kind of world we live in. In order to do science at all, the scientist must subscribe to a set of beliefs, either held consciously, or more usually taken for granted. These *presuppositions* — things assumed beforehand/taken for granted — include beliefs in the scientist's own *rationality* (powers of reason — a necessary assumption for *all* discourse), the world's *intelligibility* (that it can be understood), its *orderliness* (that there are patterns to be discovered) and its *uniformity* (that doing the same experiment produces the same results). None of these beliefs are capable of scientific 'proof'; but there has to be commitment to action based on them for any activity we would recognize as science.

Both science and religion include a concern with what is conceptually difficult and with what cannot be seen. In religion, non-physical concepts like 'God' and 'spirit' can be difficult to handle, while in science, physical concepts like 'fields', 'radiation', 'action at a distance' and 'elementary particles' tax both imagination and language. For the world of so-called 'elementary particles' is quite mysterious. At this level of size, all evidence is indirect evidence for something which cannot be seen, even with the aid of optical instruments. As in other areas of science, there are various theories to explain the data. The idea that there is always agreement among scientists is unrealistic; a Cambridge biochemist — Professor Malcolm Dixon — ventured the opinion that 'there are more disagreements and apparent contradictions within science itself than there are between science and religion'. There are different theories about the origins of the universe, about the mechanisms of evolutionary change, about whether cold nuclear fusion has occurred (see 'Test-tube energy?', below) and so forth. While there is considerable consensus within science, there are also substantial divergences of view. The importance of teaching this at school level has been recognized in Science in the National Curriculum where pupils are required to 'understand that different interpretations of the experimental evidence that they have collected are possible'.

Further reading
HARRIS, J. (1990) 'Test-tube energy?', (p. 39f) and LUCAS, A. 'Interpreting Evidence', (pp. 13–17) in *Investigating the Nature of Science*, (Ed. J. Honey), + copyright-waived pupils' materials, Nuffield-Chelsea Curriculum Trust (the school science department is likely to have a copy).

Reference

POOLE, M.W. (1990) 'Science-and-religion: A challenge for secondary education', *British Journal of Religious Education*, **13**, 1, pp. 18–27 (the whole issue is devoted to science, technology and religious education).

Chapter 10

The Junior School Child: Developing the Concept of God

Elizabeth Ashton

A serious omission from much religious education has been attention to the truth or otherwise of the *content* of religious faith. This controversial aspect of faith is always present when studying religious matters, whether or not discussion of it actually takes place or even is encouraged to do so. Its neglect therefore is serious. The procedures for handling religious education in the classroom have been rather too neatly and tidily organized so as precisely to avoid controversy, focusing not on what religion is centred on — its raison d'etre — but on what religious people do, say and think.

A recent conversation I had with a polytechnic lecturer drew attention to the hostility of students towards the subject of religion. One lecturer emphasized that this arose because of students' experiences of Christianity from early childhood. The solution of this particular institution was to present the students with a study of Islam: this to help them focus upon an alternative way of expressing religious belief. He went on to say that the aim of this study was to help students step outside of the Christian zone which was so familiar, and wherein their negative attitudes had developed and taken form, to enable them look upon religious faith from another perspective. The objective for this, he said, was to enable students to investigate the phenomena of religious activity quite impartially. Having realized this could be done, they would then understand the possibility of studying Christianity from an impartial stance to be both realistic and helpful for work in the primary school classroom.

Quite apart from his over-optimistic faith in the possibility of such impartiality, the scheme of work he showed me, though commendable in many respects, neatly avoided discussion with the students concerning the reasons why they were, in fact, reluctant to take up study of a religious nature in their training course for teaching. There was no engagement in depth with the kind of experience the students were bringing to their studies, the insights they had accumulated or the misunderstanding which barred the way to fresh exploration.

With these students, or groups of any others from infant classes through to any group of adults in discussion, the usual area of controversy which emerges if one talks with them is doubt about whether they believe in a transcendent power. This is the fundamental concept in understanding what religion is about — the belief in a transcendent all-embracing and all-controlling power within the universe which in most religions is given a name such as God or Allah.

It is necessary to begin dialogue with the students whatever their ages (and this chapter concerns mostly children of primary age) about what they understand by such terms. Whether one does, or does not, believe in such a transcendent power one must have formed either a concept or concepts concerning it, for it is undeniably extremely foolish to profess disbelief in what one knows nothing about!

Reservations about the whole area of religion nearly always stem from misunderstandings. Young children (and possibly many adults too) frequently hold concepts of a transcendent power as being an old man in the skies, white-bearded and dressed in a long white robe, something in the tradition of Santa Claus. Such ideas, as well as being ludicrous, are extremely unhelpful for serious reflection upon the subject of religion.

The most important priority I see therefore, for the teacher in the classroom, is to address the problem of naive literalism which plagues the development of religious understanding. This needs to come first because without it there can be little hope of children becoming aware of the spiritual dimension which lies at the heart of religion, or of being able to relate this to their own experience. The expression of the spiritual dimension necessarily relies heavily on symbol and metaphor, and if these are misread and discounted from the start, children are cut off from any help from religion as they seek to make sense of their own lives.

It is essential that children are taught how to interpret religious modes of expression and particularly the use of metaphor. Much damage can be done for example by allowing children to think of God as Father unless the metaphor is explained in depth. To teach the Lord's Prayer is not enough, for when Jesus spoke of God as Father he was speaking metaphorically: he was helping his hearers to understand God in terms of their familiar experiences of father. Yet people's understanding of this word raises all sorts of questions today. Problems in religious education are multiplied many times therefore unless the literal understanding of a metaphorical expression is made the subject of a thorough investigation.

No matter which world religion one discusses, the concept of transcendent power is both relevant and fundamental and needs studying fully if the debate or course of study is to reach any level other than superficial. This suggests a further advantage in adopting such a priority for religious education: it avoids the problems which can give rise to heated debate as to which religion should be taught, whether teaching of religion in schools should be biased towards Christianity or whether it should be multi-faith. For what is being emphasized is the reality of religious faith through the world, no matter which religious ideas and cultural practices have refined it and given it form. Thus the apparent impasse is avoided by studying what is behind all religion.

Adopting such an approach will also help to place the teaching of the phenomena of religion within a proper setting of religious *education*. Otherwise children are likely seriously to misunderstand and underrate religion which will tend to be seen just in external sociological or psychological terms as what some people or some groups happen to do or believe.

There is an urgent need for teachers of religious education to consider just what their subject really concerns. A study of any religion, be it Islam, Christianity or any other faith, avoids being *education* if it explore only what religious people do, and what artefacts they use in their rituals and/or private worship. If a lesson, say with 10-year-old children, affords them the opportunity of handling crucifixes, rosaries and candles, and even studies the architecture of the local parish church, and yet fails to engage them in an active discussion about *why* Christians use and create such things, the lesson will be one of Christian anthropology, or sociology, rather than religious *education*.

Many readers may raise an eyebrow at this. Surely we know by now that children lack either capacity or interest in serious thinking or discussion involving more than concrete matters of fact? This objection has so exercised the minds of teachers in the last thirty years that I shall devote the first section of my chapter to my response to it. I shall then move on to discussing how a teaching programme, designed to explore students' own understanding of this transcendent power, may help them to relate their ideas to the wide field of metaphorical usage and thereby deepen their reflection upon their own faith or lack of faith.

I shall then, in the final and longish part of the chapter, share ideas for presentation which I have actually used with 9- to 10-year-olds during the last two years. I hope that these suggestions may generate in readers ideas for development in what is a very rich and exciting area to explore.

Children's Cognitive Capacity

Goldman's researches published in 1964 and 1965 and based on the work of Jean Piaget has had a most pervasive influence on religious education in schools. His conclusion was to relate intellectual capacity closely to biological age. Yet he never questioned whether the children had ever had an opportunity for acquiring the skills which he had been testing. His findings are now heavily disputed. Points made by Ken Howkins (1966) at the time, which have been largely unheeded until recently, are now being taken on board. Robin Minney (1985) has questioned the psychology of Piaget pointing out the zoological background — his doctorate concerned an investigation of molluscs — and the undeniable fact that the development of anatomy is quite distinct from the development of intellect, as a comparison between a university professor and a primitive herdsman might reveal!

Important research by Margaret Donaldson (1978) has shown how children learn from their experiences, attempting to 'make human sense' of the world. Intellectual development must always be seen in relation to the environment against which it takes place. Conclusive evidence for the overthrow of Piaget's conclusions, and hence of Goldman's prohibitions, is presented in the research of Dr Olivera Petrovich (1989). Her work with 3 and 4-year-old children has indicated that even at that age children are capable of abstract thinking and of handling metaphors. Literalism in understanding God, she concludes, is learnt from adults rather than being something which is intrinsic to childhood.

Teachers may no longer, therefore, feel justified in linking children's biological age with their capacity for theological thinking, for this assumption is not supported by most recent research, nor is it supported by everyday experience. The fact that children are able to cope with symbols may be demonstrated by reference to the many 'pretend' games which very young children enjoy playing: for example when one child pretends to be father, whilst another is mother! Children frequently make themselves a symbol in imaginary games: it is very common in the junior school to see boys pretending to represent a whole nation in war games!

The assumption that children are unable to think theologically is unsupported. This is quite a revolutionary development, for the whole area of theological enquiry is thereby opened up for the junior school child, and the prospects for the classroom work that may be carried out is extremely exciting.

There is no need therefore for the continuous use of simplistic notions concerning God; some real beginning can be made at helping children to acquire the skills needed to understand religious concepts, and in this way reach a deeper and more personal engagement with religious truth-claims.

What Goldman's research undoubtedly drew attention to in an important way is the *difficulty* of religious concepts. The time-honoured reading of Bible stories to children in a straightforward fashion without attempts being made to interpret their meaning was, and still is where it is practised in many schools, unsatisfactory. For with regard to understanding the scriptures children suffer from a double handicap, being normally distanced from any meaningful religious background, and removed in time and culture from the metaphors which had meaning centuries ago but have now lost their relevance for most people and have become 'dead'. How far, even in the original context, the teachings were understood at any greater depth than the literal is open to speculation, but certainly literalism is a persistent problem in religious education today.

I have found in my own work with children that the Bible should, along with other examples of religious writing, be used in the education of even very young children, who find the style of writing, and the powerful imagery used, very stimulating for reflective thought. What is important, however, is to ensure that biblical material is introduced through planned schemes of work which encourage the children to investigate meaning and practise interpretation. To do so necessitates the teaching of the skills which such investigations require.

Unfortunately there is little sign of encouragement to do this in most of the Agreed Syllabuses which govern the teaching of RE in state schools. The objectives they outline will enable children, it is hoped, to begin to explore religious beliefs and their effects and grow to recognize their relevance to human morality and global responsibility. Implicit within the Syllabuses, is the hope that the young will, at least, afford religious believers respect and toleration, but there is little attempt to grapple with the real problems of religious diversity, or the secularizing tendencies of life in the modern world.

Such an approach fails to relate to some of the most significant aspects of children's experience. It is disturbing to notice, for example, the total absence of a few words which are unfailingly found within the vocabulary of the young child. One of these words is 'why', and I draw particular attention to it because this is the word with which most children, if not adults too, begin to ask questions.

As an example of what I mean by this absence of the word 'why' in religious education today, here is a fairly typical statement of attainment:

Describe what it might be like to experience and know about God.
(Metropolitan Borough of North Tyneside, 1990)

The point to notice is its air of detachment: the experience and knowledge referred to seem to depend upon *observation*, rather than upon personal experience and reflection upon it. The key to unlocking the underlying tone behind this requirement is the word 'might', followed by 'be like'. Empathy with someone else's experience, rather than an exploration and development of one's own, form the criterion by which the child's understanding is to be judged. I am reminded of the detached attitude which St Paul found among the Athenians upon his first visit to them, which caused him to depart from among them!

Had the statement of attainment been worded differently, say as follows, quite a different picture would emerge.

Investigate why people throughout the world have faith in the existence of God,

or, even better:

Investigate evidence for God's existence.

This would encourage enquiry which takes evidence seriously: evidence of faith, evidence concerning existence and evidence about God. What kinds of evidence are there in the world which point towards a controlling power which we call God? What kinds of evidence strengthen, or weaken, faith? What is faith? A wealth of theological enquiry of a genuine nature becomes possible with opportunities for discussion and reflection based upon personal experience.

Cognitive development should go hand-in-hand with encouraging awareness in children of a spiritual dimension in human experience. It is not a question of advocating something intellectual which ignores emotions or genuine involvement. In fact there are plenty of starting-points in experience from which to begin such intellectual work.

Methodology for the Primary Classroom

First of all it is necessary to be clear about the kind of meaning we attach to the word *spiritual*. I see this as fundamentally concerned with an insight, or sudden flash of understanding, that this material life here on earth is part of a greater metaphysical dimension which is outside of time, space and the limitations of human expression, including language, but to which we feel a call to respond. All that can be communicated of the awareness is therefore limited, but nevertheless will be recognized by those who have had similar 'stirrings' causing reflective thought, and in education they should be used as a means of opening up the reality of this mysterious dimension which we call spirituality.

One summer recently I was occupied with a class outing — of 9-year-old children — to a wild part of the Northumberland coast. It was a perfect summer day and we were walking on the cliffs overlooking Dunstanburgh Castle (which was once painted by Turner). I heard a boy nearby murmur half to himself:

and last year, these flowers, and this sky, and this grass, were not just like this. They are here now, but next year they will be gone.

The child had been affected considerably by the beauty of the moment, and had attempted to verbalize his thoughts. What he had been thinking was quite profound for his thoughts were upon the mortality which he sensed upon that instant in time, mysteriously confused with a rudimentary awareness of immortality.

As we walked along I suggested to him that time itself would still exist, as would the new flowers which took the place of the present ones, and asked him to consider why such things as flowers, pleasant views, enjoyable days out, etc., are part of our lives. I remember that at that point another child from the group came up upon a different errand; the conversation stopped, but hopefully the boy's reflection would continue.

I offer this anecdote from my own experience, as an example of a young child's spirituality. Upon this occasion the child managed to communicate his thoughts which became fully conscious because of the physical beauty of the occasion. One is left wondering how often other children have similar experiences of a spiritual nature but are too shy, or unable for one reason or another, to share them, or at least attempt to communicate them. The taboo against any attempt to articulate such feelings is powerfully operating in our society as David Hay (1990) shows, and it is precisely at this point that religious education needs to make a most important contribution.

The true function of religious education, I believe is to provide some form of stimulation to spiritual awareness, that is, stir into recognition however rudimentary the sleeping spirituality which lies in each of us awaiting arousal. There are numerous ways in which the class teacher may attempt to do this, and what affects one individual spiritually may not touch others. Well known experiences which may bring about such spiritual awareness are many and varied: for example seeing aircraft take off, especially Concorde, are known, to have a spiritual effect; music affects many deeply, including young children, as may poetry, prose, the natural world ... no list can ever be complete, but what is important is to recognize any expression of spirituality and be able to handle it sensitively through progressive, speculative thought and perhaps at the appropriate time encourage the child to communicate his/her experience in some art-form.

Above all else, it is important to ensure that the child realizes his/her experience is something universal: he/she is not odd because of having these insights, for such are essential for spiritual growth. It seems to me that the experiences should then be used as 'starting points' for religious education teaching children how to *recognize* the *expression* of spiritual experience in a religious dimension.

Failure to develop this aspect of the human psyche results, in all probability, in the individual not being adequately able to refine emotion and see human mortality in the light of eternity; the outcome seems to be a superficial understanding of life which lacks the power to sustain in times of personal crisis other than at a superficial level. The opposite of this sad possibility can be very stimulating and exciting to the child and adult alike. How, then, can it be activated and used as the basis for religious education in the junior classroom?

I suggest that one way of doing this is to select a few examples of metaphors of transcendence; how far the nouns 'metaphor' and 'symbol' are interchangeable is debatable — I use 'metaphor' when considering linguistic materials and 'symbol' for other devices, but both terms relate to a presence rather than an absence! Such devices are necessary because this 'presence' is usually elusive to the five senses and therefore necessitates symbolic or metaphorical interpretation in its communication. Many writers have expressed the opinion that this transcendent power cannot be communicated at all, such is its immensity and incredible powers — Anselm is quoted (in Soskice) as saying 'God is that than which nothing greater can be conceived' (p. 138). The best mere humans can do, therefore, is to attempt to use linguistic devices and symbols in art to 'point towards' that reality in which they have faith. The world religions provide a rich abundance of examples and a fascinating fact about them is how they are found in common: this transcendent reality which, apparently, underlies religious experience and faith, has common facets which may be depicted by means of such metaphors and symbols as fire, light and darkness and rocks and stones.

The theme of light and darkness, for example, is commonly found in world religions. The significance of this metaphor for religious education is that all human beings, from birth, have extensive experience of it. Young children are frequently afraid of darkness, and a useful exercise can be to discuss with them their fears, and develop the lesson by encouraging them to rationalize their thoughts by means of comparison with what they see and feel when the light is switched on, or when dawn breaks and light floods the earth. It is not difficult to see how both children and adults may be helped to understand the idea of transcendent power being like light: such is a metaphor of the presence of God, Allah, or the centre of faith of whichever culture one is investigating; darkness may be then understood not as the absence of such a power, but rather of failure to perceive its presence.

When the use of metaphor has been explored and understood in this way, students should be in a position to study at depth how religions use the theme of light and darkness in their teachings and rituals. The Jewish/Christian tradition of light as a metaphor of God is evident in the opening lines of the Creation narrative in Genesis.

> ... darkness was upon the face of the deep. And the Spirit of God moved upon the face of the waters. And God said let there be light.
> (Genesis 1[2f])

Even more, this Judaic account sees God as the creator of light itself, and therefore even greater than it: light, then, as a metaphor of God is not attempting to depict God *as light itself*, but rather in some respects as having similar effects as light. This transcendent power supersedes all attempts of description and therefore metaphor is only able to 'point the way' towards what is being imperfectly described.

In a similar way, Christ is referred to powerfully and effectively as 'the light of the world' (John 8 [12]). The metaphor is powerful because it uses the experiences humans have of light to enable them understand something of the function of Christ: the mind is led to consider the illuminating powers of light and from this understanding flow multitudes of thought-levels concerning the role of Christ and the nature of God.

The Hindu festival of Divali is often called 'Festival of Light' and the masses of lights which are placed in temples, homes and other kinds of buildings represent the traditional way of celebrating the birthday of the Hindu mother-goddess Kali. There are obvious associations here with the Christian Christmas time which may be developed with children to help them understand the significance of the metaphor and symbol.

The Judaic festival of Chanukka, celebrating the repossession and cleansing of the Temple in the second century BC by Judas Maccabeus and his people involves each Jewish home lighting a light on the first, and each subsequent, night of the festival, until all eight lights are ablaze: light, here, is used not only as a symbol of celebration but also of the triumph of good in the world.

Properties of rocks and stones have, from ancient times, provided suitable metaphors and symbols for the perceptions people have experienced of a transcendent power. Suitable aspects seem to have included their durability and strength: hence the use by Christ of 'rock' as a metaphor for St. Peter (Matthew 16 [18]). When a rock is broken, spiritual forces of a life-giving nature are believed to come forth: Moses strikes the rock which then provides water (Exodus 17 [6]): the piercing of Christ's side begins a flow of blood and water of the renewed Covenant (John 19 [34]). The cycle of a rock's geological passage may be understood as a metaphor of Christ's resurrection: the igneous rock is gradually broken up by natural forces, that is, wind and the action of water, but is reformed eventually into the new form of sedimentary rock.

An ancient Muslim story concerning the building of the Ka'ba tells how Ibrahim (Abraham) requested his son Ismail (Ishmael) to give him a stone which would be placed in the Ka'ba to mark the exact spot where pilgrims were to begin their ritual 'walking around' during their great pilgrimage to Mecca. This was done and the black stone (which is really a dark red colour) is still there marking this Islamic holy place: the stone has become the symbol of the centre of the Islamic faith to which all Muslims are encouraged to travel at least once during their lifetime.

The properties of the stone in religious symbolism may, perhaps, be enlikened to the Kara (bracelet) made of steel which ought to be worn on the wrist of all Sikhs as a symbol of eternity and unity. These qualities may be discussed at depth with students, enabling reflection and ultimately new insights to develop. Rocks and stones hold a fascination for many people who search for them, frequently polish them, and use them as ornaments both for the person and the home. Jungian psychology sees the stone as a symbol of the centre, or core, or one's personality: hence its immense power as a symbol of the divine. Children are always fascinated by stones and delight in cracking them open in a search for fossils or crystals which may have formed inside: such activities may easily be linked with Christ's resurrection from the rock-enclosed cave on Easter Sunday.

Examples of the Method at Work

The work schemes which follow are, as required by the Education Act of 1988, reflective of the fact 'that religious traditions in this country are in the main Christian', but of equal importance, as I shall illustrate, both educationally and culturally, is the fact that the schemes should also be used to help children understand both why and how these symbols are used in the great world religions.

The purpose of these teaching schemes, as they were originally used, was to help children understand the way in which people of religious persuasion attempt to communicate their beliefs as a result of their interpretation of individual experiences. Accordingly, it is important to understand that the children's work which follows is illustrative of their *capacity to reflect*: in no way was indoctrination attempted within *any* particular religious faith. Without exception, the comments of the children were the results of their own spontaneity both to the experiences upon which the work was based and also to the archetypal images which provided suitable symbolic forms of expression. What I myself found fascinating were the many insights which the children revealed that were fresh to myself!

The ways in which these teaching schemes could be developed throughout the primary school are illustrated diagrammatically (Figure 10.1).

Symbol A: Light and Darkness

One needs to begin by exploring children's experience of darkness and light, before moving on to develop the idea of their symbolic nature thus helping children to apply their experiences of them both to incidents in their own lives. This may begin by encouraging children to talk and write about occasions which were either pleasant or unpleasant. The following are pieces of writing done by children between 9 and 10 years:

> When my mam is late from work and the front and back doors are locked I worry. I think that something has happened to her. Sometimes she is ten minutes late and my brother and I get very very worried.

> I think everyone gets worried but they do not like to say.

Such ideas show signs of development when associated with symbols. These children in the same class wrote:

> Some people are in darkness because of where they live.
> Windows are always getting broken and people use bad language.
> Old people live in darkness because nobody visits them. I think darkness is like evil because when it is dark you cannot see clearly.

The children were able to use their understanding of darkness metaphorically and this skill had been developed by discussion. Others wrote:

Figure 10.1:   Developing Concepts of a transcendent power

The pre-school child

The child's understanding of differences between natural and man-made phenomena should be developed. Discussion should be encouraged with the children of problems which they encounter, as well as more pleasant experiences: for example, catching cold, enjoying a meal, etc., to encourage questioning and thoughtful reflection.

The Infant Child (Year R, 1 and 2)

An introduction to the use of metaphor: How might God be thought of as a good father; the wind; water; a good shepherd; a guide in times of stress, for example, Joseph and his Brethren. Developing concepts should be linked with appropriate Biblical/other religious ideas and developed from the child's experiences. The children should be encouraged to question such topics as why there are unpleasant things in the world: this in an attempt to counteract unhelpful sentimentality and also because such reflection is important for the development of deeper questioning later.

Transcendence and power

The Upper Junior Child (Years 5 and 6)

Development of children's understanding of metaphor, explicitly applied both to personal experience, collective experience and spiritual experience as well as to religious symbolism and imagery. The child should be helped to understand *why* imagery is necessary in religious communication, exploring as examples Christ/God like a rock; the rock, or Ka'aba Stone of Islam; the Jewish idea of Yahweh the all-powerful, especially as described in the Book of Psalms. Iconography in religious art, including and investigation of mandalas.

The Lower Junior Child (Years 3 and 4)

Further investigations of personal experiences, leading to explorations of concepts of a transcendent power: for example, how is God like fire (both Christian and Jewish); how is God like treasure (all religions); how is God like electricity (all religions if God is perceived as a power); the religious symbols of darkness and light (Christian, Hindu, Jewish). An investigation of the ninety-nine names of Allah.

(These ideas are not considered to be exclusive; many more variations are possible).

The development of theological understanding may be envisaged as a spoked wheel; at each revolution the momentum and depth of thought and variety of experience should increase. The hub of the wheel should be the quest to understand the transcendent power which is at the heart of religious experience throughout the world.

Darkness is like not understanding. Understanding is like light and when you are not afraid. Light could stand for peace and darkness for war and fighting. Light could mean hope and darkness giving up.

Darkness is when a cat is killed or when people are horrible to each other. Darkness is when someone dies in your family and everyone is sad.

In the following examples, light, too, is used metaphorically:

Light is after the night and it is having friends and being happy.

Light is like when you get your work right and you know what to do.

Light is like winning a football match, or it being your birthday or Christmas.

In these pieces of writing the children used at least two experiences upon which to base their ideas: their 'life experience' and their experience of darkness and light which they had been able to use symbolically. The effect of this is to increase the quality of both their thought and written expression, because extra depth has been given to their understanding of what happened. It is more meaningful, for example, to say 'light is like winning a football match' than 'it is good to win a football match'.

The next step shows how the children were able, after discussion of their work, to associate the idea of light being *like* God and Jesus, and darkness being the failure to perceive God.

The following comments on two biblical extracts (Genesis I, VI–4, and John 8, v. 12) reveal how the children, after discussing these extracts in small groups, were able to express their understanding:

Light is like Jesus and God, and light is happiness and joy.

Light stands for God. Light is a sign of God. If there was no light there would be complete darkness.

One child made the following observation, offering an additional symbol (there is a lighthouse near school)

Lighthouses can save people's lives when they are at sea.

A lighthouse guides them to shore.

Upon discussion, the group decided that Lighthouses were good symbols of God, for the reasons given in the child's statement.

These children were ready to be led forward in their thinking because they had grasped how at least two symbols were used in religious writing. The lesson series had arrived at this point near to Easter, and we studied the Last Supper. The children drew pictures of the event, after having discussed the story, and they were asked to show, without words, who was Jesus and who was Judas in some pictures they were drawing. There were numerous ideas, including colour-coding. One child showed Jesus with a halo 'because he is like light', whilst Judas was shown by the dark cloud around his head: his evil is represented by darkness.

Symbol B: Searching for Treasure

The idea of searching for treasure is always stimulating for children, and may be used as a foundation upon which to build their ideas of God.

Young children usually associate treasure with pearls, and they are keen to draw their own treasure-trove maps with grid references and frequently even attempt to give them an antique finish! These may be accompanied by letters written by imaginary pirates which direct treasure-seekers to their hidden hoard, and poems and stories which relate the efforts made by searchers to reach the treasure — the teacher always making the teaching-point that treasure is worth searching for.

Literalist ideas concerning treasure need to be exposed to help deepen understanding of treasure as a symbol-particularly the notion that treasure is anything which means much to an individual and often that which cannot be bought with money. The story of *King Midas and the Golden Touch* illustrates this point perfectly.

The children were then helped to reflect upon things which they regarded as being very important to them. Here are a few examples of what 9-year-olds described:

> My treasure is an old pair of slippers. Because my grandma was ill in bed she died but just before this she gave me some slippers. When I got a new pair I did not think they were a treasure as much as my other ones.

The slippers acted, in the mind of the child, as a reminder of her grandmother whom she would not see again: they had become a symbol of her.

One child's mother had suffered a severe permanent disability as a result of a surgical operation which went wrong. The child wrote:

> One of my favourite treasures is a photograph of my mam when she was well. My family is a treasure that money cannot buy.

Pets are frequently mentioned as being like treasure because 'you cannot replace the one you love' by just going into a pet shop.

There are countless examples of such ideas which could be given, all of which show that the children had come to understand that treasure is anything which is important to them and which cannot be replaced.

This principle may then be developed further by applying it to religious concepts. These children were given the texts of *The Pearl of Great Price* (Matt. 13, v. 45–6) and *The Treasure Field* (Matt. 13, v. 44) and asked to discuss the stories with their friends. They were able to see that the stories were *likening* the Kingdom of Heaven to treasure. These comments show additional thoughts which crossed their minds whilst they were in discussion:

> I think that the stories are about people trying to get, or find, love and care in their hearts.

> The stories mean that people love God and they will give all they have to stay near him.

The concluding session of this scheme of work involved the children watching a radio-vision programme about 'Baboushka'. They were asked what kind of treasure the Magi and Baboushka were seeking, and everyone agreed the treasure was Jesus Christ. A number also mentioned that Baboushka could not find Jesus because she had not understood that he was somehow inside of her.

The following is an example of a story written by a boy considered to have only limited ability. It illustrates his understanding of treasure as a theological symbol, or metaphor.

> About 2000 years ago some people went to search for the treasure of God. The treasure was the belief, or love, of him. Jesus had hidden the treasure. The people who knew about the treasure were some believers in God. When they set off for the treasure they found it was easier said than done. They had to climb high mountains and go into the deepest valleys. When they got there they knew it was the treasure because they saw something like a dove. But it was not a dove. They waited and they saw, or felt, something in their hearts and they knew it was God.

Here he has begun to write symbolically, using symbols already encountered; for example the dove had been remembered from the story of *The Flood*, and the hills and valleys which they mentioned had featured in some work which we had done a few months previously concerning the prophecies of Isaiah. He told me that he meant God was like the dove, hopefulness was the mountains and feeling 'fed up' was the valleys. What is of interest and significance is that he had begun to reflect himself about God, and was doing so symbolically. The idea of an internal God was beginning to make sense to him.

I could give many other examples. The process of reflection upon treasure was having the effect of encouraging the children to focus upon spiritual matters, and, because they were learning to use metaphor themselves in connection with their own experiences, their writing and thought was beginning to deepen.

Symbol C: Stones and Rocks

The children whose work is used in this section live near to the sea and they frequently have outings to the beach. On one such outing, which had been largely conceived of as a geological exercise, the children showed fascination at the different types of rocks, their textures, colour, shape and weight. Many were brought into the classroom and some limestone samples were split open, many of which revealed fossilized twigs, much to everyone's delight!

The children, all 10-year-olds, wrote imaginative stories about stones and rocks. Some children mentioned 'treasure' hidden inside the stone itself:

> I grabbed a stone. It began shining and a figure came half out. 'Help' he cried. Emma began to chip the stone away. I put my fingers in a crack and out he came.

They had been provided with a metaphor which they had been able to use with creative effect. To begin to use metaphor is to begin to see the old in a new way and by doing so to transform, or illuminate it.

> The process is also a dialectic of imagining new frames and contexts for our ordinary worlds, of seeing a new world which is also the old world. Metaphorical movement insists that the dream turn toward and renovate reality, not escape from it. (TeSelle, 1975, p. 58)

I wished to reinforce the idea of stones and rocks having eternal qualities, and being possessed of strength. A story familiar to the children for many years was *The Three Little Pigs*. I re-read the story to them.

I then gave the children the biblical text of the House Built on Sand (Matt. 7, vv 24–9) and we discussed why the storm was able to destroy one house but not the other. We related it to the story of the little pigs and they were able to understand with no difficulty that the house built on a rocky foundation was much stronger than that built on sand.

We then discussed people: did we know any people who were like rocks and stones? The children mentioned their friends and parents whom they could trust. Did they know people who were like sand? They said people were like this who 'did not keep their word and did not call for you when they said they would', or people who 'let you down when you thought you could trust them'.

Having established with the children the symbolic use of rocks and stones in stories, I wished to investigate how far the children were able to transfer the work done about the symbolism of stones and rocks to specifically theological religious material and in addition to assess their capacity for weighing up evidence and coming to conclusions as to what meaning the symbolic writing was pointing towards. I gave them this biblical passage, telling them that this has been written about Jesus Christ. What did they think this means?

> Jesus is like an important foundation stone in a building. If you believe in Jesus Christ, you will never be beaten. (1 Peter, 2 v. 6)

I suggested that before writing down answers, it would help if they asked themselves how Jesus could be like a stone. What are stones like?

In response they wrote:

> It is very difficult to move a stone, just like it is very difficult to move Jesus from you because he is true.

Jesus is like a stone because he is powerful.

A foundation stone is the main thing in a building, just like Jesus is the main thing in your heart. (all 10-year-old children)

One child wrote at length about what was turning over deep inside her thoughts:

It is true that you can build things with stones and it is true that stones are strong and heavy. It is difficult to break a rock and you cannot take the goodness out of Jesus. Jesus' power is trying to get inside you and give power. He is like a stone because he is strong. He is not strong in strength but he is strong in love and happiness. We should try finding Jesus' love most of all, and if we do we have found Jesus himself. What people should try to find in themselves in their lives is the joy they might never have had if it hadn't been for God and Jesus. (10-year-old)

The foregoing was written spontaneously by a child with no church connections whatsoever; she told me she had 'just thought it out' for herself.

Because the children had worked extensively on a theme, namely rocks and stones, they were able gradually to work towards an analysis of quite sophisticated biblical material, and were able to see the significance of what was written and relate it to their own experience of life. They were beginning to think, and had begun to acquire the skills of interpretation necessary for understanding religious language.

Conclusion: Helping Children to Think Theologically

I consider the most important aspects of the work were, firstly, the children were able to share their thoughts with others, including the teacher; secondly, they were extending their own thoughts beyond the basic image itself; and thirdly, I could perceive that their conception of God was moving towards a greater sophistication: the anthropomorphic ideas which had been revealed earlier had become transformed and this largely because the use of symbols had been studied in depth and applied to complex religious writing. Because of their developing skill and increasing maturity of thought, the children were able to 'make human sense' of the material.

The spirituality of children is probably profound and awaits activation by appropriate symbols and images. I have shown how the symbols of light and darkness, treasure seeking and rocks and stones may be developed from an experiential foundation, but this is, and must be, understood as being a *foundation in spirituality* only. It is a foundation because these are symbols of an image deep in the human psyche which provides children with the potential for deeper insight into their own spirituality as it is interpreted within a religious dimension.

What I would like to underline, however, is that no matter how creative their work may be, unless this capacity is explicitly linked to some theological enquiry, true *religious education* will not be achieved.

To unify personal experiences of childhood with the theological interpretations which have been perceived within them by the great world religions is to help children see beyond their daily routines and to deepen both their thought and their quality of perception.

> To call a parable a metaphor does not mean that it 'points to' an unknown God, but that the world of the parable itself includes both the ordinary and the transcendent in a complex interaction in which each illumines the other. (*ibid*, p. 46)

Thus, helping the child grow to understand and interpret the form and meaning of theological writing is to enable the growth of understanding which allows him/her to see the miracle within the everyday, or as once stated:

> To see myself within the perspective of transcendence; to perceive ordinary life in a new way, to see the strange within the familiar. (Lealman, 1982, p. 59)

This may have been what happened to the child on his visit to Dunstanburgh; the succeeding work on rocks and stones was an attempt to develop this experience and those of the other children who were on the outing. Spiritual experiences and theological perspective need to illuminate each other.

Such an approach to religious education frees both the teacher and the pupil from the trap of relativism which is so frequently what is actually communicated to children today; the subject may then be allowed to become an exciting, creative area of the school curriculum which heightens children's insights and helps them gain not merely knowledge of what religious people do, but understanding of how theology offers possible interpretation of their own experience of life.

References

DONALDSON, M. (1978) *Children's Minds*, London, Fontana.
GOLDMAN, R. (1964) *Religious Thinking from Childhood to Adolescence*, London, Routledge & Kegan Paul.
GOLDMAN, R. (1965) *Readiness for Religion*, London, Routledge & Kegan Paul.
HAY, D. (1990) *Religious Experience Today: Studying the Facts*, London, Mowbray.
HOWKINS, K. (1966) *Religious Thinking and Religious Education: a critique of the research and conclusions of Goldman*, Bristol, Tyndale Press.
LEALMAN, B. (1982) 'The ignorant eye: Perception and religious education', *British Journal of Religious Education*, 4.
METROPOLITAN BOROUGH OF NORTH TYNESIDE (1990) *Agreed Syllabus of Religious Education*, Metropolitan Borough of North Tyneside.

Elizabeth Ashton

MINNEY, R.P. (1985) 'Why are pupils bored with RE? — The ghost Behind Piaget', *British Journal of Educational Studies*, October.
PETROVICH, O. (1989) 'An examination of Piaget's theory of childhood artificialism', DPhil thesis, University of Oxford.
SOSKICE, J.M. (1989) *Metaphor and Religion*, London Longman.
TESELLE, S. (1975) *Speaking in Paarables*, London, SCM.

Chapter 11

Teaching Discernment: An Overview of the Book as a Whole from the Perspective of the Secondary School Classroom

Michael Donley

Just over a decade ago, having changed career, I sat down as a mature entrant to secondary-school teaching to rewrite the syllabus of my RE Department. What were my priorities?

I knew, to begin with, that I had no wish simply to paddle in the shallow waters of multi-faith sociology. Instead I focused on the question, 'What *is* religion?' — not 'religions' in the plural — that is, organized systems with observable phenomena — but that which constitutes the essence of them all. For it seemed to me, quite reasonably I believe, that religious education ought to concentrate not on morality or law and order (although these are the issues which one suspects primarily motivate Parliament to legislate) but on religion. I opened my introductory paragraph as follows: 'The Department considers the *spiritual* (rather than the moral or the sociological) to be the basis of religion'.

I recall how gratified I was to have had, in formulating my ideas, the support of a book which had recently (1978) been published. It remains to my mind the best available on the subject (that is, the philosophy of religious education) and is unlikely to be surpassed in the 1990s. It has never, however, received the widespread recognition it deserves. It is satisfying, therefore, to find the ideas put forward in it being espoused in the present collection of articles and being disseminated to what one hopes will be a wider public. Slee indeed refers to it (see p. 42) The book is Raymond Holley's *Religious Education and Religious Understanding*.[1] Among the contributors here, the most common theme seems to be precisely Holley's concern with the *spiritual*.

Michael Donley

The Meaning of 'Spiritual'?

Since the expression 'spiritual development' is among the very first words of
the National Curriculum itself, we might be tempted to think that the argument had been won. Yet difficulties with defining the concept of *spirituality*
(see Slee, pp. 43–6; Wilkins, p. 75f) remind us that such is not the case.
Holley's chapter 3 will assist those wishing to go deeper into the matter. But
those involved with religious education would also do well to recall that the
word 'spiritual' in contemporary Western usage is as likely to be found on the
lips of an atheist as of a believer. Indeed, in many instances it seems to mean
little more than 'uplifting'. However, once this has consciously been allowed
for, we are quite entitled to insist that in our own subject area the concept be
given a more technical definition, just as the Science Department expects
pupils to understand words such as 'mass' in a special way.

Yet even within our own subject area, we must make one further
distinction, one that only Wilkins (p. 76) among the present contributors
points out. So indoctrinated with materialistic secularism has our society
become that probably the majority of people instinctively feel that the word
'spiritual' automatically connotes something good and beneficial. How many
of those who now use the word 'spirituality' so freely actually believe, one
wonders, in the reality of the spiritual world, in the world of spirits both
good *and evil*? One gets the impression that, for many, the term simply refers
to the inner feelings of a given individual. Hence, indeed, the use of the term
'experiential' to describe such currently fashionable approaches. There is here
the possibility not simply of a certain naivety but of considerable danger.
Before tinkering with techniques of which one has little experience, especially
with children, one ought to think twice. The danger is, in fact, potentially
more serious than that that posed by the old bogeyman 'indoctrination'.

Traditions such as my own (Russian Orthodox), that have as their very
essence — although from the textbooks now appearing (of which more
later) one would never suspect this — the pursuit of spiritual advancement,
know what they are talking about when they offer warnings and advice! ...
Never experiment without an experienced and trustworthy guide. Mistrust
'images', especially those that seem 'good'. It is relatively easy to distinguish
between good and bad at the level of morality; at the level of spirituality, it
takes many years of hard-won experience.

A further note of caution is required. One possible reason why the 'spirituality' approach is becoming popular is that it fits in with the rather
common relativistic, do-it-yourself approach to religion, offering what seems
to be a way of side-stepping issues of theology. In what other discipline would
such an amateur approach be tolerated? Spirituality cannot be restricted to
matters of style and manner, as opposed to content. Spirituality *is* content! It
is understandable that, because of the general divorce between theology and
spirituality in Western traditions, there should be a move to correct the im-
balance; but success will not result from simply switching the focus of attention
— from theology to spirituality — *while maintaining the divorce*. Theology
without spirituality is sterile; but spirituality without theology is suspect.

Despite these caveats, the stress in my own approach has always been, as stated, on the essence of religion as being the spiritual. Among other things, this means bearing in mind at all times that the observable phenomena that still take up so much space in even the best textbooks (and on GCSE question papers) are of minor importance. I have come to be even more aware of this problem now that my own tradition has recently begun to figure in some of these textbooks. From the typical emphasis on ritual, icons and beards one would hardly guess that the heart of Orthodoxy is inner prayer. Outside a context of prayer, icons, for example, cease to be icons, becoming mere art objects.

It is good, therefore, to see the present contributors helping to drive a few more nails into the coffin of phenomenology and linking RE, via a more *responsible* emphasis on spirituality, to pupils' own personal development — which is our prime concern. They would all seem to agree that the 'sleeping spirituality' (Ashton, p. 171) that lies in all of us must be given the chance to develop, and that any education which does not cater for this is 'defective' (Ashraf, p. 82). This 'responsible' emphasis further involves focussing on what Ashraf calls 'virtues' (p. 82) but which might be better termed 'spiritual values'. It is important, too, to discriminate between these and 'moral' values, despite the overlap (Holley, 1978, p. 108ff, is particularly useful here). Again, it means provoking and challenging in such a way that even in the classroom — and not simply on class outings (see Ashton, p. 170) — pupils might have momentary flashes in which they see things in an entirely different way, standing outside both themselves and the hurly-burly of the typical school day. It is not surprising that the arts and the imagination should have found a place on the best syllabuses. Slee's article is a useful resumé of recent thinking in this area. The link between art and religion is of obvious interest to me, since orthodoxy has always viewed icons not as illustrations which happen to have a religious subject-matter, but as theology itself 'in lines and colours', as valid as the 'verbal icon' of scripture. (Although they can only properly be 'written — as the Greek and Slavonic put it — by someone who has experience of the spiritual truths they symbolize.)

It should perhaps be added that Slee — like the authors she quotes from — gives insufficient attention to the dangers of an over-dependence on the imagination, which most Christian tradition, for example, sees as 'fallen' imagination in need of 'cleansing'. Although Slee (p. 50) does admit that the imagination can be misused and 'channelled into self-indulgent fantasy and delusion or more sinister and destructive acts', she limits these dangers to the level of '*human* invention' alone.

Moreover, if we are to use vocabulary such as 'soul' or 'spirit', we should not ignore the original meaning given to these terms, for they are *not* synonymous. Christian anthropology views the human being from *three*, not two, angles: the material body which has senses to perceive physical phenomena; the *soul* (or life-force) which, in the case of human beings, possesses the faculties of *imagination* (and reason); and the *spirit* (*nous* in Greek, or *intellectus* in the older Latin sense). It is this, not our imagination or reason, which constitutes our supreme faculty and which is capable of allowing us to have direct apprehension of the celestial realm.

Michael Donley

Slee considers that 'the aesthetic imagination moves to a point of convergence with the religious vision' (p. 48). Yet this convergence can also produce confusion. Philip Sherrard has written an entire book — *The Sacred in Life and Art* (1990) — to examine this very problem in considerable depth. It deserves to be read by anyone interested in this area. Sherrard correctly points to the *spirit* (in the above sense) as being our 'original organ of vision' (*ibid*, p. 134).

Religion and Truth-Claims

'Nothing is real' (Strawberry Fields', The Beatles)
'Cause we're living in a material world,
And I am a material girl' (Madonna)

RE should focus on religion primarily, not on morality or any other related but separate areas, and should be linked to spirituality; but is there any more that one can say by way of definition? Any dictionary tells us that religion is in essence belief in a transcendent being and all that flows therefrom. It seems reasonable therefore that in the limited time allocated to RE in state schools, the syllabus should reflect this primacy by concentrating on what is traditionally called 'theology' — though not, of course, in the arid sense referred to earlier. This involves homing in on certain fundamental concepts (and here I welcome Hulmes' quotation and discussion of Buber on 'religious concepts', p. 137f). This cannot, of course, mean that one concentrates one's teaching at the conceptual level! Yet it does mean getting one's priorities right, and letting the rest naturally develop around the key issues. In a healthy religious tradition, it does not matter at which outer point on the wheel one starts from; any spoke will lead to the hub, if pursued far enough. Sadly, it is my experience that people active in the RE world all too often abandon the journey a couple of inches in from the rim. Yet whatever the age or ability of the pupil, one ought to be able to put before him/her the very heart of any religious issue. If we are not able to do this, should we be teaching the subject at all? Those who object that pupils cannot possibly understand such things have failed to take into account that *no-one* can 'understand' them in that sense! Indeed, that is part of the very message one would hope to communicate!

Such objectors fail, in addition, to do justice to young people themselves. For experience repeatedly shows that basic religious concepts do intrigue pupils. If given the opportunity, they ask the profoundest questions of all. (One ever popular topic, for example, is death — a subject of discussion which frightens most adults today.) They are ever ready (as should the teacher be, cf. Ashton, p. 169) to pose the question, Why? In fact, a good part of any course should derive from the questions, comments and criticisms of the pupils themselves — in all years, not just with seniors. This is one of the reasons why I welcome Poole's contribution (see his p. 144).

Without being exhaustive and without wishing to repeat Hulmes' list or that of Ashraf (p. 82) exactly, some reference will now be made to the kind of issues that should be given priority in *any* RE course. What, for instance, does the concept 'God' mean, to believers of various sorts, and also (perhaps more interestingly!) to non-believers? Does such a being exist?

At this point, having used the word 'God', I should perhaps indicate a very commonly used red herring, one that is also referred to by Ashraf (p. 91). What of a *non*-theistic religion such as Buddhism?

To begin with, the question of whether or not Buddhism is or is not 'theistic' is far from resolved, and makes for an interesting discussion in itself. Yet even if one follows the strictest of Theravada lines, it remains the case that Buddhism is, like other religions, concerned with the nature of reality. Whether or not Buddhism posits a *personal* supreme being, it is certain that the Buddha himself believed in something permanent beneath the shifting appearances of the visible world. Another anti-phenomenologist, we might say, and someone who would not have agreed with Madonna. Yet nor would he have sided with The Beatles, despite what is often fancied. He believed in and searched for the eternal, the immortal. Interestingly, his comment that there exists an 'unoriginated', an 'unmade', an 'uncompounded' uses identical negative vocabulary to that used by the Greek Fathers.[2]

Another fundamental issue that can so easily be overlooked is whether evil is primarily external or internal (cf. Ashraf pp. 83–5). Politics and sociology tend to imply that the causes are purely external. Yet are *all* people from bad housing estates trouble-makers, *all* poor or unemployed people criminals, *all* children from broken homes delinquents? What an insult to even suggest as much! Yet how do we explain the difference? Children will warm to these issues, sensitive though they are, if the teacher has provided an atmosphere of security which they have come to recognize.

One final example concerns the priority which O'Keeffe wants to see in schools, that of developing responsible attitudes towards the environment. This is of considerable relevance to today's 'green' youngsters. It necessarily however brings in its wake the question whether humanity needs saving. Few would disagree that in some sense it does. Yet can people save themselves? Is care of the planet just a matter of people 'pulling up their socks'? Children are genuinely interested in these matters, so let us not castrate RE lessons on such topics by limiting them to being poor copies of Blue Peter, with a dash of Victorian sentimental religiosity thrown in for good luck.

In all this we are, in Wilson's words, 'helping (pupils) become reasonable in the sphere of religion' (p. 11); or, to quote Priestley on the true function of education, we are helping 'to produce thinking people' (p. 35). As Hulmes rightly remarks, many attacks on religion are 'irrational' and 'ill-informed', 'the educational task (being) to challenge the irrationality' by developing pupils' 'critical faculty' (p. 128).

Many pupils — whose heatedly expressed views one depends on, in fact, for lively and meaningful lessons — are of the opinion that whereas atheists are 'thinking people', believers have been unintelligent. There may be very good reasons why they have come to such a conclusion; yet who, if not the RE teacher, is to encourage them to probe below the surface? As a member of a tradition that still, quite naturally and habitually, sees Christ as the incarnate Logos, I have no hesitation in claiming that true Christianity is 'logic-al' and, if not rational (in the sense of being fully graspable by human reason alone) certainly reasonable. Adherents of other religions will doubtless wish to make similar claims. Educators do well to recall that when Justin the Philosopher (and Martyr) became converted in the second century, he did not discard his philosopher's professional garb; he considered Christianity to be the 'true philosophy'.

Although I happen to agree with him, it is not the adjective 'true' that I wish to stress here (as if to denigrate other faiths), but rather the noun 'philosophy', understood not as an arid logic-chopping process but the love, and pursuit, of wisdom — a process which is surely not so remote from what we mean by 'education'.

RE as De-indoctrination

Yet one cannot conduct RE in the above manner without being, as I have admitted, personally committed. Ashraf (p. 83f) and Nichols (p. 118f) make a valid and indeed crucial point here. Could a tone-deaf person teach music? How then can someone not attuned to the spiritual dimension, or who denies its very existence, hope to teach meaningfully in this area of the curriculum?

There is no need, however, to make too much fuss over the possibility of indoctrination. To begin with, anyone genuinely committed to the spiritual finds the zealot's approach as distasteful as the bigot's. Indoctrination, in fact, runs counter to the tenets of maturely-held religious convictions themselves — the inviolable freedom of each person being axiomatic. Then again, any attempt to indoctrinate today's children would be self-defeating and counter-productive. I have never ceased to be amazed at the facility with which some critics (have they themselves recent classroom experience?) are ready to invest the RE teacher with Svengali-like powers. Any teacher foolish enough to embark on any such attempt would need anyway to be even better equipped than that, requiring at least a cupboardful of miracles.

In truth one has no choice but to be committed. Even the desire for neutrality — still quaintly fashionable in some quarters — is itself a commitment! I say 'desire', for — as most thinkers today, even in purely scientific disciplines, agree — it is an illusion. Why one should wish to pursue this grail-like search for some mythical entity I do not know. All one can do is be aware in one's own mind of what it is that one is committed to (even if that be humanism or agnosticism, which are of course no more 'neutral' than any other stance) and, secondly, to make no secret of one's commitment to one's pupils. This does not mean saying, 'I think X is a load of rubbish!' It does mean being prepared to admit, if pushed to it, that, although X has many points in its favour, one tends for such-and-such a reason to prefer Y. It does not mean saying that Y is the only answer. It does mean being prepared to admit, if pushed to it, that Y is the answer that best satisfies you.[3]

If pushed to it? There is little doubt that, if pupils have been encouraged to question and debate, they will certainly push one to it! (It should be noted too that it is very frequently the children of supposedly lesser academic ability who are most gifted in this area.) Yet even if pupils have not been encouraged to probe in this way, they will, with the skill and unceremoniousness of tracker dogs, sniff out any pretence at neutrality within minutes, and surely throw the ball back into the teacher's court with a 'But what do *you* think?' If they daren't even do that, there is something seriously wrong with one's teaching.

Total honesty and openness is what children deserve, and all they will respect. Putting one's cards on the table in this way betokens not dogmatism, but vulnerability. In no other subject area does one have to strip oneself bare so frequently. Yet this approach makes things fun, exciting and 'real', even when one has to admit that one doesn't know the answers to all their probings.[3] There is, I believe, a sense in which one can claim that a good RE lesson, at whatever age-level in the secondary school and whatever the nominal subject-matter of a given lesson, is *de*-indoctrinatory. As one 14-year-old commented quite recently in my hearing to a friend: 'I like RE because we can argue without getting told off!' I would have preferred the word 'discuss' or 'debate', but approved of the sentiment.

Religion and Social Harmony

'Sit up and eat like a Christian!'

The above comment made by an elderly aunt (now dead, but possibly not 'sainted') has given me many moments of pleasure.

To begin with, I enjoy the way in which it puts on the spot those of a sociological bent who claim that Christianity (or, *mutatis mutandis*, any other religion) can be reduced to the way in which its adherents behave. Secondly, it acts as a constant and graphic reminder that religion, properly understood, has no aim external to itself — improved table manners or whatever. It cannot be used in this utilitarian way, although — as I have said — governments are keen that it should be. I am pleased, therefore, to see Nichols (p. 114) warning against mistaken attempts to put religion 'at the service of social harmony'. For this very reason I have certain reservations about what might come over to readers as Hulmes' overemphasis on religion as something that will prepare pupils 'to cope with the complexities of a divided society' (p. 124). Anti-racism, social harmony, a clearer knowledge of the difference between right and wrong — even, who knows, improved table manners — may all result from an involvement with religion, as its 'fruits'. Yet there are many other fruits, some less easily classifiable as observable and measurable social phenomena, but equally important. The point is that one cannot artificially engineer these results in a predictable manner. Nor, more importantly, should one be tempted, in my opinion, to give religious education or education in general what Hulmes admits to be 'an *explicitly* (sic) instrumental purpose' (p. 125). Such purposes anyway represent a short cut, and may even produce a short circuit which is very far from what I suspect Hulmes has in mind because of what he says on p. 00.

No doubt my aunt considered that improved table manners constituted not just greater social harmony but increased *personal* development as well. Now the development of the *person* of the pupil (which is not to be confused with PSE, or whatever these sessions of social engineering are timetabled as) is the fundamental aim of all true education and of all true religious education. Moreover, despite my above strictures, it is paradoxical but true that it does have a social dimension. It cannot, as Ashraf (p. 81) and O'Keeffe (p. 96f) point out, be dismissed as something 'private'. Strangely, the arbiters of our society today seem to want to have it both ways: they both wish to bottle religion up as a 'private' concern and yet wish to reap the law-and-order benefits which it is deemed to afford.

The words of Nicolas Zernov, written on the eve of the Second World War and in the wake of his experience of the Bolshevik revolution, remain just as true today:

> It was generally accepted in the past century, and still is in ... sections of Europe and America, that what really matters in a man is his conduct, and that religious belief is a private affair of no great importance because it has no direct bearing upon social or national issues.... In reality, men act, feel and think under the influence of innumerable factors, both spiritual and physical, but the most powerful among them being their belief (or disbelief) in God. (Zernov, 1939, p. 92)

Is Your Teaching Subject-centred or Pupil-centred?

Let us turn now to some of the more practical suggestions put forward by the contributors.

The above question with its false dichotomy — when will we escape from the either/or straitjacket? — is frequently heard on the lips of those who advocate what have come to be called 'active learning strategies'. The present authors understand, however, that there is *no* learning which is not 'active'. They see, too, that there is no need to fight shy of the 'subject', through fear of losing the pupils' interest and attention. All their suggestions aim at depth and therefore quality.

If one aims at quality and depth, however, then selectivity is essential. Slee's remarks (p. 38f) are particularly relevant to today's situation. Selectivity is not a 'dodge'; it is essential to the art of good teaching. I am concerned, however, that the laudable attempts of SACREs to draw up Attainment Targets, whilst giving teaching greater rigour, might in fact encourage teachers to plump for the easy option of superficial breadth, in an attempt to make sure everything is covered. I am somewhat dismayed by the letter (dated 18 March 1991) by Mr Chamier of the DES to Chief Education Officers and the National Curriculum Council. This document — offered as legal advice — suggests that no legally adequate agreed syllabus can 'exclude from its teaching any of the principal religions represented in Great Britain.' Any ? ... Are we to be plunged back into the mish-mash of the discredited Cooks Tours of the 1960s and 1970s? A case of 'Never mind the quality, feel the width'?

Against this background, it is to be hoped that the ideas in the present collection of articles will steady teachers' nerves and encourage them *not* to abandon the attempt — if they are already making it — to take as their starting-point fundamental religious principles and skills, which can then be applied by pupils to *any* phenomena they come across, whether in the class-room, or — better still — outside it. To focus on the 'essential principles common to all religions' (Ashraf, p. 87) — all the contributors would agree — is the best *educational* way of complying with legal requirements such as the above, simply because it does allow one time to engage in work of qual-ity and depth and thus to promote genuine understanding. Surely the West-ern world is becoming punch-drunk with 'information'; How much better to equip pupils with specifically religious skills to enable them to sift through the phenomena, discriminating between what is genuinely a religious issue and what is not, between the authentic and the hypocritical or parasitic. For this reason the practical suggestions of Poole and Ashton in particular are of especial value. If we had to content ourselves with helping to get rid of the 'naive literalism' that Ashton complains of (p. 166) — and which infects not just the primary and junior school but the secondary school, sixth form colleges and beyond — that would be a major achievement. Perhaps we might even get people to see that 'fundamentalists' are in reality more often than not 'superficialists'.[4]

Education for Personal Development

'In a sense, individual and person mean opposite things'
(Lossky, 1957, p. 121)

The term 'individual' is a curious one. Our education system and our general culture seem to value individuality, 'doing your own thing', self-fulfilment — even though these seemingly good aims may bring in their wake an uncomfortable amount of aggressiveness and selfishness. An 'in-divid-ual' is really an automatic bit of society, the smallest bit it can be divided up into, a quantitative, numerical social unit. Is this the sort of thing as educators, as religious educators, we should be promoting?

A 'person', on the other hand, recalls the classical term *persona*, or mask, through which one faces and communicates with others. The individual is turned inwards; the person looks out at those around him, but in doing so becomes more integrated himself. The Christian tradition speaks of God as three 'persons', not as three 'individuals', in one — the Trinity being a model of personal interaction and integration. (And in all this discussion of 'spiritu-ality' how one longs for more mention of the Holy Spirit.)

It is good, therefore, to see Priestley reminding us that true education is itself religious (p. 33). Holley ended his book with the claim that RE is the 'lynchpin' (p. 151), being 'logically central to all educational activities' (p. 169) in that it is especially concerned with insights into patterns of relationships, and with the self-integration and wholeness of persons. Priestley makes much the same point, seeing RE as the 'hub' (p. 37) of the National Curriculum. He will surely approve of the fact that Holley quotes from Whitehead (often at length) on some half dozen occasions. Nichols (p. 121) also sees RE as a 'potentially unifying principle' and Poole provides the clearest practical demonstration of the principle.

Although it is not necessarily what the legislators had in mind when they framed the National Curriculum, we may justifiably emulate the above positive line and end by asserting that if RE is in the *Basic* Curriculum, in a special category of its own, it is because — as all the contributors to this volume have shown in their various ways — it is the *basis* of everything else.

Appendix

I add a list of the priorities that I have worked with for some time, and which preface my syllabus. It is encouraging to note the general convergence between the points it contains and those sketched out in the above articles.

General Philosophy

The department considers the *spiritual* (rather than the moral, the sociological or the ideological) to be the basis of religion. Instead religion is presented as what it claims to be, that is, the response of humans to what they experience as the sacred, a dimension of reality that is felt to have objective existence. The central concept, thus, is what is traditionally called 'God'.

It is in this context that related concepts, and the secondary task of imparting some understanding of religious phenomena, should be conducted. Yet even here we are concerned less with content (with 'what facts pupils ought to know') than with equipping them with the *skills* required to answer the following six core questions. This ability can then be applied to any content, perhaps much later in pupils' lives. Much misinformation (and disinformation) abounds; what is needed is basic *religious literacy* Someone who has this may be said to be 'religiously educated', whether or not he or she is a believer.

The six core questions (from Watson, 1987, pp. 138–41)

   (i)   What is religion (not religions)?
  (ii)   What does religious language mean?
 (iii)   How do actions and visual symbols express belief?
 (iv)   How can one tell whether a given person, action or issue is genuinely religious?

(v)   Are religious beliefs true?
(vi) How do I view Religion, and why?

Objectives Common to all Years

To enable pupils:

(i)   to conceive the possibility of a spiritual level of reality;
(ii)   to perceive that religion and the urge to worship (in one form or another) seems to be universal;
(iii) to discover that religion is intellectually demanding, stimulating and controversial (and not necessarily hostile to science);
(iv)   to perceive that religion is not a 'subject', but a total view of what it means to be a human being;
(v)   to understand basic religious concepts in a more mature and technical manner, and to appreciate that our grasp of such concepts should develop continually rather than fossilize at the infant stage;
(vi)   to acquire an interested but open and honest attitude to such religious texts as the Bible, and to acquire the skills necessary to read them, with their differing uses of language (including the symbolic);
(vii) to acquire the skills of thinking clearly and of reflecting thoughtfully and honestly about religious issues and about their own attitude to religion;
(viii) to appreciate the necessary relationship between belief and a way of life, that is, the practical relevance of religion as a contemporary living experience;
(ix)   to take seriously the inner experience of believers and thus to develop increased respect for personal inwardness and awareness.

Principal Aim

Through an understanding of the true nature of religion (see above), to help pupils to become 'persons' rather than mere 'individuals'; to help them realize their capacity for 'wholeness'; and to help them discover patterns of meaning in life and in their own experience.

Notes

1   It did not even score a single footnote reference, for example, in the *British Journal of Religious Education* summer 1985 issue, which was entirely devoted to spirituality — even though early drafts of the book had appeared in that magazine when it was still called *Learning for Living*.
2   Nor is Nirvana some negative annihilation into non-existence. Rather is it the 'dying-out' of passions or desires, and can be positively viewed as an ideal state of

bliss. Viewed thus it has affinities with beliefs in other faiths, and is not unlike the Greek Patristic term *apatheia*.
3 I have often had to own up to possibly being an atheist — that is, if God really is the way some pupils describe Him as being!
4 Here I disagree with Ashraf, who seems (p. 00) to frown on 'intellectual discussion'.
5 I regret that no contributor attempts to clarify the confusion that exists in most textbooks and Agreed Syllabus between SYMBOL and SIGN.

References

HOLLEY, R. (1978) *Religious Education and Religious Understanding*, London, RKP.
SHERRARD, P. (1990) *The Sacred in Life and Art*, Ipswich, Golgonooza Press.
LOSSKY, V. (1957) *The Mystical Theology of the Eastern Church*, Cambridge, J. Clarke.
WATSON, B. (1987) *Education and Belief*, Oxford, Blackwell.
ZERNOV, N. (1939) *St. Sergius — Builder of Russia*, London, SPCK.

Postscript

The concerns voiced in this book map out an agenda for RE well into the twenty-first century. I like to think that the various priorities can neatly come together like the spokes of a wheel, and that the greater the depth with which each is pursued the nearer to the others it moves and the more stable the result is. This metaphor was quite independently used by two contributors and taken up twice by Donley. Amid all the confusion and change, complexity and ambiguity, disturbance and challenge of today's educational world, perhaps we should try to stay close to the centre of the wheel — to quote T.S. Eliot: 'At the still point of the turning world' (Eliot, Burnt Norton, *Four Quartets*, 1935).

The twelve priorities listed in Appendix 1 have been arranged in the shape of a wheel in Appendix 3 and focussed on what pupils may gain from RE which adopts them. Never far below the surface of what we see as a priority, is an awareness of some widespread misunderstanding, or something serious which is overlooked. I have therefore indicated what I think is the particular danger of which each contributor is especially aware. There is obvious overlap in some, but I think it is clear that they are all interrelated. All the authors are aware of the pull of forces which marginalize religion in today's world.

It may be helpful to see the priorities chosen within their contexts, so I have added round the edge of the diagram the major area of concern for each contributor. The widest differences are apparent here. The religious persuasion of the contributors includes Orthodox Christian, Roman Catholic, Evangelical Christian, Muslim, Liberal and what may be termed the Loosely Attached. At this level the possibility of coherence may seem remote and actually be so. Can Muslim and liberal educationalists, such as Ashraf and Wilson, really join hands, or is there an unbridgeable divide between them? The sciences and the arts appear to talk different languages, as a glance at Poole's and Slee's chapters may show. Schools to nurture Christianity seem to be far removed from the serious engagement with pluralism for which Hulmes asks. The questions here seem to be unlimited and unanswerable. Appendix 2 suggests themes for discussion on some of these.

I personally can see the very different concerns of the writers coming together in a number of ways and will discuss four of these.

The Nature of Religion

The first priority to emerge for me clearly from the book concerns the importance of clarity about the nature of religion. I think a measure of accord is reached which can perhaps be summarized in this way: religion is centred on awareness of mystery (stressed especially by Slee and Poole) which, in its emotional impact leads to worship and awe, (Wilson, Priestley, Ashraf) in its intellectual aspect relates to concepts of God (Ashraf, Ashton, Wilkins, O'Keeffe, Nichols. Hulmes and Donley); in its practical aspect leads to moral integrity (Ashraf), responsibility towards the environment (O'Keeffe) and affirmation (Hulmes); and in its sociological or communal aspect becomes associated with ways of behaviour and authority-structures (most current RE and acknowledge by all authors).

This understanding of religion therefore gives substance to the idea of the common Religious Tradition voiced by Ashraf and made the main object of exploration by Hulmes. This can be maintained despite the reality of controversy about how that which is at the heart of all religion is seen and responded to.

There are, and remain, very important differences between the writers of this book, but with regard to religious education it is important that we first attend to the enormous amount of common-ground, as Ashraf points out. This common-ground is often neglected because differences appear to be much more interesting, and yet they only gain any significance (or real appreciation of them is only possible) if what is in common is first understood.

With the limited amount of time and resources available for religious education, most of our time could and should be taken up with this. It is not a lowest common denominator approach leading to an anaemic version of religion. It is the reverse. By taking Priestley's and Slee's advice to pursue even a single point in depth, it is possible to realize an underlying unity far more significant than the multiplicity of observable forms of behaviour and belief.

The understanding of religion with which each contributor operates shows a marked emphasis either on the spiritual experience which ratifies religion, or on the source of that experience which is revealed. Nevertheless I think that probably all the contributors would agree that these are two ways of looking at the same thing — at that interaction between the divine and the human without which religion would have no meaning or truth.

Nurture and Autonomy

Yet the differences in the way in which religion is seen — what is central to it — are likely to result in a significant difference in the way that the purpose of education is seen. Broadly speaking one can say that there is a divide between the nurture concern and the autonomy concern, between the tradition-orientated and the pupil-orientated approaches. Even so there is a moving together towards the hub of the wheel. This is shown by the nurture concern of those who are clearly educational in their outlook, and the openness apparent in the concern for individual integrity of those who approach religious education from a definite tradition which they would like to see handed on. The point is of course that this dichotomy is a false one at root, because nurture is unavoidably part of any education. That is to say the principles on which education is based or around which it is organized *are* communicated in a million ways. Similarly, no tradition can be handed on via robots — all living traditions acknowledge that the young must genuinely hold the tradition and be prepared for change and development in order that the tradition can go on living and growing instead of succumbing to the forces of inertia. What people are anxious to see carried on is something living, not defunct.

So inherently there is the necessity to overcome the dichotomy. What I think the writers in this book achieve — and I am enormously grateful to them for their efforts — is that they take us a bit further on the path to *realizing* that both nurture and autonomy are involved and *can* cohere.

Deepening the Phenomenological Approach to RE

Nicola Slee, in an important article in the *British Journal for Religious Education* in 1989, noted that the time has come for a rapprochement between the so-called confessional and phenomenological approaches to religious education. It is to be hoped that this book is a step towards helping teachers to develop such a rapprochement. A possible criticism, however, could be made by some concerning the emphasis of the book as a whole that it despatches rather too thoroughly the phenomenological approach to RE, suggesting that the authors have not taken seriously enough — have not welcomed — the multi-faith scene. I do not think this is true in that firstly, all, except the Christian School Movement, argue that what is common and fundamental to all great religious traditions should receive the priority, and as Ashton says this preempts the question of competition or rivalry between particular religions. Secondly, insofar as one religion is referred to, the understanding of it is not narrowly-conceived but in a way inclusive of the insights of others.

Yet because this *could* be the impression that some readers get, I would like to underline here how such dialogue can, and should, develop from the priorities here given, and can and should be shared with children. All the priorities with the exception of the one which is described, not argued for as such, refer to a broad, unifying role for religious understanding. Exclusiveness is, in most, explicitly guarded against especially in 2, 3, 4, 5, 6, 7 and 8. The other four, namely 1, 9, 10 and 11, are concerned with skills which are basic for any progress in multi-faith understanding.

A critique can indeed be made of the phenomenological approach, and this appears several times in this book. It is a critique however based on awareness of its many merits and that the superficiality with which it is often associated is not inherent to it but the result of many other factors, especially the conditioning of society. Such a betrayal of phenomenology has become so widespread because it seems to answer a need. Many people required to teach RE — especially in primary schools — are *not* specialists, and do not have the resources to tackle the dangers and complexities of the subject. Phenomenological RE appears to offer relatively safe sailing in a controlled harbour for such novices.

The question is whether this will do — can RE stay there? Religion itself points to the necessity for journeying — for crossing the ocean. It raises awkward questions such as, is religion true? and how can we live with diversity? Such questions cannot be engaged with by staying in the harbour, because we cannot get to know what the ocean is really like that way, and because the real world is tossed by the tempestuous waves of real religious conflict. RE must help pupils to accept the risk venture which RE needs to be, otherwise the idealism of a larger more personalistic approach will go unheeded.

Some kind of kit enabling pupils to learn to navigate the ocean in as safe a way as possible is needed. I suspect it will include most of the priorities argued for in this book. Questions can be raised concerning all of these. Nevertheless it is hoped that some progress has been made in appreciating the complexity of the issues involved and seeing the possibility of a realistic and creative way forward.

Teaching Discernment

It is extremely important that pupils learn how to discern what is genuinely religious from what is not and on that basis become better able to reflect realistically about the truth or otherwise of religion. Donley alludes to this several times, and at least four of the objectives for RE listed on page 193 relate to concepts and interpretative skills. Such discernment depends on a willingness not to take things at face-value but to delve deeper. It involves the priority which Ashton has identified of helping pupils to transcend literalism, meet up with the depths in their own experience, and trust their intuitive capacity to sniff out the real from the sham.

All the contributors would I think agree that this capacity is basically present in children, although they imply it in different ways, whether as a basic rationality to be appealed to, an inner personal perceptiveness, the capacity for imagination which can transcend the mundane and purely external, or as the intuitive moral sense and so forth.

What they also agree on is that whilst in a sense this quality of perceptiveness is natural, it very easily gets overlaid, forgotten, buried or ignored by the pressures of society and modern life, by the dangerous outcome of various — isms conditioning people and through erosion from sheer non-use.

So what the teacher needs to do is not so much try to give something not already present in children, but to awaken and develop what is there.

Some of the contributors may be unhappy to put it like this in case it is understood as implying a humanist assumption that human nature is fundamentally good and we can achieve wholly good ends through endeavour alone. This is a common enough assumption today in education circles, for example, this quotation from Peter Kutnick — 'teachers must be aware that children are inherently *good*, and this goodness should be allowed to develop'. (Kutnick, 1987, p. 77). Many, and perhaps all, the contributors would be unable totally to agree with this, for it tends to underestimate the powerful forces of evil — however understood — which profoundly affect how people see, and which can become internalized. We *are* dealing with something deadly. Life is dangerous it has been often observed, and so is the inner life. The warnings that Donley, Slee, Wilkins, Hulmes and others have given need to be heeded. Religion can go badly astray.

This is why teaching geared towards helping pupils gain skills of discernment is crucial, enabling false and demonic forms of religion to be exposed. The reader may ask whether the various contributors have actually taken this point with sufficient seriousness. Perhaps the references by Wilson, Slee, Ashraf and others need to be developed further.

Fear of intolerance has been a major reason for the failure to encourage the evaluative aspect of RE. Yet concern for clarity and for truth ought not to result in intolerance. It is never the truth that is the trouble, but rather the attitude of possessiveness, of misunderstanding of dogma, of thinking of truth as an entity which we have and somebody else does not have. That is why if we follow Priestley who powerfully draws attention to the falseness of a static, self-concident attitude to knowledge, we shall be able to combine a concern for both tolerance and truth.

Notes

BOLTON, A. (1991) *RE: Values and Pluralism*, NAVET Discussion Paper, spring.

HARVEY-JONES, J. (1991) interview recorded in *Management Week*, May, **4**.

KUTNICK, P. (1987) 'Autonomy: The nature of relationships, development and the role of the school' in Thacker, J., Pring, R. and Evans, D. (Eds) *Personal, Social and Moral Education in a Changing World*, Windsor, NFER-Nelson.

SLEE, N. (1989) 'Conflict and reconciliation between competing models of religious education', *British Journal of Religious Education*, **11**, 3.

Appendix 1

Priorities Argued for in the Book

(1) The need for clarity as to what 'religion' means, and the development of qualities enabling pupils to become more reasonable in religion and the handling of emotions (John Wilson).

(2) The need to challenge the secularist assumption which separates religion from education, and to work towards seeing things whole, adopting a fluid and constantly fresh approach to teaching (Jack Priestley).

(3) The need for the education of spirituality through a more pupil-centred, personalistic approach encouraging an awareness of mystery, the development of creative imagination and the stimulation of artistic capacity within the student (Nicola Slee).

(4) The need to take seriously the religious understanding and experience which pupils may bring to school and to recognize their positive contribution to pupils' educational development (Richard Wilkins).

(5) The need to cultivate the religious sensibility of pupils through exploring the Religious Tradition and developing moral integrity and respect for others without succumbing to relativism (Syed Ali Ashraf).

(6)* The need to help pupils understand Christianity in such a way as to take seriously the possibility of commitment to Christ (The Christian School Movement).

(6) The need to explore religious perspectives on environmental concerns (Bernadette O'Keeffe).

(7) The need for faith-commitment and cross-curricular enquiry as an expression of the way in which religion can offer a potentially unifying principle (Kevin Nichols).

(8) The need to take seriously, within the controlled environment of the classroom, the *possibility* that beneath the outward forms of religious and cultural diversity a hitherto unsuspected, and therefore surprising, degree of unity may be both recognized and affirmed (Edward Hulmes).

The numbers refer to chapters in the book

*   There are two priorities discussed in chapter 6, the first, marked with an asterisk, is described, the second argued for.

(9)   The need to question the supposed conflict between science and religion, by appreciating the nature and limits of science, and the importance of discernment in religion (Michael Poole).

(10)   The need to counteract the literalism which acts as a block against development of children's own spirituality and capacity to relate in a meaningful way to religious traditions (Elizabeth Ashton).

(11)   The need to encourage reflective thinking about religion, and the capacity to distinguish between what is authentic and valid, and what is not. (Michael Donley)

Appendix 2

Questions for Discussion

On the Priorities as a Whole

1 Do you consider that there are any misfits amongst the priorities discussed in this book?
2 Are some more fundamental than others?
3 Would the age of the pupils make a substantial difference as to which priorities might be pursued?
4 Can you identify your own personal priorities regarding RE amongst them?
5 Would you wish to add to them or substitute any with a priority you consider more important?
6 Do you feel strongly that any should *not* be there?
7 Compare the list of priorities with the list of objectives given by Donley on p. 193.

On the Nature of Religion

8 Is religion, as Wilson sees it, primarily a matter of emotions which need to be rationally understood?
9 Would genuine education be religious, as Priestley argues, or can the wholeness of which he writes be reached by other means, bypassing religion?
10 Does Slee's understanding of the 'spiritual' successfully include how secular humanists and religious believers use the word? Do you consider it might be helpful to retain the traditional distinction between 'soul' and 'spirit' to which Donley draws attention?
11 Is it the case that only certain forms of Christianity or of any world religion allow the possibility of 'spiritual development' being on the agenda of state schools? (This is based on the question with which Stewart Sutherland concluded his chapter in O'Keeffe's book of essays *Schools of Tomorrow* (Falmer Press, 1988).

203

On Commitment

12 What kind of commitment, educational and/or religious, do you consider a teacher should have in order to teach RE.
13 Does rootedness matter, or can children be educated without any sense of belonging to a tradition to which they have a provisional commitment? Can such commitment be distinguished from conditioning or dogmatism or prejudice?
14 Wilkins stresses the importance of out-of-school pupil experience of religion. Might it be legitimately argued however that *some* of this might be damaging and unhelpful? If so, how should RE relate to this?

On Indoctrination

15 Can it be said that all education is manipulative unless this very problem is shared with pupils? If so, what are the implications of this for RE?
16 Should education — and especially religious education — carry a health warning? Does it necessarily change people?
17 How can the dilemma posed by the Johannesburg van-driver's religious education, as cited by Wilkins, be overcome without teachers exercising undue pressure on pupils?
18 Slee speaks of the dangers of 'a bland and lazy relativism'. Do you agree? If so, how can RE avoid reinforcing this if it tries to be fair to many traditions and not teach dogmatically?

On the Importance of Discernment

19 Do the major religious traditions of the world have much in common so that we can speak of 'the Religious Tradition' as Ashraf does?
20 What do you understand by the 'fluency in the language of affirmation' to which Hulmes points? Why does he refer to it as an important stage on the road to religious literacy?
21 Is the principle of reciprocity one that can help resolve the problem of defining the limits of tolerance in a pluralist society?
22 Donley refers to the 'fallen' nature of imagination. Do you consider that human-beings are basically good, so that, encouraging pupils to be creative is automatically beneficial?
23 Has enough been made in this book of the way in which religion can go dangerously astray and constitute one of the most potent forces for evil in the world? How ought RE to tackle this problem?
24 Has religion anything specific to add to the environmentalist movement? Can religion indeed be anti-environmental, and, if so, does this necessarily disqualify religion from any role?

On Practical Classroom Work

25 Is Priestley's emphasis on centredness in the present moment feasible in the light of the requirements and pressures placed on teachers and schools today?

26 How far do you see the suggestions for work given by Poole on science and religion as adaptable for younger pupils?

27 Are young children capable of distinguishing between different uses of language, as Ashton maintains, and appreciating the way in which religious language in particular operates?

28 Can we talk about children's spirituality? Should we assume that they have the capacity for spiritual discernment, and if so what difference might this make to teaching?

An Educational Wheel

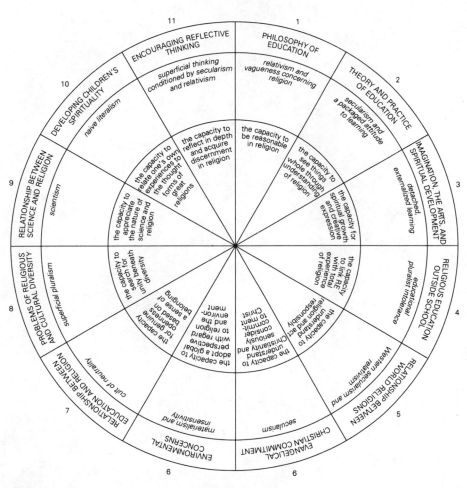

Key
OUTER SECTION:
A MAIN AREA OF INTEREST OF EACH CONTRIBUTOR
Middle Section:
Current dangers which each has particularly identified
Central Section:
Priority focus — on what it is hoped pupils may gain from RE

Notes on Contributors

PROFESSOR SYED ALI ASHRAF is Director General of the Islamic Academy, Cambridge and a member of the Faculty of Education, University of Cambridge. As a Professor of English he has taught at Harvard University and in Pakistan and Saudi Arabia. He is the author of many books on Islamic education including a Teaching Manual for Westhill Religious Education Centre. He is currently working on a GCSE book for Stanley Thorne.

ELIZABETH ASHTON has been a primary school teacher since 1972 in North Tyneside. She has an Open University degree, and in 1989 gained an MA (Durham) for a thesis on *Religious Education and the Unconscious* relating it to 7–10-year-old children. She is currently engaged on further classroom-based PhD research with the University of Durham. In January 1992, she became a lecturer in Religious Education at Durham University.

MICHAEL DONLEY is Head of RE and Music at Cotswold School, Bourton-on-the-Water, Gloucestershire. After a career overseas, which included some lecturing, he became an RE teacher in this country twelve years ago. He is a member of the County's SACRE, representing the Orthodox Church, and is *starosta* (Warden) and Choir Director of the Russian Orthodox Parish in Oxford.

DR. EDWARD HULMES is Spalding Professorial Fellow in World Religions in the Department of Theology, University of Durham, where he has recently introduced the study of comparative theology. He is an experienced teacher who has taught courses in religious studies in Britain and in the United States. His most recent book is on *Education and Cultural Diversity* (Longman, 1989).

FATHER KEVIN NICHOLS formerly a teacher and student Chaplain, served for six years as Advisor on Religious Education to the Roman Catholic Bishops of England and Wales. He has written widely on education and liturgical questions and is now a parish priest in County Durham.

DR. BERNADETTE O'KEEFFE is a sociologist who is currently Fellllow at the Von Hugel Institute, St. Edmund's College, Cambridge. As Senior Research Fellow at Kings' College, London, she wrote *Faith, Culture and the Dual System: A Comparative Study of Church and County Schools* (Falmer Press, 1986) and she edited *Schools for Tomorrow: Building Walls or Building Bridges* (Falmer Press, 1988).

MICHAEL POOLE is a lecturer in science education at King's College, London. He has published extensively on the interplay between science and religion, with special reference to its education context. He was a Director of the Farmington Science and Religion Project, and his most recent book is *A Guide to Science and Belief* (Lion, 1990).

DR. JACK PRIESTLEY has spent his whole career teaching and training teachers. After many years as a Lecturer and Senior Lecturer in the University of Exeter School of Education, he has since January 1991, been Principal of Westhill College, Birmingham. He has written extensively on most aspects of religious education.

NICOLA SLEE is Lecturer in Theology and Religious Studies at the Roehampton Institute of Higher Education, and currently seconded to the Southwark Ordination Course where she is engaged in training adults for ordained ministry in the Anglican, Methodist and United Reformed churches. She has wide-ranging interests in theology and education and a number of previous publications in the areas of religious education, feminist theology and Christian spirituality.

BRENDA WATSON is currently Academic Consultant to the Farmington Trust. For eleven years she was at the Farmington Institute in Oxford and was its Director from 1982 until 1988. She had earlier spent eight years teaching and eleven years lecturing at Didsbury College of Education in both the History and Religious Studies Departments. Author of *Education and Belief* (Blackwells, 1987), she has published widely on religious education.

RICHARD WILKINS is General Secretary of the Association of Christian Teachers. He taught for twelve years in further, primary and secondary education in that rather eccentric order. His last teaching post was for eight years as Head of Religious Education in a comprehensive school. He has written many articles and papers on religious education.

JOHN WILSON is currently Fellow of Mansfield College, Oxford, and Lecturer in Educational Studies. He has held teaching posts at the King's School, Canterbury; Trinity College, Toronto; and the University of Sussex. He was Director of the Farmington Trust Research Unit, Oxford, and has written widely on education, moral philosophy and the philosophy of religion.

Index